THE CHALLENGE

Also by Chay Blyth

A Fighting Chance
Innocent Aboard
The Impossible Voyage
Theirs is the Glory

THE CHALLENGE

The Official Story of the British Steel Challenge

CHAY BLYTH
and
ELAINE THOMPSON

HODDER AND STOUGHTON
LONDON SYDNEY AUCKLAND

First published in 1993
by Hodder and Stoughton Ltd

10   9   8   7   6   5   4   3   2   1

British Library Cataloguing in Publication Data
Blyth, Chay
Challenge: Official Story of the British Steel Challenge
I. Title   II. Thompson, Elaine
910.4

ISBN 0-340-59190-0

Maps devised by Captain Spencer Drummond and drawn by ML Design
Typeset by Hewer Text Composition Services, Edinburgh
Printed in Great Britain by Butler & Tanner, Frome, Somerset

Hodder and Stoughton Ltd
A Division of Hodder Headline PLC
47 Bedford Square
London WC1B 3DP

CONTENTS

A NOTE FROM CHAY BLYTH

In 1971, when I sailed round the world, I never saw myself as the one who was taking the risk, I saw the British Steel Corporation as the risk takers. Equally, I believe that with the British Steel Challenge it was the men of vision, that is, the board of directors, who took the greatest chance. Without them taking that chance, this race would never have happened. I also owe a debt of gratitude to the sponsors of all ten yachts, those which were members of our Business Club and all the others who helped – too numerous to mention.

A personal thank you must go to the management team, Greg Bertram, Helen Wybrow, Andrew Roberts, Mike Kay and the rest of the staff, and a very special thank you to Elaine Thompson for her help with this book.

PHOTOGRAPHIC CREDITS

All the photographs were supplied by Pickthall Picture Library Ltd. Individual photographers who are credited by their initials are as follows:

PRB Peter Bentley	DB David Branigan
PB Paul Buchanan	AC Andrew Chamberlain
PE Paul Egan	SE Suzanne Emerson
RH Rob Haine	H *Heath Insured*
HL *Hofbräu Lager*	SL Simon Littlejohn
MO'R Mike O'Regan	MP Mark Pepper
BP Barry Pickthall	AR Adrian Rayson
CR Cedric Robertson	NS Neil Skinner

FOREWORD

Those of us who have long relished the excitement and the rigours of yachting will understand and perhaps even feel a twinge of envy on reading of the joys and the deprivations experienced by the crews of the British Steel Challenge yachts as they circumnavigated the globe. As patron of the Challenge and president of its official charity, The Save the Children Fund, I followed their progress with great interest from the start.

What has impressed everyone associated with this bold adventure is the degree of dedication and sacrifice which imbued the 140 volunteer crew members: all are amateurs and many had never before sailed when accepted by Chay Blyth to participate in the race.

I feel certain that all the competitors will in some way have found their lives to have been changed as a result of the opportunity to take part in this unique endeavour and hopefully their achievements will serve as an inspiration to others to rise to similar challenges in the future.

HRH The Princess Royal

1 Horseshoe lifebuoy.
2 Helmsman's seat with liferafts underneath.
3 Communications centre with radar, satellite navigation receiver (GPS), INMARSAT satellite telex transceiver and JVC camera.
4 Single wheel designed to take into account the age range of crew and relative strengths of male and female crews.

5 Compass.
6 Deep cockpit specifically designed with safety in mind.
7 Lewmar 66ST winches. The design of the boats was based on this.
8 Wind speed and boat speed instruments for helmsman.
9 Foot brace.
10 Companionway hatch. A doghouse hatch was added later.

11 Mechanical rather than hydraulic vang to reduce the chances of vang tension breaking the boom.
12 Dorade vent. The ventilation was dictated by Department of Transport (DTp) regulations.
13 Spinnaker poles. A number of these were damaged during the race.
14 Grabrails.

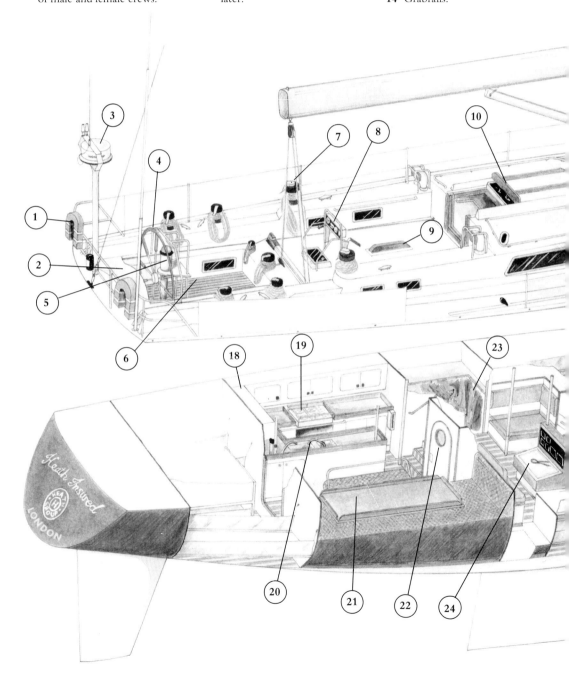

15 Raised hatch coaming to help hatch remain watertight despite continually washed with waves.

16 Guardrail height in excess of DTp and Offshore Racing Council regulations.

17 Forestay bottlescrews. This area was to cause major problems on the second leg.

18 Oven.

19 Hob.

20 Sinks. One mistake we made was to put the sinks directly opposite the cooker; they should have been offset so two people could work side by side in the galley.

21 Saloon table, designed so that all the crew could sit round it at once. It could also have been used as an operating table in an emergency. The boat was not open plan to keep it warm in cold climates and to assist resale later.

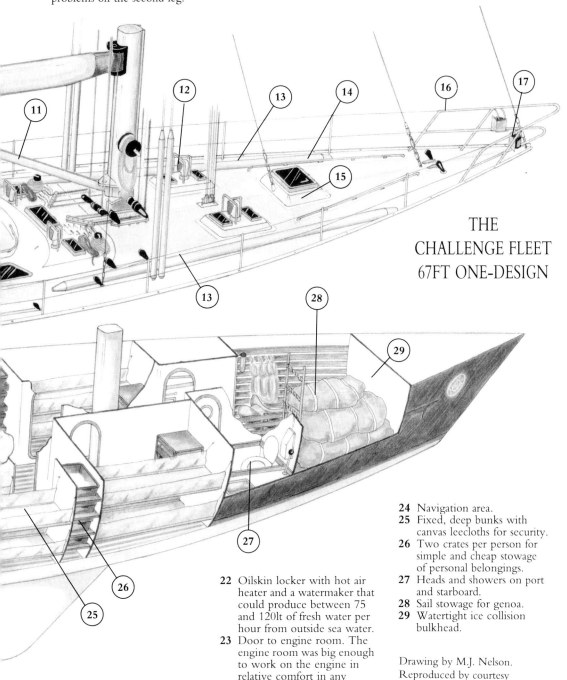

THE
CHALLENGE FLEET
67FT ONE-DESIGN

22 Oilskin locker with hot air heater and a watermaker that could produce between 75 and 120lt of fresh water per hour from outside sea water.

23 Door to engine room. The engine room was big enough to work on the engine in relative comfort in any conditions.

24 Navigation area.

25 Fixed, deep bunks with canvas leecloths for security.

26 Two crates per person for simple and cheap stowage of personal belongings.

27 Heads and showers on port and starboard.

28 Sail stowage for genoa.

29 Watertight ice collision bulkhead.

Drawing by M.J. Nelson.
Reproduced by courtesy
of *Yachting World*.

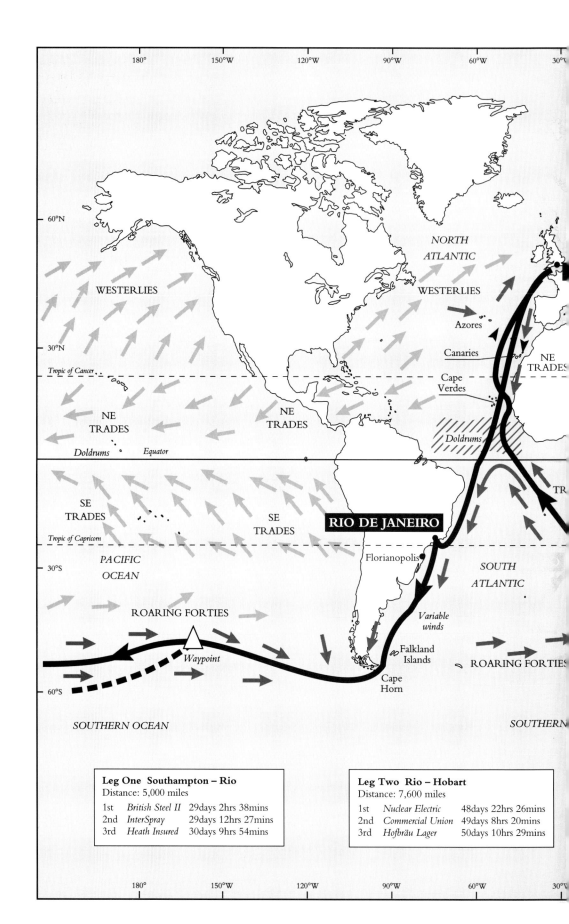

NORTH
ATLANTIC

WESTERLIES

Azores

Canaries

NE
TRADES

Cape
Verdes

Doldrums

TR

RIO DE JANEIRO

Florianopolis

SOUTH
ATLANTIC

Variable
winds

Falkland
Islands

ROARING FORTIES

Cape
Horn

SOUTHERN

WESTERLIES

60°N

30°N

Tropic of Cancer

NE
TRADES

NE
TRADES

Doldrums   Equator

SE
TRADES

SE
TRADES

Tropic of Capricorn

PACIFIC
OCEAN

30°S

ROARING FORTIES

Waypoint

60°S

SOUTHERN OCEAN

Leg One Southampton – Rio
Distance: 5,000 miles

1st   *British Steel II*   29days 2hrs 38mins
2nd   *InterSpray*   29days 12hrs 27mins
3rd   *Heath Insured*   30days 9hrs 54mins

Leg Two Rio – Hobart
Distance: 7,600 miles

1st   *Nuclear Electric*   48days 22hrs 26mins
2nd   *Commercial Union*   49days 8hrs 20mins
3rd   *Hofbräu Lager*   50days 10hrs 29mins

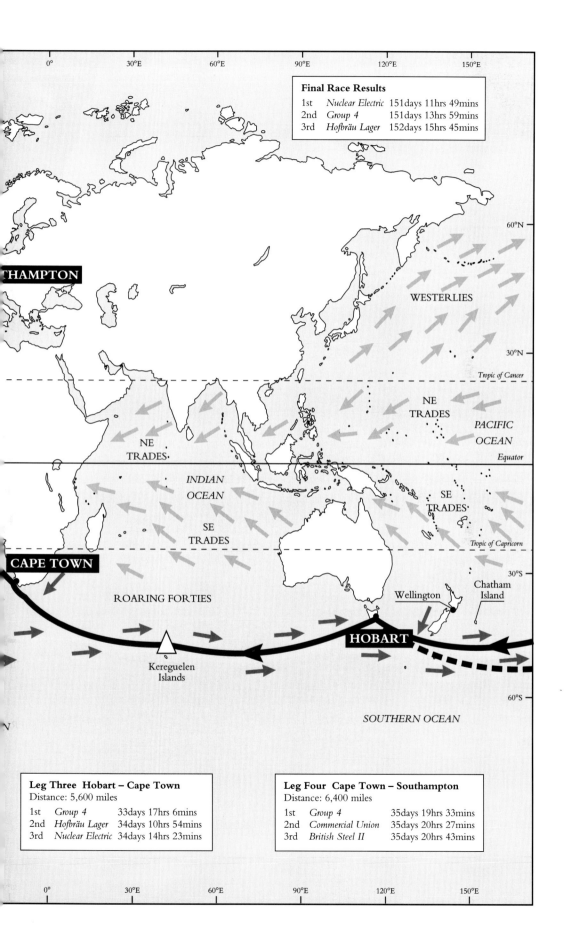

0° 30°E 60°E 90°E 120°E 150°E

Final Race Results

1st	*Nuclear Electric*	151days 11hrs 49mins
2nd	*Group 4*	151days 13hrs 59mins
3rd	*Hofbräu Lager*	152days 15hrs 45mins

THAMPTON

60°N

WESTERLIES

30°N

Tropic of Cancer

NE
TRADES

*PACIFIC
OCEAN*

NE
TRADES·

INDIAN
OCEAN

SE
TRADES·

Equator

SE
TRADES

Tropic of Capricorn

CAPE TOWN

30°S

Chatham
Island

Wellington

ROARING FORTIES

HOBART

Kereguelen
Islands

60°S

SOUTHERN OCEAN

Leg Three Hobart – Cape Town
Distance: 5,600 miles

1st	*Group 4*	33days 17hrs 6mins
2nd	*Hofbräu Lager*	34days 10hrs 54mins
3rd	*Nuclear Electric*	34days 14hrs 23mins

Leg Four Cape Town – Southampton
Distance: 6,400 miles

1st	*Group 4*	35days 19hrs 33mins
2nd	*Commercial Union*	35days 20hrs 27mins
3rd	*British Steel II*	35days 20hrs 43mins

0° 30°E 60°E 90°E 120°E 150°E

CHAPTER ONE

THE CHALLENGE DEFINED

"Above deck the wind gusts to seventy-five miles per hour. The sea spray hits you in the face as if fired from an air rifle and, as you steer the boat, waves knock you off your feet. Huge roller-coaster waves carry on top of them endless rows of short sharp smaller ones, and there is no respite. These waves are aggressive, endlessly tackling us.

"The sky is a menacing variety of grey and black. Marcus Gladwell, our bowman, described it best yesterday when he said that even at dawn it was as if someone had thrown a black tablecloth over everything. Down below, condensation drips down the walls and everything is soaking; sleeping bags are like giant sponges. Grown men, just off watch, have tears rolling down their cheeks as they wait for the blood to start circulating again to their fingertips. It takes twenty minutes to get all the layers of clothing on and off.

"It should not have been a surprise. We had been told, we had read articles but somehow we didn't really believe it. The third leg, from Tasmania to Cape Town, across the southern Indian Ocean, has been a nightmare. We have had sixteen days of non-stop gales. Storms have aged a few of us, exhausted us all and reminded everyone of the power of the sea. It would be good to slow down but this race is so competitive that somehow the idea does not enter your head. Many of us were cynical when we saw it being described as the Toughest Yacht Race Ever. Well, if there is a tougher one, you can count us out: going the wrong way across the Indian Ocean is a humbling experience."

In February 1993 the ten boats, each with a professional skipper and thirteen amateur crew on board, had sailed over halfway round the world. In the most testing of conditions, in the ferocity of the Southern Ocean between Tasmania and the Cape of Good Hope, Kevin Dufficy brought himself to describe what life was like aboard the yacht, *British Steel*

Left Learning to take all that the Southern Ocean could throw at them was what the Challenge was all about.

II. Although weary, cold and perhaps a little lonely even among a crew of fourteen, he still felt compelled to portray the daily struggle that makes a circumnavigation anti-clockwise round the world so challenging.

A few hours after he had written this report and sent it to race headquarters in Hampshire, I read it with mixed emotions. On one hand, I was reading it from the security of being on land while the fleet was bashing to windward against gales and through mountainous seas and, like all the friends and families involved, I remained anxious about the crews' well being while they were at sea. On the other hand, I envied Kevin his adventure and the crews' achievements. His message also added some elements of nostalgia to that mix of feelings; a wistfulness about the experience. The Southen Ocean, cold and inhospitable, is truly one of the last great wildernesses, and it is barely possible to convey a proper impression of its might.

I had sailed along the same route in 1970, in the ketch *British Steel*, on my way to making the first non-stop circumnavigation of the world against prevailing winds and currents. With Kevin's telex in my hand, I recalled my own passage across the Southern Ocean to conjure up an image of what the crews of the British Steel Challenge fleet were enduring day after day. I had made that part of the voyage a month later in the year and had been completely alone.

I remembered the insanity of the sea, and the boat crashing through an army of advancing waves, like legions going into battle. From trough to peak, the boat ascended through forty feet or more, then plunged towards the trough like a wild horse trying to unseat its rider. Sometimes the waves would bury themselves under the quarters of the boat and pitch her upwards, stern first. Breaking crests cascaded on top of the bow and broke along the length of the boat with such force that the breath would be pressed out of my lungs when I was caught in their path and I would have to cling on to whatever was nearby to keep my feet.

Usually, the winds were maddeningly inconstant. Endless sail changes wore me out physically and, equally, finding the resolve to keep going was an intensely exhausting mental struggle. This, I knew, was how it was aboard all ten British Steel Challenge boats. I remembered being knocked into the scuppers by an enormous weight of hissing water, feeling as if I were being scuffed ceaselessly with sandpaper, and having to scale a cliff face of wet deck to get back into the cockpit. I remembered the volume of noise below deck as the boat pounded into the face of waves and crashed into valleys beneath. From time to time, *British Steel* would emerge through a breaking peak with such a sheer face that there was nothing beneath, and the boat would fall from its height with stomach-turning velocity.

Broken sleep and chill I also recalled. I had written in my log of aching limbs and of bruises, and I had longed for a calm. The physical discomfort and mental strain were made worse by having to hand-steer the boat most of the time, for my self-steering gear had smashed at Cape Horn. Progress was frustratingly slow. In similar conditions, the people on the British Steel Challenge twenty-one years later, must have wondered why they were enduring such hardship. They did so to take part in an adventure, as I had. Like me, they were pitting themselves against the worst of the world's elements, but unlike me, who had been alone, they were experiencing how teamwork and trust have to be relied on to prevail, even in the teeth of storm Force 11 winds and huge seas. And they were also there, I suppose, to taste fear, awe and effort as an antidote to the complacency of normal life. All 140 crew on board, some of them taking part for only one leg of the race, had signed on for the adventure of a lifetime, and none was in any doubt that here was everything they had imagined, dreaded and hoped for.

My first adventure began in 1966 when I had rowed across the North Atlantic with John Ridgway. It was the same year that Sir Francis Chichester, the daddy of all pioneering yachtsmen, was sailing round the world in *Gypsy Moth IV*. The welcome John and I got when we returned to England convinced us both that the obvious progression was to go sailing. In those days I was a sergeant in the Parachute Regiment, but I recognised that sailing might offer me great opportunities as a career. Chichester had stopped once during his single-handed circumnavigation, so the outstanding feat then to be achieved was to sail round the world non-stop. I resolved to do that.

A few major hurdles confronted me, though, the principal ones being that I couldn't sail and I couldn't navigate. And there were other, well-qualified contenders. The legendary French yachtsman Eric Tabarly had expressed his intention to sail round the world without stopping. So, too, had Donald Crowhurst, John Ridgway, Nigel Tetley and Robin Knox-Johnston.

My plans changed and I decided to take part in the 1968 Round the World Race. Unfortunately, the same difficulties applied, but I was lucky in meeting Neville Woods, a former Chief Petty Officer in the Royal Navy, who at that time had a sailing school in Langstone Harbour, near Portsmouth. Neville offered to teach me how to sail. I explained to him that I intended to race across the Atlantic, and asked how long it would take me to learn enough about sailing to achieve that. "Three weeks," was his reply. "You'd know enough to get across safely by then, although you won't know enough to race competitively." I was astounded. To me, sailing was an extremely complicated business, half art, half science, and with an arcane language to match. How could anyone possibly learn all that in three weeks? Neville remained unshakeably confident, though, and I found his positive attitude infectious. Sure that he meant what he said, I set out to find a sponsor to fund the crossing, and a boat to do it in.

My attempts to find a sponsor came to nothing. I knew what I wanted to do and what benefits I could offer a company prepared to back me, but my plans lacked credibility. Invariably I would be dealing with someone with Naval experience at the interviews, or the interviewers would have someone with that kind of experience on hand. So, when they asked "Can you sail?" and I replied "No," there would be a look of surprise, followed by silence and an embarrassed shuffling of feet. Generally, that was followed by the question "Can you navigate?", to which I had to give the truthful answer, "No." More shuffling of feet and discreet coughs. Usually the meeting came to an abrupt end after that. None of my interviewers ever commented on my deficiences, they just said that they would let me know, and a few days later I would get a very polite letter turning down the proposal to sponsor me.

Without sponsorship, it looked bleak until I met Brian Cooke. Brian was a bank manager and I met him when I gave a talk about my experiences of rowing across the Atlantic to a group of his colleagues. He was a keen sailor himself, and had taken part in the Single-Handed Transatlantic Race, and Brian in turn introduced me to Mr R. A. G. Nierop from Westfield Engineering Ltd, who agreed to loan me his Kingfisher 30 for my venture. Again, Neville was positive. We fitted the boat out for the voyage at my expense, I got a few sailing and navigation lessons and Neville gave me a crib sheet to follow to enable me to work out my position from a sun sight. Before then, I had assumed I'd have to know all about astro-navigation to work out where in the world I was, but that wasn't Neville's approach. It didn't matter that I didn't understand the theory, he informed me, all I had to know was how to use a sextant and a few books of tables to arrive at the correct information.

The plan after that was simple: I just set off from the River Hamble, near Southampton. Neville sailed in front of me in his boat and when he tacked, I tacked; when he pulled the sails in, so did I. When we got past the Needles, he wished me bon voyage, waved and turned back. That evening, out in the fringes of the shipping lanes of the Channel, I was so exhausted from the exertions of getting ready and finally leaving, that I set the self-steering gear, turned on the light at the masthead and went to bed. I awoke at dawn, with the boat careering along down-Channel, and extinguished the one little white light I believed had been keeping me safe and visible to ships all night. That memory gives me a chill of horror.

On that Round the World Race, the navigational aim was to try to locate Madeira. If my navigation worked out, I would carry on; if not, I was to turn round, sail back and start looking for Britain. At Ushant, at the north-west corner of France, I decided not to pass south through the channel because I didn't know much about navigation buoys. It was a beautiful day, sunny and flat calm and, as the boat drifted listlessly offshore at the whim of the tide, I thought to myself that it would be a good idea to prepare for a gale. So, in fictitiously dreadful conditions, the wind built and I changed to smaller and smaller sails, until I was drifting along under storm jib and trysail. As I was feeling pleased with my accomplishment, a big ship passed close by and I could see the officers standing on the bridge peering at my boat with astonished interest. I can still imagine the Captain looking at this little yacht with the smallest possible scrap of sail up on a beautifully balmy, windless day and saying to his officers: "By God, chaps, he's not taking any chances!"

When I got into the Roaring Forties south of Africa, I discovered that the little boat couldn't track. She kept broaching in the huge seas and at one stage I broached three times in one hour and eleven times in one day. For a while, I thought this was normal, just part of the trials of sailing, but eventually it dawned on me that my yacht would not be able to stand up to the seas. My self-steering gear had broken countless times, until every replacement servo blade had been used, and I faced the prospect of hand-steering the rest of the way. Commonsense prevailed. I abandoned the voyage.

My wife Maureen flew out to South Africa to meet me and help me sail the boat back, but instead of an overjoyed welcome, she was angry that I hadn't done what I set out to do. "Why didn't you carry on?" she demanded. I answered that the boat couldn't sail round the world that way, to which her reply was: "Well, if it wouldn't go one way, why didn't you turn round and go the other way?" I was still so naive that I'd no idea why I couldn't have done that. To me, it was a terrific idea and I made a note to plan that route when I got back to England.

By the time we reached England, Robin Knox-Johnston had become the first man to sail round the world non-stop, so the plan was settled: I would sail the other way, against the prevailing winds and currents. The British Steel Corporation agreed to sponsor me, perhaps because I made it seem so easy. You leave Britain, I told them, sail south through the doldrums, over the equator, down the eastern seaboard of South America, turn right at Cape Horn, pass Tasmania, turn right again at the Cape of Good Hope and then you sail back home. Not particularly difficult at all, I told them.

In 1969, I began to plan in earnest to sail the "wrong way" round the world. After negotiating British Steel's backing, I left Southampton on 18 October 1970 in the 59-foot ketch, *British Steel*, to attempt the first non-stop solo circumnavigation of the world against the prevailing winds and currents. The venture was so dismissed at that time that it came to be referred to as "the impossible voyage".

The unexpected scale of the welcome I received when I returned to Southampton after 292 days at sea changed my perspective. Thousands of people cheered *British Steel* into Southampton, and the reception held for me by their Royal Highnesses Prince Philip, Prince Charles and Princess Anne, and the then Prime Minister, Edward Heath, was the beginning of an unforeseeable sequence of events and opportunities. I knew I had to capitalise on the public and media interest that had been generated.

Two years later, I sailed round the world again, in the first Whitbread Round the World Race, skippering the 77-foot ketch *Great Britain II*, sponsored by "Union" Jack Hayward, and I took with me a crew from the Parachute Regiment whom I had trained specially. We set the fastest elapsed time for a circumnavigation, sailing with the winds and currents this time, and finished in 144 days, 10 hours, 31 minutes and 29 seconds. This record demolished, just as my lone voyage had done, the cozy image that sailing is a skill that takes a lifetime to cultivate.

With hindsight, I see this race as the beginning of the ideas that formed the British Steel Challenge. Most of my crew of paratroopers had no sailing experience whatsoever before I recruited them, but they had a common denominator: they were already very fit, they were determined, and they were disciplined. The idea that this could be done with civilians did not occur to me for many more years, but the process of training and motivating them turned out to be similar.

That race had emphasised, yet again, the dangers of ocean racing. On the third leg, between Auckland and Cape Horn, one of my crew, Bernie Hosking, fell over the side. We had just changed from a spinnaker to a boomed-out No 3 yankee and had hanked on a number four in case the wind rose yet further. As Bernie helped to lash the sail, one of the sail ties got caught in the hanks. Bernie tugged at it, but as he did so, the boat fell from the top of a wave into a trough and the hanks of the yankee eased in the lull at the base of the next wave. Bernie jerked at the tie and in so doing toppled backwards over the side. In those freezing temperatures, he probably died in a matter of minutes. We turned round and searched for four hours, but never recovered him. That is one of the most searing of all my memories, and the question of what else I could have done will echo in my mind again and again for the rest of my life. From that time, safety has been almost an obsession.

After that Whitbread Race, I won the two-handed Round Britain Race with Rob James in 1978 and finished second to him in 1981, first sailing the 54-foot trimaran, *Great Britain IV*, and later a 65-foot trimaran, *Brittany Ferries*. Then, a second of the elements that were to contribute to the British Steel Challenge was forged. This time, I had *Great Britain II* again and was to enter her in the 1977/78 Whitbread Race, with Rob James as skipper. Although the notion of owning a yacht conjures an impression of easy wealth, it more accurately indicates enormous expense. There were, for example, mooring fees to be paid, never-ending and costly maintenance to be done, sails to be made or repaired, yet the money I was making as a would-be adventurer was quite small.

Thus, to enter the yacht in the Whitbread Race, I had two choices: either I found a sponsor or I worked out some other way to pay the bills. Since Jack Hayward had supported me so loyally, I was keen not to change the name of the boat, and that precluded corporate sponsorship. So instead we asked the crew to pay towards the costs. Later, this was to be another element of the British Steel Challenge.

In 1981, I sailed in my second Whitbread Race, in what had been *Great Britain II*, then renamed *United Friendly*. After that, I moved to multihulls, such as *Brittany Ferries* and *Great Britain IV*. Attempts to break records have always had a special attraction and in 1984 I set off with Eric Blunn on a voyage from San Francisco to New York to try to beat the fastest ever passage made in the great days of sail trading – the eighty-nine days and twenty-one hours set by *Flying Cloud*. Unfortunately, it ended in disaster. *Beefeater II*, our 54-foot catamaran, capsized off Cape Horn and Eric and I spent nineteen hours in savagely cold water before rescue.

I was beginning to have serious reservations about the number of people being killed on racing catamarans and trimarans. I began to be critical, too, about the high-tech way they were being developed, so that they needed bigger and bigger budgets. So, I left multihull sailing and embarked on projects that led to the British Steel Challenge. I enjoy sailing all kinds of boats and still sail, although I have had less time to do so in the last few years. In any case, I have never seen sailing as a hobby; it has always been a job and a way of life for me.

Of all the enterprises I had been involved in before the British Steel Challenge, however, it was the adventurous spirit of my solo circumnavigation and the Whitbread Race I'd sailed with my crew of paratroopers that I most savoured. They had proved something important, not just to me, but to the sailing world in general, and the idea occurred to me that I could combine what was most extraordinary about both. Fate, or whatever governs these things, eventually played its part in hastening me to do something about organising a race the wrong way round the world.

In 1987 I was asked to do some consultancy work. The task was to find out for a potential sponsor how much it would cost them to run a campaign for the Whitbread Round the World Race. The first thing they needed to know was what sort of boat was eligible and what the rules of the next race would be, so I called up the Whitbread organisers and asked for a copy of the race rules. "Yes, of course," was the reply, "just send us a cheque for £200." I couldn't believe it – I wasn't even taking part in the race. Couldn't they send me photocopies, I asked. "No, I'm afraid not. The race rules cost £200."

That attitude made me furious. I was enquiring for a potential sponsor and supporter of the Whitbread Race and I still couldn't get basic information at a reasonable price. So much for wanting to open up sailing to all! In that moment of indignation and fury, I decided to run my own race around the world.

The first people that I turned to, late in 1988, were Andrew Roberts and Helen Wybrow. Andrew had run his own boatyard in Dartmouth and it was he who worked on all my boats. He is also a very experienced sailor and racing yachtsman, having sailed thousands of miles over many years. Helen had worked with me since 1985 when she became my assistant for, as she thought, six months or so. Helen is highly qualified and a great asset to the business, and her job gradually expanded. Since then, she has worked with me on projects such as the Virgin Atlantic Challenge and the Silk Cut Multihull Challenge. She is a stickler for detail, and has always tempered my ideas.

Helen and Andrew had known me for long enough to groan when I announced that I had hatched another plan. Nevertheless, they met me in July 1989 at Mayflower Marina in Plymouth and as we began to discuss what might work and what definitely would not, their enthusiasm grew. We would follow the classic route, we decided, south down the Atlantic, round the Cape of Good Hope and across the Southern Ocean to Cape Horn before turning north to set a course for Europe.

The factor that would really set this event apart from every other in the history of ocean racing was at the heart of the plan. When I selected that team of paratroopers with little or no experience of sailing and trained them specifically for ocean racing, it had reasserted my belief that determination and single-mindedness are the qualities that matter most. No guts, no glory. This time I would apply the same reasoning.

Apart from a professional skipper on each yacht, the crews would be made up of men and women from all walks of life. To make that possible, the crew volunteers would have to pay towards the costs, but it was important to me that the main qualification for a berth would not be the ability to buy it. I wanted to open this opportunity up to people who, first and foremost, had the enthusiasm and will to go, whatever obstacles they encountered.

Andrew and I decided on steel boats. Given the exacting sailing these freshly trained crews would be doing, along a route sometimes scattered with partly submerged ice, steel was the logical material from which to build the fleet. To save money, we opted for identical boats in a one-design fleet. It is the customised gear that makes boats in the Whitbread Race or the America's Cup so expensive, as they strive to use lighter equipment to gain advantage over their competitors, and we could not afford to do that. The equipment we used would have to be standard production gear and, even at this early stage, Andrew and I decided that we would supply the builders with almost all the necessary fittings and materials.

As he considered the options, Andrew came up with a brilliant idea. He argued that we should base the design of the boat round a 66 self-tailing winch, the biggest top-action winch in standard production and the upper limit before one has to fit highly expensive coffee-grinder winches to enable crews to handle their sails. His reasoning was that the primary winches, as the powerhouse of the boats, would put in place all the other parts of the jigsaw: the maximum line rating of the winches would determine the sail size, the sail size would determine the displacement, the displacement would, in turn, determine the waterline length, and the length would define how many berths we would have. The idea was simple, yet ingenious and was to be the foundation of the design. Furthermore, a one-design fleet had other great advantages. It would mean that every yacht would have an equal chance of winning; there would be no incalculable advantage to be gained by one designer over another. Nor would there be any advantage to be gained by the sponsors with the biggest budget, who might otherwise equip their boats with the most expensive gear; the strict class rules of a one-design fleet would ensure a standard specification and level-pegging for all the entrants.

All the basic ideas for a presentation to a potential sponsor were in place, with the exception of perhaps the most vital of all – money. I contacted Greg Bertram, an accountant who was a very keen ocean racer and who had sailed with me in the Atlantic Triangle Race from St Malo in France to Cape Town, where one joined the annual Cape to Rio race before returning to St Malo. I asked him to do some costings for a fairly low-key event, explaining that not much money was going to be spent on this race; we could not ask companies to invest great sums of money to have their names on the side of our boats. We worked out that we could run the event with sponsors paying £225,000 each and crew paying a reasonable sum.

From Andrew's calculations and Greg's figures, we determined to build boats of about 65 foot: beamy, big volume yachts that would be cutter-rigged and would have a deck saloon. In order to minimise our costs and make fitting out and maintaining the boats simple, we would create an interior which, while basic, would have comforts far greater than you would ever find in a contemporary racing yacht. The engine would have to be simple, but good. A seaworthy boat was essential and we had to ensure the engine power, fuel and fresh water capacity provided the necessary self-reliance. These boats would be venturing far out into forlorn expanses of water, and there was always a chance they might need considerable reserves.

The other fundamental consideration was the resale of the boats, for this was the financial underpinning of the entire venture. The ability to find another use for the fleet of yachts after the race was vital for our business: boats that would have resale value afterwards were at the heart of the project's viability. As we thought out what we needed, we consulted brochures of the successful standard charter boats available, such as the Ocean 60 and the Swan 65, all of them long-legged cruising boats.

However, all the boats we looked at were bluewater boats and, although ours would have to be sailed with relative ease by people who would not be professionals, the design would also have to be capable of standing up to the most vicious conditions. There were lessons from the old *British Steel*, the 59-foot ketch that had been designed for my circumnavigation by Robert Clark, but she had been tailored to a single-handed voyage, whereas for the British Steel Challenge to be viable, there would have to be a fairly large crew. For this race the yachts would be bigger and Andrew and I did not feel that a ketch design would be suitable. With its second mast and additional deck gear, it would be too expensive and complicated. The design had to be a sloop or cutter.

Andrew's good ideas were crucial and he had the expertise to turn the basic idea from blueprints into reality. His experience of all aspects of design and building is unrivalled and I recognised that the British Steel Challenge was going to need the sort of innovative ideas and solutions that are his hallmark. He understood the type of boats that could withstand the pounding they would get in the race and still return at the end of the event in good condition. The designer had to be someone who also appreciated what the boats and crew would have to go through, and Andrew was keen to use someone who had experience of one-designs as well. Yet although the boats had to be sturdy and no corner could be cut where safety was concerned, we needed to produce them at a reasonable cost.

The glamorous end of ocean racing provided us with few useful lessons. Racing design had moved off into a different arena to the one we visualised, and our race required a designer who could go back to some of the basics of all-round performance and draw us a boat that would sail resolutely and be weatherly rather than fast; seaworthy and robust, as opposed to lightweight.

After Andrew Roberts and I had gone over every desired characteristic of the boat we required, David Thomas was approached and given a precise design brief. David is a respected naval architect who has some of the most enduring and popular one-designs in the world to his credit. He was responsible, for instance, for the Sigma 33, 36 and 38, which are raced in great numbers in the UK. Our one reservation was that David had not been responsible for any large one-designs, but I didn't think there would be that much difference. Andrew was not so convinced and there was a lot of discussion before David was finally given the contract and produced preliminary drawings.

Four months after Andrew, Helen and I had met in Plymouth, fate intervened. In October 1989, I had a phone call from Ron Melvin, director of information services at the newly privatised British Steel plc, who asked me to meet him for lunch to discuss a proposal that had come across his desk that day. Ron and I had first met in 1971, after I had completed the voyage in the yacht *British Steel*, but our paths had crossed only occasionally since then. What he told me when we sat down to lunch in Soho that day struck me immediately as the clearest sign that the time had come for my idea of a new race. Ron had been asked if British Steel plc would be willing to sponsor one of the yachts about to compete in the annual Round Britain Race and he wanted my views on that, as well as on the whole question of a sea-going spectacular in which the company could participate.

For more than a decade, the British Steel Corporation had laboured under the bleakest of public images, born of huge financial losses and the painful bouts of massive redundancies that accompanied them. They had fought back, however, and become one of the acknowledged leaders of industry. As a privatised company, British Steel needed to shake off its old reputation and establish a rejuvenated image. To both Ron and me, the possibility of renewing our successful association seemed like a good starting point for discussion.

The idea for sponsoring a yacht in the Round Britain Race was quickly discarded. We agreed that it was too brief and not imaginative enough to capture public attention. I mentioned that we were working on a project – a round the world yacht race – and I outlined the idea. As a former journalist, Ron quickly saw the potential of the event, even at that early stage, but as we talked the idea began to take quite a different twist. What if we turned the route of the race around and made it a contest between a one-design fleet racing the wrong way round the world? Would it be possible to follow roughly the same route I had sailed in 1970 and thus mark the twenty-first anniversary of my voyage?

The idea was exciting and the possibilites for publicity enormous. However, the question remained after the meeting had finished: could we really send people down into the Roaring Forties, the Furious Fifties and the Screaming Sixties, to sail against the wind? And even if we could do it, confident of success, would people dismiss the idea as an impossible, crazy idea? No-one besides me had ever done a "wrong-way" non-stop circumnavigation, and for a very good reason – it is still the toughest, most arduous and longest route round the world. Could we convince anyone that this race really could be done?

I returned to Hampshire and talked the new proposal over with Andrew and Helen. The boats we had already envisaged were well capable of the trials they would have to endure on this route and when we examined the logistics of such a race, we all agreed: we were sure that it could be done. I believed that the reality of sailing into the prevailing winds would not be such a battle as it seemed. After all, when the idea of the Single-Handed Transatlantic Race from Plymouth to Newport, Rhode Island was first discussed in 1958, the question that caused most debate was: could yachts race across the Atlantic to windward? The perception of adversity was so great that only five boats entered the first race, and when the ace French yachtsman Eric Tabarly took part in – and won – the second, his comments were a surprise to everyone who had followed the race. He had not been sailing on the wind most of the time as expected, he reported, but had been able to close reach much of the time, making better speeds and being able to lay the shortest course along the Great Circle route to Newport. I thought it would be the same in the Southern Ocean. Casting my mind back, I didn't remember being hard on the wind all the time, tacking back and forth interminably to cover the distance in the right direction. My memories matched with Tabarly's experience: the wind varied enough to let me make good progress, even when its prevailing direction was exactly opposed. Yet if the race was perceived to be impossible, then quite simply it was. What we had to do was to convince sponsors that the race was difficult, but achieveable.

Another issue we discussed in depth was the stopovers along a different route. Three criteria were important, first that the ports should be sheltered and safe havens for the yachts, secondly that they should be interesting, lively places that would appeal to everyone's imagination and, thirdly, that they were places where the companies involved could do business. We had to try to keep the lengths of the legs roughly equal, so the first stop had to be in South America, before the boats rounded Cape

Horn. São Paulo was the ideal place to stop from a business perspective, it had no proper port. I wanted the race to stop in Rio, where the Whitbread Race used to go, because it was exuberant and exotic, with Copacabana Beach, the statue of Christ on Corcovado, the Sugar Loaf Mountain and the excitement of Brazil.

There might be problems with stopping in Rio, however. We had all had a good time there, but the Whitbread Race had ceased to stop there since 1973. The Yacht Club is massive by British standards, and stands on a thirty-acre site in the shadow of the Sugar Loaf Mountain, but it is more a social club than a sailing club. There are dinghies, racing yachts and sport fishing boats, but the members' interests also include backgammon, chess, bridge and rally driving. They have their own bank, souvenir shops and restaurant in this haven from the sometimes grim reality of the city.

In 1973, the stopover coincided with the carnival, and all the crews of the Whitbread boats were invited to buy discounted tickets to what the club called a "Hawaiian Night". Strong drink and samba music raged by the poolside that night, with the race crews getting more excitable by the hour. All except the Commodore was in song. He presided over the gathering, resplendent in his uniform of white shirt, white trousers, white shoes, white socks, a white naval tie and a cap adorned with gold braid.

As he walked past the poolside table I was sitting at, a crewmember from another boat rose up and tapped him hard on the shoulder. The Commodore was walking at a brisk pace and, with the momentum he was carrying, slewed off and went full tilt into the pool. I will never forget the expression on his face as he surfaced. The party hushed as he came up and the club members looked aghast as he bobbed comically in the water with his white hat round his ears. After he hauled himself out of the pool, streaming water from every crease of the white suit, the commodore went berserk, screaming and shouting until security guards with dogs came running into the compound to restore calm. The image of international racing yachtsmen has been tarnished ever since and to bring the race to Rio, we envisaged ourselves having to take great pains in presenting our crews as the very best of Corinthian sailors. We need not have worried. When we approached the Rio Yacht Club to discuss hosting the race, they were very keen and easy to deal with.

From Rio, we decided we should go to Auckland, the self-styled "city of sails". New Zealand is the first land mass after Cape Horn along the route our fleet would be taking, and a stop here was logical. From Auckland, we considered a stop at Perth before going on to Cape Town, but on later reflection we decided that if this was to be the toughest yacht race ever, the distances between stopovers had to be at least 6,000 miles. Mauritius was explored as an alternative. However the tourist authorities in New Zealand were not helpful and this, combined with the re-admittance of South Africa into the arena of world trade, caused us to finalise the stopovers to Rio, Hobart and Cape Town. To give the most favourable conditions of the all the hostile options along this route, we decided the start should be in September 1992.

The basic proposal now existed, and Ron Melvin set up a meeting for us with his colleagues at British Steel, but before we could talk to them, every detail of the costs had to be estimated. Once Greg had worked them out, right down to figures for our company's overheads, we were ready to take them to British Steel's headquarters, on the banks of the Thames, in London. We knew that all the ingredients of the race would appeal to British Steel, at least in theory, and the uniqueness of the basic idea and the public relations potential it represented was sure to be alluring. British Steel could capitalise on their long association with me and, as the boats would be constructed from steel, they would obviously benefit from an irrefutable demonstration of the strength and versatility of their product.

We figured that, provided British Steel were prepared to make the necessary contribution to kickstart the event, we could then seek to market the crew places and sponsorship of each competing yacht. Every potential crewmember would have to raise about £15,000, (it actually worked out at £14,850 for the complete voyage) but it would be a unique adventure and I was certain that the people I wanted the race to attract would find some way of raising the money. In addition, though, we would also need to sell sponsorship packages for all the boats.

With the number of sponsorship deals around these days, one would think it was easy to get sponsors, but today's market makes them more difficult than ever to obtain. Marketing directors are not satisfied with just a name on a boat or a billboard at a football match, they are continually looking for extra benefits to go with publicity. One needs to offer business-to-business opportunities, benefits for company employees, or team-building and corporate hospitality. Our strength would lie with being able to provide four of these requirements: publicity, corporate hospitality, employee participation through allowing the sponsoring companies to send some crew of their own choosing, and business-to-business opportunities. We had a potentially excellent product to market, and my previous business enterprises and contacts in industry made me comfortable with the prospect of selling the sponsorship.

The proposal to Ron's colleagues at British Steel was received with a great deal of interest, but they had their reservations about our ability to raise the rest of the money we needed. They accepted that we could persuade other businesses to sponsor the yachts, but what they found difficult to believe was that we could persuade 130 people to pay so much of their own money! We, on the other hand, suspected the reverse: that finding the crews would be the easy part and that the difficult part would be the sponsorship of the yachts. What none us us knew then was that the economies of the developed world were about to lurch into the longest and deepest recession since the 1930s. If I had suspected that, or others had, the entire venture would probably have foundered then and there.

We were by now at a stage where we could afford to leave nothing to fate. I've learned that the people who decide on a project may be people you've never met before. In other words, you may have convinced one board member your project is marvellous, but other board members who haven't met you and have a less detailed idea of what you are proposing, are likely to turn the board around to say no and once the refusal has been given, there is seldom any redress.

A board meeting had been arranged to discuss the sponsorship and I was extremely nervous about the outcome, but at the end, I was asked to meet with Dr David Grieves, the Vice-Chairman of British Steel. In this I was fortunate, for Dr Grieves was one of the principal architects of the company's recovery from near extinction to record profitability and was therefore familiar with the benefits of public relations. He had immediately seen the advantages of getting involved. All the same, there was no doubt that my meeting with him, arranged to answer other questions he wanted to put to me, was to be the most crucial of all. If this failed, the Challenge would never happen.

The lunch meeting was to be held in the City of London late in 1988 and I left early – and anxiously – to get there. On my way to the appointment from Hampshire, however, there was an accident on the motorway ahead of me and I was completely stuck for over an hour. That was one of the most frustrating and infuriating hours I've ever spent. Here I was, hopefully about to clinch the biggest sponsorship deal I had ever struck, knowing that if any aspect was seen to fall short – including me – the whole thing was off.

By the time I arrived in London, three hours after I'd set off, I was practically shaking with annoyance and embarrassment. I didn't bother to find anywhere to park, just stopped outside the restaurant, left the car there and ran in. Dr Grieves and Ron Melvin were still there, quietly eating dessert, as I came in puffing and panting. About half an hour of detailed, penetrating questions followed, which I answered as carefully and professionally as possible, but at the back of my mind was the fear that being late would be held against me.

At the end of the lunch, however, Dr Grieves shook my hand amiably. We had the authority to go ahead and organise the British Steel

Challenge, he said. They would be happy to renew the association we had formed twenty years earlier and I could rely on their backing. They were going to be cautious, however, and a clause in the contract that was subsequently signed specified that if less than twenty-five people had signed up within nine months of the announcement of the race, they could withdraw. Our estimate of the number of boats we could find sponsors for ranged from ten to twenty. Our contract with British Steel released them if we could not fund more than five. Nevertheless, I was cock-a-hoop; the wild idea was no longer an abstract fantasy.

Dr Grieves left me outside the restaurant and, as I watched his car disappear into the city traffic, I saw the slow, calculated progress of a traffic warden towards my own. I shot across the road, leapt into the driving seat before the man had a chance to bring out his pen and drove off.

Back at Petersfield, I reflected on the success of the venture so far. The British Steel Challenge was going to be not just a race, but a major event, and would demand withdrawal from all my other business interests. Thanks to Dr Grieves's endorsement of the plans, I no longer thought it risky to put all my eggs in one basket, nor would it be too difficult to postpone lesser projects. But what about the other people I wanted to join the Challenge team, Andrew, Greg and Helen, for example? I would also be asking them to take calculated leaps of faith.

It was clear to me that I needed Andrew Roberts on the team and, to be honest, it never occurred to me that he mightn't want to join. Andrew, however, had different ideas. He had just finished selling his business and, after years of working incredibly long hours, was looking forward to a well deserved six months off. When I asked him to become part of the team, he didn't respond with the enthusiasm I'd expected; he just groaned and shook his head. For the second time in less than a week, the project's foundation looked a little shaky.

I've never been one to take no for an answer and wanted to know how on earth he could turn down a project as exciting as this. I think Andrew believed that this would be another seven-days-a-week job, but I convinced him to come and work for the term of the British Steel Challenge. I suppose now that it is over, I owe Andrew an apology, for, like everyone else involved – the race team as well as all the crews – it most definitely has been a seven-days-a-week commitment!

Now all we had to do was to find the companies to sponsor each boat and, most importantly of all, to find men and women adventurous and determined enough first to learn to sail and then to sail round the world. I had talked myself into running the toughest yacht race ever, but it was not just the riskiest and most exciting venture of my life – it would be the same for everyone who chose to take part.

CHAPTER TWO

GETTING IT TOGETHER

On 3 January 1989, the day before the London Boat Show opened, the British Steel Challenge was announced on the lunchtime and evening television news on ITN and the BBC. The announcers described the race and the boats, and explained that we were looking for people who wanted to take part in the adventure of a lifetime. What they didn't include in the story was the contact telephone number, and the following day the media switchboards were inundated with callers wanting to know how to apply. Even the Royal Yachting Association received enquiries, although they were nothing whatsoever to do with the event.

Carol Randall, a journalist from Peterborough, was at a friend's house when she saw the News at Ten. "I was captivated by the thrill of such a trial of endurance and competitiveness," she recollects. "That was it. I got on the phone to British Steel the next morning to find out all the details." Don Deakin was staying in a hotel in the course of doing business, and when he heard the news story his reaction was even more immediate. "I phoned my wife and asked: 'Did you see the story about the round the world race on the news?' She said: 'Yes, I did. And yes, you can.'" At eighteen years of age, Justine Cotton was one of the youngest applicants. She was then at university, but as soon as she saw the news, she telephoned her father, who had some connections with British Steel. Her question was not whether she should do the race but how to go about getting selected. "I thought it was great," her mother says. "Not knowing much about sailing or the perils involved, I was enthusiastic."

Simon Clarke, a director of a small skiing holiday company, had been reading the autobiography of Sir Ranulph Fiennes when he heard about it. "At the time, I was disillusioned," he comments, echoing many other volunteers' sentiments. "I didn't like London. The work I was doing was monotonous and I could see myself doing the same thing in ten years' time." Anxious for an adventure to emulate Fiennes's, Simon applied.

When, eventually, we got all the enquiries through British Steel and sent out application forms we had almost a thousand potential crewmembers. We weren't going to need more than 200, even allowing for people who signed on for just one leg of the race, or for those who dropped out during training. We immediately whittled the list down to about 250 people, all of whom I would interview. Once we had sorted them out into geographical areas and arranged to interview them at central locations, I then had to address the problem of how we would choose between all the applicants. Clearly, it would be subjective and I accepted the fact that one's mind is made up about people within the first few minutes of a meeting. But I was also concerned to get across what the Challenge meant. These interviews were to be a two-sided exchange, after all, and I wanted everyone I met to understand straightaway something of what they were letting themselves in for. It was as much a chance for them to ask questions of me, as for me to interview them.

I realised that I couldn't treat these meetings as if they were job interviews. Some people just don't interview well, and allowances had to be made for that. What I was really looking for above all was enthusiasm for the project. It didn't matter to me one iota whether they had ever sailed, or had even been on a boat before, but somehow they had to infect me with their enthusiasm.

I remember interviewing Lisa Wood, a former Wren who had been invalided out of the service after she had been severely burned and spent eight months in hospital. She was working as a care manager in an old people's home when I interviewed her. The meeting was held at the Royal Ocean Racing Club in London and within a short time she had convinced me of her determination and suitability. While I was waiting for the next candidate to arrive, I heard frantic shrieks and cries from the street outside. I looked out, and there was Lisa jumping up and down and whooping with delight, to the bemusement of businessmen in the offices nearby.

One of the more unusual interviews was with Mark Lodge, who fitted suspended ceilings. Mark lived in Essex but, as he was self-employed, it was not easy for him to take time off work. So, I agreed to meet him near his home, and we held the interview in his van, in a car park just off the M25 motorway. Like Lisa, Mark struck me within minutes as just the sort of person we wanted on the Challenge and the meeting was short.

When it came to people I didn't think suited, I made an early mistake that I learned not to repeat. The first man I decided not to offer a place to, I foolishly told so. There followed an argument that became more and more heated. Why was he not right for the Challenge? What were my reasons for turning him down? Did I not realise how suitable he was? There really were no satisfactory answers to these questions; it was simply a case of instinct. From then on, if I felt comfortable with someone, I offered them a berth there and then. If not, they were told they would hear from me by post.

When I had considered all the people who had applied, I found I had turned down thirty or forty for various reasons. In some cases it was a perceived lack of commitment; in others a shortage of time to spend on training. One or two gave me the impression that they were too highly qualified and experienced in sailing, and wanted to step on at the end of the training programme and give us some advice on how to do it. That attitude made me wary, as I knew that it would be a continual disruption for the rest of the volunteers.

In a couple of cases, I turned people down because of money – not that they couldn't get the sum together, but that it came a little too easily. One man, a banker, just wanted to pay the cheque, turn up and go off on the voyage – the money was almost irrelevant to him. Much more often, volunteers admitted they didn't have a clue how they would raise the £15,000, but I invariably accepted their applications. Tenacity, determination and resourcefulness impress me, and those attributes we needed in plenty. All the same, at every interview I tried to make it plain how difficult it was going to be to make the payments. For many of the crew volunteers, it was as much of a struggle as I had feared. Lisa Wood, for example, sold most of her possessions, piece by piece, to make the instalments until she had reached components of her car. She tells the story of raising the money to get down from Surrey to Plymouth for a training session by selling the spotlights of her Mini.

At the interviews, I tried to prepare everyone for the enormous difficulties they would inevitably face in saving the money, getting sponsorship or making sure their families would be provided for while they were at sea. Perhaps the warning was of some use; in any case, a worldwide recession bit in 1990 and money was scarce. In one year, Lisa wrote over 200 beseeching letters to companies for personal sponsorship. There were examples of managing directors who contributed £10 or £50 from their own accounts, being unable to donate any of their companies' money, but most requests were politely rejected. Justine Cotton also wrote scores of letters asking for assistance, realising how unfair it would be to press her parents. "In those pre-recession days we were fairly well placed and we felt we could help out with the money. As it happened, we needed to," her mother admits. Justine raised as much of the £15,000 as she could, and had to cope with living away from home, studying and training at the same time.

A few people were extremely apprehensive about the interview. They worried about what I might ask them, believing that I would want them to tell me the answers to all kinds of technical questions, or that I was going to test their sailing knowledge. But my questions were rarely technical. Mostly they were personal, and drew some amusing answers. A husband and wife applied to go on the race and when I asked the man if he would want to go to sea on the same boat as his wife, his reply was; "Oh yes, very much indeed." When I interviewed his wife, however, her reply to the same question was: "Like hell I do!"

Scores of people had turned up to apply at the Boat Show, at the small stall we had taken at International Paint's stand. After watching our video, an Irishman called O'Connell came over and said he would like to sign up. I looked at him with interest; he had long hair and a pony tail, and was of slightly larger build than me. Trying to determine whether or not he would be right for the Challenge, I asked him if he had ever done anything gung-ho before. He stood still and looked thoughtful for a minute, then replied in a deadpan voice: "Well, I've ridden in the Grand National three times." I burst out laughing and said: "Right, you're the man!"

Roy Meakin's story was also unusual. Roy was from Nottingham, twenty-four years old, quiet, shy and not especially well-educated. He was certain he'd blown it when he met me for the first time at his interview. Roy had long hair and an earring, and when he walked into the room he came face to face with a yachtie in a reefer jacket. We talked for three-quarters of an hour or so, and I felt that this was something he could do. Even so, I knew it would not be easy. Roy had been a lifeguard, but he had endured a long period of unemployment and all the ebbing morale that accompanies it. Saving the money was an obvious hurdle, but I thought that if Roy could somehow be given a kick start, he would manage.

It so happened that I had been asked to give a lecture in the Nottingham area, an invitation I had to turn down, but I phoned the club and told them that if they would pay a lecture fee of £500, I would come and give a talk. They agreed, and the arrangement was that the fee would be given not to me, but to Roy, and that he would come along to be awarded a bursary. It was not until Hobart that Roy learned from talking to a *Daily Mail* journalist how the £500 had come his way. That award gave him the confidence to raise the rest of the money, but I believed that if he had known how it really came about, he might never have made it to the start.

Roy made phenomenal progress and threw everything into preparing for the race. He gradually gained in confidence through his determination to learn more about sailing. Still, there are pitfalls when you start with no knowledge of boats at all. Roy got completely the wrong end of the stick when we sent training manuals to all the crewmembers. We explained how and why sail area is reduced as the wind speed rises, stating that our boats would carry a number one jib in 15–20 knots of wind, a number two jib up to 25 knots of wind and so on. Roy was then so naive that he interpreted this as advice on how to achieve the boatspeed you wanted: hoist the number one jib and you'd go at 15–20 knots!

Once he had mastered the basics, he became a very good hand on a boat, and before our race started was invited to sail in the Round Britain and Ireland Race on *Ocean Leopard*, an extremely fleet 80-foot racing boat. He was fortunate, too, in ending up with John Chittenden as his Challenge skipper, for John saw the same virtues I'd seen and set about encouraging him and a fellow crewmember, twenty-one-year-old Nigel Janes. "Kind of selfishly I wanted to bring those two on and make them watchleaders to build up their confidence," he told me. "If they could walk off the boat with the same self-respect a couple of youngsters from my boat in the Whitbread Round the World Race had gained, I knew I'd feel it was better than any trophy we might win."

Whatever obstacles the younger crews faced, they were of a different order for the married volunteers, and those with families. In some cases, the money came more easily, yet the sacrifice was greater. Most still had to pay the mortgage, even though they would be forfeiting eight months' income. Husbands might be leaving their wives alone for eight months to keep the home fires burning and cope with the strains of caring for children. The fortitude each partner would need was going to be huge, but what amazed us, as we looked on dispassionately, was the loyalty and devotion that went with every decision to take part in the Challenge. Wives, in particular, became very involved and enthusiastic during the four years of the build-up to the start. In many ways, the partners and families of the crew volunteers are unsung heroes of this story.

Employers took a variety of attitudes. When some crewmembers told of their intention to go on the race, their bosses took a positive approach and viewed it as a good way to help them become better people. Others didn't see it that way at all and pronounced that a job would definitely not be kept open. Yet others warmed to the idea that taking part in the race was a demonstration of loyalty; these were the companies that sponsored boats in the race and sent employees to sail in a leg of the event. For them, the benefits in terms of public relations, internal as well as external, were potentially immense.

As we selected the crews, the plans for the yachts were shaping up. It had already been decided that the race would be run with ten competing boats, but Andrew and I agreed that eleven yachts had to be built, the first as a prototype. The first boat, named *British Steel Challenge*, could be used for training and, as it carried the same name as the event, would give the race three years' publicity. Another benefit was that we could assess the prototype boat over 20,000 miles of training. There is always a list of minor improvements and items to be thought out again when you launch a new design and we knew that this one would be no different. There would be no great changes to the overall design, but when a crew of fourteen finally got a chance to sail the boat in all weathers, there might be deck gear to change, or equipment below deck to be altered, as well as small things Andrew's team could tinker with to improve efficiency.

Another consideration was the level pegging of the boats. If we built ten and the first were used for crew training, all the gear on that boat would be used harder and be more fatigued than on the brand new yachts. Also, as the first boat would have to be built two years ahead of the others, it would be impossible to guarantee the production and quality control of the fleet would be uniform, all ten precisely the same weight, exactly the same quality of build. There were a host of variables to consider and the necessity of the boats being absolutely equal was fundamental to the concept of the event. So, we planned for eleven boats.

The next stage was to find a builder. The contract was put out to tender to fourteen yards, then shortlisted to four. Finally, we selected Devonport Management Ltd, which operates from Devonport Dock-yard, the Naval yard in Plymouth. Apart from their very competitive tender, the greatest attraction of DML was the size: this was a boatyard on a grand scale. There are draughtsmen, certificated welders, quality control personnel and engineers all on one site, and they had the re-sources to complete the boats on time.

One thing that worried Andrew and me was that they were a Navy yard and had never built any yachts. We weighed this up and considered that, as this was a straightforward engineering job and DML had skills for tasks which were far more complicated, they could easily construct eleven yachts. We visited the yard and saw examples of their steelwork, with which we were very impressed. As it turned out, their work was excellent; I don't believe anyone else could have done a better job.

Because of the Ministry of Defence environment, we were required to undertake a contractual obligation to supply accurate drawings before any work started. This was fine by us. Many yacht designers like to add refining touches to a design as it progresses, but by having this ruled out for us, we avoided an escalation of costs. So Thanos Condylis of C&S Yacht Designs and his assistant, Nick Pike, used their experience and considerable computer-aided design skills to develop detailed ideas and quickly generate the many drawings required.

The first yacht began building in September 1989, in a special jig system developed by DML to allow three hulls and two decks to be constructed at one time within the tight tolerances we needed. Once the hull was constructed, it was placed on its keel and moved into a portable building so that the steelwork could be shot-blasted, faired and painted.

Early on Andrew instigated rigorous inspection procedures and the final handover checklist amounted to over fifty pages. Safety considerations had always been paramount, for we had to consider that the race was potentially dangerous. Every aspect of the design and fit-out was examined and re-examined to reduce the risks. We paid particular attention, for example, to the problems of moving around at sea, on deck and below, for there was potential there for injury. The result of that concern was a large number of grabrails, handholds and "fences". Likewise, the safety inventory had to be considered and tested thoroughly. By the launch of the fleet, we had an inventory of safety equipment far in excess of Department of Transport, Whitbread or Offshore Racing Council regulations; indeed, it was probably more comprehensive than has ever been specified for any other true ocean race.

On 5 April 1990, Her Royal Highness The Princess Royal, who we were lucky to have as patron of the British Steel Challenge, gave the first boat the name of the event. We now had a boat and were ready to train the crew. We had chosen the 160 crew we needed for the race (see Appendix II) and to cover for anyone who had to drop out. They were from all manner of backgrounds, with very different personalities and abilities, and from twenty to sixty years of age. There were surgeons, farmers, students, company directors, and over seventy per cent had never sailed before. The one thing in common was that these were ordinary people with a desire to do something extraordinary.

We advertised for a skipper to follow through the crew training and were lucky to get Pete Goss, a former Royal Marine commando who had taught sailing at the Joint Services Sail Training Centre in Plymouth. He had sailed the Two-Handed Transatlantic Race in 1986 and the Single-Handed Transatlantic Race in 1988, and was clearly an accomplished ocean racer. Pete is also a natural leader and one of his most impressive qualities is that he exudes confidence; he was to gain instant respect for his knowledge and seamanship from everyone who sailed with him. He is also the best person I have seen handling a yacht under power, with the possible exception of Andrew Roberts. His being an ex-Royal Marine did not impress me, as a paratrooper, but I was prepared to overlook the misfortune!

Pete's task was truly formidable: he had to familiarise the volunteers with sailing and with the boat, and train them to a basic but sound level of competence. "What I wanted to do was to teach them seamanship," he recalls, "not just how to do knots, but the philosophy of it." That philosophy evoked self-sufficiency within a team and a need always to look ahead and plan for what might happen next. That ethos was essential for the testing conditions that lay ahead in the Western Approaches of Britain in winter, where they would be doing their training, let alone in the race itself.

First, though, the basic skills had to be imparted. There was a whole new vocabulary to acquire and even apparently straightforward things had to be learnt. The toilet had to be referred to as "the heads"; after that came the instructions on how to flush it! Pete had to teach the volunteers the correct way to get on board a yacht, and why you shouldn't arrive with a suitcase because there is no way of getting it below deck and nowhere to stow it.

Over the winter months of 1990, Pete took groups of crew out from Plymouth, round a triangle in the Western Approaches for five days at a time, working from a training brief that we had compiled together. The training was intense because Pete wanted to simulate ocean passage-making, introducing everyone to watch systems and giving them an idea of how a boat handled at sea and what it was like to live aboard. In the race, there would be no stopping because of bad weather, and the intention was to start as we meant to go on. A lot of people maintain that there's no tougher weather anywhere than when deep winter depressions sweep westwards across Britain, and winds occasionally as much as 55 knots, lumpy seas and piercing cold were a fitting introduction to what was in store during the race. "I was a firm believer that they ought to get out there and taste rough weather when we could get it for them," Pete says. "I had one course that started with an introduction alongside in the marina and we went straight out into a Force 12 in January."

While sailing presented the crew volunteers with a steep learning curve, it was very much harder for uninitiated friends and relatives to appreciate. For the crews, training to race round the world became ever more central to their lives, to the extent that, as one put it: "I eat, drink and sleep this race. I don't care about anything else." Often the experience could not be shared and it took them, little by little, into a different world. One story, possibly apocryphal, was repeated among the crews with relish. A woman crewmember, asleep and in the grip of a dream, muttered: "Are we tied up yet?" Her bemused husband replied, "No, but we can be if you want!"

Pete knew he had to tread carefully. He understood that he was dealing with something far greater than just job training. It may sound melodramatic, but he recognised that in most cases it was people's lifetime's ambition, and under the tremendous enthusiasm there was awe of what they had taken on and, to some degree, fear of failure. His response was a distillation of the RAF Parachute Training School's motto that knowledge dispels fear.

Each time crews went out they would sail in different groups, as we wanted everyone to get to know each other. Once they had left Plymouth behind, Pete ensured that there was a sail change or course change every twenty minutes, so that sail handling and trimming would be practised again and again. "I remember one day when we did thirty spinnaker gybes and, I think, fifty reefs," he told me. Every time, the emphasis was on safety above all else. Here, Pete found he benefited from having a crew of novices, who had no blasé preconceptions about what you could get away with on a boat. If it was windy or dark, the automatic reaction was to wear a lifejacket and harness. Man overboard routines were gone over repeatedly, so that everyone knew instinctively the procedure to follow. In port the working of the boat was examined in detail: the location of all the seacocks, where every wire and hose in the boat ran, how the engine worked, how the watermaker worked, how to strip a winch, how to repair a sail. Pete's opinion was that it was not only a matter of maintenance; the proper, seamanlike attitude was to have pride in one's boat.

At the same time, he worked on building a confident, positive attitude. Tasks and repairs had to be done as soon as they were needed, no delaying. He kept a book of record times taken for various manoeuvres, such as reefing or gybing, and each successive crew worked to beat the fastest time set by the last. There were inter-watch races to foster a competitive spirit and to add incentive and a feeling of pride to difficult, strenuous jobs. And everyone had to learn to trust the other crewmembers. This Pete did by sending people to the top of the mast in a bosun's chair when the boat was rolling unpredictably at anchor. A chilling fear of heights might have to be overcome and everyone had to learn to put complete trust in the colleagues who were at the other end of the halyard that held them aloft.

Fitness was essential. By Pete's own admission, there were a few overweight people that "really needed knocking into shape – except that they weren't quite aware of what shape meant". Everyone got a copy of guidelines on getting fit and Pete's Plymouth sessions grew notorious, for he gradually intensified the training by getting everyone out of their bunks at 0600 and forcing them to take a swim in Plymouth Sound, even during the winter. Everyone got the message that it was not a holiday as he pushed them as hard as he knew they would be pushed in the Southern Ocean. "I used to let them go and get to sleep for their four hours off watch, wait about forty-five minutes until they were into a really deep sleep and then go and give them a shake and tell them to come on deck to do a sail change. It would be cold and wet, and they would get terribly, terribly tired. Suddenly, then, they realised that they did have to get fit.''

The crews took turns at elementary navigation, such as putting a plot of the yacht's position on the chart and learning how to work it out by dead reckoning. Over the training period, some went on to become quite highly qualified. The regulations laid down by the Department of Transport require two people on each boat to be qualified, so we paid half the costs for some of the crew volunteers to study for the Royal Yachting Association's Yachtmaster Ocean exam. Others also studied seamanship and navigation on formal courses, gaining other RYA certificates.

Throughout Pete looked for leadership abilities and noted skills in learning tasks such as sail-repairing or engine maintenance. A combination of technical sailing ability and leadership was something that Pete had to mark particularly, because people who combined them were to form a nucleus from which watchleaders for the ten boats could be drawn. These would be people each skipper could trust to take all but the most important decisions while he or she was off watch. Everyone took turns at acting the part of watchleader and it produced some surprises; quiet people sometimes came to the forefront and grew in stature, while other seemingly confident people didn't stay calm in their position of responsibility. To our surprise as much as Pete's, the training advanced quickly. One of the first lessons we all learnt about the British Steel Challenge was that this was by no means an ordinary group of people; they needed little stimulation and it was they who pushed the pace.

We were all aware that we were trying to teach a whole new way of life and values that were partly at odds with the throwaway society ashore. In the early days of training a crew would go through the entire ship's supply of water in twenty-four hours – the tankage that was intended to last for two to three weeks at sea. Slowly, everyone began to realise that they couldn't just turn on the tap and let it run while they brushed their teeth, and that you couldn't waste gas when you were cooking. Another element we had to try to get across was that the skills of living in a confined space with thirteen other people have to be learnt, too. Hygiene was extremely important, from the perspective of safety as much as of seamanship. They had to learn to consider their crewmates, to be as tidy as possible, not to be greedy or selfish about food, and they had to learn that the skipper's word was law, whether or not they agreed with it. In short, they all had to comprehend and bow to a different social order aboard the boat, and people who came from a hierarchical or disciplined job possibly found those rules easier to accept.

In October 1991, Ron Melvin retired from British Steel and was succeeded by Charles Lewis which gave me a moment of trepidation in case he lacked Ron's enthusiasm for the Challenge, but I need not have worried. We could not have had a better person to deal with, nor one so supportive. Charles had the knack of involving himself when necessary and of staying away when his presence was not necessary. Even on the second leg of the race, when there was a series of rigging failures and pressures on us were at their greatest, Charles phoned and said, simply: "Look, there's not much I can do, but if you need me I am here. Just tell me your plans and your strategy and I'll let you know what I think." In fact, the rest of the British Steel team: Mike Hitchcock, Brian Richards and Phil Wolfinden, were likewise a pleasure to deal with, and they were tremendously keen to do a good job. We were very fortunate to have had their support.

Early in the summer of 1991, we advertised for skippers and embarked on the lengthy procedure of selecting suitable people. We advertised in all the UK yachting magazines for three consecutive issues, so that no-one who might be suitable could reasonably miss it. The criteria were straightforward: I wanted people who had an RYA Yachtmaster Ocean certificate and who had crossed an ocean as skipper. They had to have some racing experience, and although we recognised that the merit of various types of racing was quite subjective, we wanted candidates to demonstrate some solid evidence of tactical ability. Above all they had to have proven leadership qualities. We were sure we would get plenty of applicants, because it represented a springboard into the world of top professional racing for plenty of keen able sailors.

Within a month, we had had eighty-seven replies. We decided to interview forty-four, from which we began to form an idea of their qualities. I wanted to judge leadership qualities at first hand, and was looking for men or women who had already been in charge of a team. It didn't matter if that team was not a yacht crew; we just wanted to be sure each applicant could bring together diverse people and motivate them to work as one. In the case of Vivien Cherry, for instance, experience as an environmental engineer proved that she was used to leading a team.

Each applicant was asked a series of questions in an interview that lasted about an hour and a half. As I had looked for enthusiasm from the crew volunteers, so I now looked for eagerness from their skippers. With a few people, I was disappointed, for the main interest seemed to be in money. Several appeared to think they were going to be handling a team rather like that of a Whitbread Round the World Race yacht and therefore they should be extremely highly paid. One man actually asked for a salary of £100,000, which I thought was really very funny. Needless to say, he didn't get a job.

Following on from the first interviews, we settled on fifteen candidates. After we'd seen them lead a team of volunteers on a leg of the publicity tour of Britain which we did in *British Steel Challenge*, we narrowed it down to ten. The skippers we chose were Vivien Cherry, John Chittenden, Adrian Donovan, Mike Golding, Pete Goss, Alec Honey, Paul Jeffes, Ian MacGillivray, Will Sutherland and Richard Tudor.

Vivien Cherry, a thirty-two-year-old environmental engineer, was possibly one of the most qualified of the skippers from a racing perspective, but we were later to find that an abrasive leadership style sometimes didn't go down well with her crew. Technically, though, she was sound and nobody questioned her sailing ability or her judgements.

John Chittenden was then fifty-one, a Master Mariner who had won the cruising division of the 1989/90 Whitbread Race. He became the "father" of the skippers and was both very professional and very experienced. His leadership qualities were excellent and he majored on safety. Throughout the training and the race, his crew would have followed him to hell and back.

Adrian Donovan, thirty-three years old, was also a Merchant Navy officer, as well as a Naval architect. He was, without doubt, the most relaxed skipper of the team. He always gave the appearance of being totally at ease and in command, and his crew, like John Chittenden's, worshipped him. The record his crew adopted as their theme tune was Frank Sinatra singing "Nice and Easy", and it seemed to sum up his laidback approach. At the same time, Adrian was indisputably a professional.

Without question the best organised skipper was Mike Golding, a thirty-one-year-old watch commander from the Royal Berkshire Fire and Rescue Service. His boat was always immaculate, his crew well briefed on what they had to do and detailed to get on with their jobs. Mike was to see himself in a supervisory role, which his crew liked.

Alec Honey, forty-eight years old, was a former Paratroop captain and my number one on the first Whitbread Race. He owned a sailing school in France, and I knew from past experience that he was very professional and competitive.

Paul Jeffes, a thirty-nine-year-old naval architect and managing director of Silvers Marine boatyard in Scotland, was also a good leader. As a Naval architect he was well qualified. He had done much inshore racing, and had been successful at it. Paul is a likeable person and crew and corporate guests alike warmed to him.

The quietest of the skippers was Richard Tudor, a thirty-two-year-old sailmaker and rigger from Pwllheli, North Wales. Richard was very competent, an excellent leader and never made a fuss. I always saw his crew doing things as a group, for he had the ability of getting them together as a team on land as well as at sea.

Will Sutherland was forty-six, a former teacher who ran management and leadership training activities, such as sailing and skiing. Will was to prove first-class at corporate hospitality, but failings I had not anticipated began to reveal themselves before and during the race. I'm sorry to say that, by the first leg of the race, my own management skills had been shown to be at fault in choosing him, but it was not until much later on that the facts slowly unfolded. His weaknesses in performing under pressure and in dealing at close quarters with interpersonal conflict were clear by then. In retrospect, I think it may have been part of his teacher's background which made him seem to talk down to his crew.

All the while, we sought sponsors for the ten boats, but even when companies were very nearly at the contract stage, not all our negotiations proceeded according to plan. Our first presentation to Coopers & Lybrand, the accountancy and management consultancy firm, went well and left me feeling reasonably confident. When I was asked to meet again in London three weeks later, I was sure we would have an agreement, because if the answer is no, people usually don't want to see you a second time. So I was astonished when I was told that Coopers & Lybrand had decided not to sponsor the race. The reason, the executive told me, was that they had taken advice from a BBC TV producer, who said that the event would get very little publicity, certainly none on television, and that she thought it unlikely all the necessary crewmembers would part with £15,000. I am still not sure what expertise a producer has to make this analysis, but I'm glad to say that Coopers & Lybrand had the foresight to take the research further.

An even stranger turn of events happened with International Paint. As manufacturers of yacht paints, they were keen to sponsor a yacht in the race, but didn't get the consent of their parent company, Courtaulds plc. By chance, I had to go to Japan on some unrelated business, and I met with an International Paint representative there. During that meeting, he pointed out that his company was deeply disappointed that British Steel hadn't even asked them to quote for the paint needed for two ships being built for British Steel in Japan. Already one ship had been completed and the steelwork was being done on the second of them, but the contract for the painting hadn't been signed. I asked what would happen if International Paint could be put on the quoting list. The representative said he thought it might help us with sponsorship.

When I got back to Britain, I contacted the appropriate person at British Steel, who saw no reason why International Paint should not be on the quoting list. In turn, he contacted someone in Japan, and the outcome was that not only did they get on the list, but eventually were awarded the contract. What little experience I have of Japan led me to interpret it thus: the shipyard took the instruction to include International Paint on the list as a tacit command to favour them and, not wishing to lose face, gave them the contract. That, in turn, meant that we eventually got sponsorship for a yacht, *InterSpray*.

For some time, I had felt sure that an area of business I should go into was pubs in waterfront areas. The best example I have ever seen is Bertie's Landing, at the new Victoria and Alfred Waterfront development in Cape Town, and after seeing it I began to fancy the idea of a Chay's Landing. At the 1992 London Boat Show I went to Teesside Development Corporation's stand to look at the plans and model for the new marina in Hartlepool. It was the perfect place for the pub business, I thought, and the upshot was I also managed to persuade Teesside to sponsor a yacht in the race.

Similar discussions took place with other potential backers until finally we had the ten needed for all the boats. British Steel would sponsor a yacht themselves, to be named *British Steel II*. Commercial Union, the largest UK insurer in Europe, sponsored *Commercial Union Assurance* (shortened by us to *Commercial Union*), Coopers & Lybrand had a yacht bearing their name, and the security organisation Group 4 Securitas sponsored *Group 4 Securitas*. The independently owned UK insurance brokers, the Heath Group, named their yacht *Heath Insured*, and another independent company, brewers Hall & Woodhouse named a boat after their draught lager, Hofbräu Lager. International Paint's entry was *InterSpray*. Another sponsorship agreement was made with Nuclear Electric plc, which owns and operates the commercial nuclear power stations in England and Wales, and an agreement was made with French-owned chemical and pharmaceutical company, Rhône-Poulenc, for a boat of that name. To carry their name across the world, Teesside Development Corporation named their boat *Pride of Teesside*.

Late in 1991, we set about marrying skippers with the ten sponsors. We knew we would have to choose carefully. Training the skippers somehow to accommodate three different sets of demands was going to be difficult. Firstly, each of them was employed by us, yet was leading a crew to whom they had to remain loyal, with complete trust on all sides. The crews never saw themselves as paying clients, but we were aware that they were just that and appreciated that the skippers could well be torn in different directions. And now we were adding the understandable demands from sponsors to pull them in a third direction. So compatibility was going to be important. Hall and Woodhouse were very keen on Pete

Goss, for example, and since they are West Country brewers and Pete a West Country man, we found a link. Mike Golding, we decided, was ideal for *Group 4* (as the name became unofficially shortened to): being a fireman, he would be familiar with the disciplined work in which they were involved. Paul Jeffes was managing director of Silvers Marine, a boatyard in Scotland that specialises in international paint treatments, so he was an obvious choice as skipper of *Interspray*. Coopers & Lybrand wanted a woman skipper, so we assigned Vivien to their boat.

By December 1991, we had assessed every one of the crew volunteers through the training programme. Because we had mixed them as much as possible, everyone had got to know each other, and we were able to build up a profile of each individual and their skills. To foster harmony we let everyone write a list of who they would most like to sail with, and who they would least like to sail with. A few people gave us a long list of people they didn't wish to sail with and we discovered that it was less an indication of how difficult the people on the list were, than of how much that person themselves could be a problem!

Finally selecting the crews took Pete and Helen four days, with some involvement from me later on. We tried to build crews whose strengths and sailing abilities were roughly equal and when we had finished, we put each team into a separate envelope.

Late in December we invited all ten sponsors to join us for Christmas drinks at British Steel's headquarters in London and, like presenters do on all the best game shows, I shuffled up the envelopes and said: "Right, here you are. Come and choose your crew." The skippers were already allocated, now they picked their teams absolutely at random, choosing their envelopes, opening them, not knowing if they would get an engineer, a housewife, a lorry driver, a baker, a photographer or a doctor. I remember that moment as one of the most exciting of all because, from then on, it was up to the sponsor and the skipper together to make the very best use of the opportunites their team offered.

By March 1992 the boats were ready to be launched. The building process had been a culture shock to us as well as to DML; we were a small, hands-on team dealing with a huge industrial company used to Ministry of Defence and Naval procurements, and our contract had been less than one hundredth of their annual turnover. However, the determination of a number of DML employees, especially project manager Andrew Maltby, meant that the boats were completed and launched on time. It was quite an achievement for us all.

At Easter the crews and skippers met for the first time in a marine environment. I don't think any of them will ever forget it. The event signified the beginning of the work-up to the race and everyone knew it was where the characteristics of each crew would be formed and the hard work of fine-tuning each boat and crew would begin in earnest. The launch took place in Brixham, and the atmosphere was unmistakably tense. For one thing, the skippers were nervous, not only about meeting and leading their crews, but about getting behind the wheel of their own big boat for the first time. The boats were larger than some of the skippers were used to, and close-quarters manoeuvring was necessary as they took them over to the fuel berth to fill up with diesel. Vivien Cherry was at the far end of a long jetty, and the task called for her to back the boat all the way down the pier to get room to turn. It was not easy; there was a strong cross wind that was firmly encouraging the bow to fall away, so Andrew Roberts offered to take the boat for her. To Vivien's credit, she graciously refused, but sensibly asked Andrew to come aboard just in case.

Chaos and confusion added to the tension. It was extraordinary that although we had ordered equipment, in some cases almost twelve months beforehand, a number of items still didn't arrive on time. Putting all the equipment on the boats was good experience for the crews; they had to reeve the halyards, sort out mooring lines, blow up the fenders and find a place for everything on their yachts' inventory. That done, the boats left Brixham and made for Southampton. On the way, we planned to get a publicity shot of all ten sailing in close formation off the Needles.

If the first morning at Brixham had been nerve-wracking for the skippers, the day of the publicity photograph was even more so for the organisers. From various points of the compass, the ten yachts converged to a position off the Needles at the appointed time, but as they closed on the western point of the Isle of Wight, a dense bank of fog rolled over the fairway buoy. I had a disturbing vision of ten boats careering towards the buoy in opaque mist, conditions where the chances of an accident were really quite high, but at the last minute, just as they reached the entrance to the Solent, the fog parted. A few minutes after, sunshine broke through the fog bank, and the helicopter carrying a television crew arrived to capture a perfect shot. It augured well.

From that time on crew volunteers turned up for training during their holidays, at weekends and at times when leave from their jobs could be granted to them. Others gradually gave up their jobs to devote all their time to it. I tried to discourage such single-mindedness and wrote a letter to all the crews, exhorting them to keep working until the last minute, knowing full well they would need as much money as possible.

They were all resourceful people, though, and novel ways of raising money for the crew kitty were found. One very successful idea came from Suzanne Emerson, a twenty-eight-year-old computer programmer, who painted a picture of her boat, *Rhône-Poulenc*, and had the painting made into a card. Her plan was to sell the cards to anyone who would support the crew, and send them back from each port of call with a short report of what had happened on the leg. As a result, she got two commissions to paint other people's boats and added more money to the funds.

In the first few months after their assignment to their boats, the crews had to learn quickly to be totally self-reliant. Yet although their confidence continued to grow, it was interesting to observe the reactions to them of more experienced sailors. Gara Hampton, a repair specialist and Naval architect who looked after the maintenance of the boats, found the crews exasperating from time to time.

"They were trying to help," he says now, "but hopelessly lacking in experience of the little things which mean so much to the running and safety of a ship. At first they couldn't understand why the boats couldn't be driven straight out of the showroom, but soon they began to realise that maintenance is an on-going thing. They really didn't know much about the working of the boats. For example, I found one person stripping a galley foot pump to make it work, when all it needed was the valves to the water tank turned on."

As the summer of 1992 progressed, crew volunteers were sent to train with manufacturers in the marine industry to learn more about the equipment on the boats, the maintainance of the sails and all the systems that keep boat and crew going and which count towards winning. Among the companies that helped were Hood Sailmakers, who taught at least one person from each of the boats how to repair sails. Lewmar taught others how to maintain winches and McDougalls ran excellent courses showing how to get the best from the freeze-dried food that we would ship for the race.

By the summer, with two years of intermittent coastal sailing experience behind them, the crews were ready for the long offshore race we had planned. It was time to pit the boats against each other in proper ocean conditions. Apart from the Round Britain and Ireland Race, the most testing and notorious ocean race of them all in British waters is the Fastnet Race, and we chose a variant of this. By setting a 820-mile route from Southampton to Ushant, at the north-western tip of France, round the Fastnet lighthouse off the south-west coast of Ireland and back, the crews would have an ideal chance to prove themselves, sailing on all points of the wind. It was, at the same time, an ideal opportunity to test our equipment and whet the appetites of the press, both those members of the yachting press who had been so sceptical and so volubly dismissive of the whole concept of the Challenge, and the media in general.

Later our plans altered. Perhaps a training race would be better, we reasoned, so that the skippers could concentrate on instructing their crews and not feel there was any pressure to go flat out. But we had under-estimated the competitive resolve of skippers and crew to win and, the night before the race, we found that Mike Golding had added a top sailor from the Whitbread Race on his crew list. He argued that we had said it was not really an official race. So we stuck to our original decision that it was a race, under the auspices of the Royal Ocean Racing Club, and run to International Yacht Racing Union rules, and Mike had to leave his expert on the quayside.

Unbeknownst to us, however, Alec Honey on *Rhône-Poulenc* set off with top French yachtsman, Leon Péan, stowed away on board. In the early hours of the morning before the start, *Rhône-Poulenc* had stolen off to a jetty well away from the rest of the fleet and picked him up. Leon's secret mission was to train the crew in race tactics and strategy, which he had done effectively but it meant the crew had been learning sailing skills, not seamanship skills, and when you are on a long voyage it is seamanship that counts. Later that day, after the boats had cleared the Needles, I called *Rhône-Poulenc* on the radio telephone with a routine question and who should answer but Leon, in an unmistakable French accent. I knew Leon well from the 1985/86 Whitbread Race, when he sailed *L'Esprit d'Equipe*, and there was no disguising his identity from me – the game was up; they were immediately penalised.

In addition to testing the crews during the race, we wanted to try out our contingency plans. We had drawn up a list of exercises so that a fictitious emergency could be given to each crew. Before the skippers left, each was given a sealed envelope with a number on it. Inside were details of an emergency situation that would put them and their crew to the test, and show us how effectively they reacted to the standing orders for such circumstances. Once at sea, we sent the appropriate numbers to each skipper on their telex and, at that moment, their emergency situation began. No-one knew the others' situations, as each skipper carried codes for any messages we didn't want the world at large to know.

One of the situations was the injury of the skipper and one of the crews had to race their boat unaided from the Scilly Isles to the Fastnet and back, which they did successfully. In another fictitious situation, a man had fallen overboard and the crew had to carry out search and rescue drills. To the yacht whose duty it was to maintain communications with race headquarters, we sent a message that all their communications had gone down. In the race proper, a different yacht would be nominated by us every twenty-four hours to take on the responsibility of maintaining communication. On the duty yacht the crew would be responsible for the radio schedule between the fleet, they would relay positions and pass on useful information. Each boat's position would be sent back to us

Richard Tudor and the crew of *British Steel II* were shaping up as one of the most
competitive teams and were definitely out to win the training race.

automatically via their satellite navigation equipment, so the duty yacht's
crew didn't have to worry about that, but they would have to maintain a
constant watch on the international emergency and contact channel,
2128MHz. Most importantly, from our point of view, they had to make
the daily sitrep, or situation report. In this they would report their position, course and average speed, the weather conditions, lists of problems
or defects and anything newsworthy about life on board. Nominating a
duty yacht in this first race meant that we could find out what it would be
like to cope with the predicament of their telex going down in, say, the

middle of the bleak Southern Ocean. The reactions of all the crews to their various "emergencies", however, were proof to us that they could all cope with everything we threw at them in a competent way.

Meanwhile, Richard Tudor and the crew of *British Steel II* were already shaping up as one of the most competitive of the fleet. Richard didn't at all see this as a training race, he wanted to win it. Maybe this was the most effective way of preparing his crew psychologically, of inculcating a winning attitude, but I discovered afterwards, when *British Steel II* were confirmed winners by a large margin, that Richard had helmed the boat for most of the way back from the Fastnet Rock, in heavy downwind conditions. To our minds, however, the name of the game should have been to give the crew practice.

Back on land I found that the Ushant/Fastnet Race had added pace to the preparations for the race proper. It had sharpened competitiveness, but with that came, for the first time, mistrust between crews. The business with *Rhône-Poulenc* and, to a lesser extent, *British Steel II*, had an enormously negative effect on the other crews. *Rhône-Poulenc*'s were looked on as cheats and the subterranean mumblings that came back to us asked: "If they are doing this now, what will they be prepared to do on the race?" Some sponsors also felt aggrieved and complained that the allocation of skippers had been rigged in *British Steel II*'s favour. We tried our best to resolve the ill feeling and banned contributed tactical advice and weather routing during the race.

I also became aware of some bad feeling on *Coopers & Lybrand*. Vivien had a very able crew, which included people like Matthew Steel-Jessop, Neil Skinner and Robert Faulds, who were fairly experienced, and Vivien seemed to feel that they were having trouble taking orders from her. She is a determined person and very competitive. Her leadership style is tough and she demanded high standards when the crew was racing, with an approach that rubbed them up the wrong way. I knew her to be well qualified, however, and I was sure she had the ability to focus her team completely on the race, so I talked to them all, separately and together, to try to promote better communication between them and develop confidence. By the end of the first leg skipper and crew did, indeed, find an equilibrium, but it continued uneasily throughout the race.

Some weeks later I was called upon by Alan Green from the Royal Ocean Racing Club, under whose auspices the Fastnet/Ushant race and the British Steel Challenge itself were being run. He told me that some of the flag officers of the club had heard reports about the inadequacy of the crews in terms of seamanship and were worried that they were ill-prepared for sailing round the world. My hackles rose immediately, for assumptions seemed to have been made, even though none of the detractors had ever sailed with the crews. I offered to meet with Alan Green and one of the RORC's flag officers, Stuart Quarrie, a well-known and respected racing yachtsman, and I pointed out that the crews had just sailed on an offshore race much longer than the Fastnet Race, which is run every other year by the RORC for its members and was the longest race that they ran at that time. Did these crews not, therefore, have the same sort of skills as RORC members, I asked? I also pointed out that many of the crews had Royal Yachting Association qualifications, including a number who had Yachtmaster Ocean certificates, one of the highest qualifications awarded by the RYA. Stuart conceded that the information he had been given was wrong and I left the RORC that day with full backing from the club.

For me, one of the biggest setbacks came a matter of weeks before the start, when Alec Honey resigned from the job as skipper of *Rhône-Poulenc* because his wife had become ill. Oddly, although I had anticipated some of the crew leaving, I had not foreseen any of the skippers quitting, for whatever reason. But the skippers laboured under exactly the same pressures as anyone else, and I had made a big mistake by not lining up replacements. Many well-qualified skippers who had not been selected were now busy elsewhere and I was faced with the first real chink in my vision of how the race would run. With less than two months to the start I had to look for a replacement.

I found just the man in John O'Driscoll, a distinguished Naval officer well used to team leadership, a bomb disposal expert who had earned an MBE. John was embarking on a civilian career and agreed to skipper *Rhône-Poulenc*, but with the proviso that he would take the post subject to the first leg going satisfactorily. I hoped the relationship between him and his crew would be a harmonious one but, as the first leg later proved, the style of command needed was very different to that which John had been accustomed to in the Royal Navy, and it did not suit him.

Most of the crews had given up their jobs by the beginning of September 1992 and were wholeheartedly preparing for the race. Tremendous tension overshadowed the boats as the start got closer. As is always the case in small spaces such as boats, flare-ups and short tempers arose from the most trivial things. Expectancy and optimism existed, but as time passed they were sometimes buried beneath an oppressive air of anxiety. Not for one moment did the crew volunteers imagine, nor did they suggest to friends or relatives, that they had any real notion of what the next eight months would bring. All the same, the books that appeared on a number of the boats told a tale: *Heavy Weather Sailing*, *Survive the Savage Sea* and my own book, *The Impossible Voyage*. Maybe these accounts, they hoped, would hold some clues as to what lay ahead.

CHAPTER THREE

LEG 1:
SOUTHAMPTON
TO RIO

For three years we had all been preparing for that instant at noon on Saturday, 26 September 1992, when Her Royal Highness The Princess Royal would fire the starting gun. A week's festivities in Southampton, with special dinners given by sponsors to their crews and the round of parties and celebrations that are some of the traditional high points of sailing events, masked the anxiety – but only just.

Last minute worries took hold of the skippers as well, as they made sure again and again that their boats were ready for sea. There was fevered work to be done adding chafe guards, checking rigging and provisioning. In the midst off all this, the crews and their families prepared to say goodbye, most of them for eight months. In the atmosphere of tremendous excitement there was also nervousness and some inevitable misgivings, particularly from the men who were leaving behind wives and children. There was the anxiety of setting off into unknown conditions, and there was no turning back.

The day before the race I gave a public briefing to the skippers and crews, as I was to do at every stopover. I reminded them all about the importance of safety, of all they had learnt from Pete Goss during their training and from their own skippers. I told them about the route and the conditions they would experience and went over all the details of the start. All the crews had practised starting in the preceding weeks, and they had refined their techniques together four times, but then there had been no narrow, buoyed corridor down the Solent, bordered by hundreds of spectator boats, as there would be this time. It was impossible to prepare in advance for the distraction of hundreds of boats, and spectators calling out to them. Yet with the eyes of so many on us all, it was vital that everything should go smoothly. I urged everyone to think of the consequence of all their actions. "Stay in your station," I told them. "Watch your skipper for instructions and don't get carried away. Enjoy the atmo-

Left Murray Findley, the only American among the crewmembers, loading stores on *Coopers & Lybrand* at Ocean Village.

sphere, by all means, but keep alert." I emphasised the importance of the foredeck crew in the close-quarters manoeuvring that would be called for and said: "Your skipper will want someone up at the front of the boat and yours is an important job – to judge the distance between your boat and others and let the skipper know." I also gave them three pieces of advice that I was to reiterate at each stopover: "Remember that the shortest distance is invariably the fastest, that races are won and lost in light winds and that you should always go for speed, not course. Go that little bit faster if you can, particularly when you're on the wind and don't just hug your compass course."

We were blessed with unusually good weather. The day was fair: hazy but with a cloudless sky, and a light, warm wind promised to change to a sea breeze in the afternoon to hustle the fleet out of the Solent at Hurst Narrows. The race officer, Captain Spencer Drummond, gave a briefing in the morning, in which he spoke of how a postponement of the start would be shown and privately we told the skippers to expect a few minutes' delay at the start. We talked about the corridor west along the Solent as well. We wanted to involve spectators as much as possible and break down some of the barriers to watching big-boat racing. People would want to see the start from their own craft at sea and from on land, so we devised this lane to take the competitors through narrow gates off Gilkicker Point marked by the sail training ship *Sir Winston Churchill* and then on a dog-leg to Cowes, marked by the training ship *Malcolm Miller*. With so many boats around, the fleet would never be able to spot small racing marks, but these tall ships would be easy targets to aim for.

The corridor would be kept clear of spectator boats and would channel the boats close to the shore at specified places where spectators could be sure of a good view. At each of these we put up a cash prize of £2,000 for the first boat through and £1,000 for the second boat so there was an incentive to put everything into the start. We did not want the crews to take the easy option of hanging back in the hope of clearer wind or less congestion. A good, crisp start would imprint the image of a closely run race on every spectator's mind.

My thought when we devised this route was that if the boats were close on the wind the positions would change after the first gate and two different yachts might claim the prizes at the second gate. But as the wind was going to be behind the boats as they sailed down the Solent that looked less and less likely.

Her Royal Highness The Princess Royal, the race committee, the main sponsors and 400 VIPs were invited aboard the Brittany Ferries ship *Armorique*, and I felt great pride that the potential for commercial synergy was so good. We left early, for *Armorique* also had on board the fourteen members of the Royal Ocean Racing Club who were to start the race. By late morning, as the crews were becoming fraught with understandable anxiety and our guests were finishing the last of the buck's fizz and croissants, the boats began to emerge into the Solent from Southampton Water and the huge spectator fleet started to gather in anticipation.

Stage fright had to be quelled, manoeuvres perfected, crews had to be reassured that they did, indeed, know how to make a brisk, clean crossing of the line when the starting gun was fired. I could see the skippers practising long before the start, while every minute more and more spectator boats emerged from the marinas and harbours that fringe the Solent, obliging them also to deploy their skills threading through the mêlée to the start. The wind was a light easterly, and the course was going to send the boats west down the Solent, so it would be a spinnaker run. Here was an ideal chance for them to put up the promotional spinnakers, the most flamboyant sail in the wardrobe, and the one that would shout out the sponsor's corporate logo to everyone watching.

By 1100, the start area off Gilkicker Point was thronged with vessels of all kinds. From the *Armorique* down, there were barges, all sizes of yachts, sailboarders, jet skis and inflatable boats, all of them milling around within feet of each other for the best view. The ebb tide had begun and was running at one knot, slightly dragging the boats towards the start line. If they got too close, there was little enough wind to help them back. With a few minutes to go before the start, *Commercial Union* began to get their spinnaker ready. Just at that moment, we fired a postponement gun. The reason was that BBC Radio 2 had agreed to cover the start live on Ed Stewart's programme, but they had to broadcast the midday news first.

In spite of this five-minute postponement and our earlier advice to the skippers, *Commercial Union* crossed the starting line early, in obvious disarray. "What do you think they are doing?" The Princess Royal asked me. I honestly did not know. What was Will Sutherland playing at? We had allowed each boat to take on board a journalist or someone from the sponsoring company, so long as they got off before the boats left the Solent, and Peter Ward, Commercial Union's managing director, was on board. Not until Peter contacted me a couple of weeks later did I get the first-hand information that Will had taken the boat over early and given panicky, contradictory information to his crew. Then, as he lost steerage way after prematurely crossing the start line by a whole minute, Will had disappeared below in anguish. Not being a sailing man, Peter naturally thought that Will was below doing the navigation, but when he went to look, he found the skipper in the saloon with his head in his hands.

"What on earth is going on?" Peter demanded. Will would not reply. "Look," Peter continued, "we're in the middle of the spectator fleet and we're drifting sideways. For God's sake go up on deck and take charge!" At that Will did go up and ordered a headsail to be hoisted, and a 360° turn made, rather than restart. There is a phrase in the Merchant Navy Act that says it is the irrevocable responsibility of a captain to ensure the safety of his vessel and his crew, and to my way of thinking, Will had utterly shed that responsibility.

While this was happening, *Heath Insured*'s crew were trying their best to free their boat from the ground tackle of the outer limit buoy, which they had accidentally sailed over. Adrian Donovan had misjudged the tide, understandable considering how fast it was running and how fickle the wind. The rope beneath the buoy had wrapped round their rudder and all efforts to sail off failed. In the end, they cut themselves free with a knife. In fact, one of the crew stabbed it, so that the buoy immediately deflated and, to my annoyance, I was faced with a surprisingly large repair bill afterwards!

Mike Golding on *Group 4* had read the start signals correctly, but did not judge the conditions quite right, so he, too, was over the line when the starting gun fired. By the time they had a chance to answer the recall gun we fired to indicate to him that he had started early, *Heath Insured* was slowly towing the limit mark behind them, which made the rule of re-rounding the mark rather difficult to follow. Mike and his crew made their attempt to go back, as David Cowan explains: "A forest of boats had turned out to give us a rousing send-off – and to impede our progress. Mike ploughed our comparatively huge craft through them, bawling out ancient seafaring blessings as they criss-crossed our path. It was breath-taking, both in terms of excitement and apprehension."

Assessing that he would be unable to go back round the mark without endangering his own boat and others, Mike resumed the course down the Solent. However, *Group 4*'s ill luck was not yet over and, as the crew hoisted the spinnaker and made their way west to the Needles in the wake of other boats, the two snapshackles holding the corners of the sail flew open and the sail billowed free. To their credit, the foredeck crew sorted out the problem quickly, and by the end of the day the boat had crept up a few places to seventh place.

Group 4 had still not completed a penalty for starting early, though, and the race committee decreed that two hours should be added on to her elapsed time. Mike Golding felt that was unjust, and lodged a protest with the race officer, Captain Spencer Drummond, writing: "We have already paid the penalty of a slow start and I can say that, had it been possible to have rounded the ends, we would have done so. It would be irrational to do otherwise.'' The race rules allowed a skipper to protest about anything at any time, but we discouraged frivolous protests by putting a deposit of £500 on each, which the skipper forfeited if he or she lost the appeal. The cases were heard in each port by a protest committee that included two International Yacht Racing Union judges and three others unconnected with The British Steel Challenge. The protesting team might give evidence, but would play no part in the hearing or judgment. In Mike's case, he convinced the protest committee in Rio, using on-board video footage, that the hundreds of boats bearing down on him prevented him from going back to the start line and he succeeded in getting his penalty reduced to thirty minutes.

In the meantime, Ian MacGillivray and his crew on *Pride of Teesside* had made a terrific start, getting their spinnaker up quickly and gybing down the course towards the first mark with practised skill. They were followed by John Chittenden's *Nuclear Electric*, Pete Goss on *Hofbräu Lager* and Richard Tudor on *British Steel II*. Vivien Cherry's crew on *Coopers & Lybrand* were close behind and I have to confess that I was urging them on under my breath, for Viv was an aggressive starter and I had a £100 bet on her to be the first out of the Solent. Futher back were *Rhône-Poulenc*, *Group 4* and *InterSpray*, with *Commercial Union* trailing despondently in last position.

Pride of Teesside cut just ahead, past each of the other boats to go through both gates in first place. It was a moment of triumph for Ian, who was a Southampton sailor and knew the vagaries of Solent winds and tides well and whose friends were all watching and cheering him. "Four grand, four grand, four grand", her crew chanted uproariously to their support boat. Their supporters matched their high spirits with the music of a live jazz band.

As the boats reached down towards the exit of the Solent at Hurst Narrows, a squall came off the Isle of Wight. On *Coopers & Lybrand*, Viv smartly dropped her promotional spinnaker and changed to a headsail as the wind headed her. In the lead, Ian MacGillivray had his light spinnaker up, and his experience told him that the stronger winds would blow it out in a matter of seconds, so he turned downwind and went up the north channel. Most observers thought this a canny strategy, but I knew he had some doubts about whether or not his crew could react quickly enough to save the spinnaker. In any case, Viv's decision paid off and my bet was safe: *Coopers & Lybrand* led the fleet out to the English Channel.

As *Coopers & Lybrand* took the lead out of the Solent in the failing afternoon light, with the daunting first night at sea ahead, many of the crew were experiencing mingled emotions. David Cowan summed it up

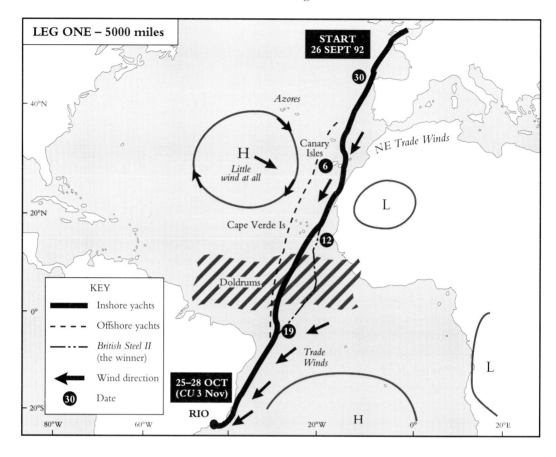

best: "We've all had difficult moments dealing with the sadness of sailing away from family and friends, and for a lot of us that became the most powerful emotion of the start of the race. Suddenly, it was irrevocable; here we were on one boat and there they were on another. Their boat would be turning back at three o'clock, but we were going to be cut loose from that world . . . Why had we done it? Why had we done it to them? So, while it was wonderful to have family and friends keeping pace with us down the Solent, calling out good wishes, waving and blowing kisses, it also created a sense of folly and guilt in many of us."

Such feelings did not last long. Once out of the Solent, everyone left the pangs of high emotion behind and began to get on with the business of racing. All other distractions banished, the common focus of attention on all the boats was only this: to be the first to cross the finish line in Rio de Janeiro. With that in mind, they settled into their various watch systems that gave each person perhaps four hours on watch and four hours off continuously or maybe gave everyone one day off watch and on maintenance duties every third day.

After the unusually balmy weather of the Solent, the boats found themselves in heavy weather less than a week later. By then they had rounded Ushant, at the corner of France, and the tactical battle had begun. Each morning boats reported their positions by high-frequency radio to the duty yacht, so everyone knew where everyone else was. It was also a chance to exchange news or information. Hence these radio schedules were referred to as the chat shows.

When relative positions and distances had been calculated, the crews could see who was their nearest rival and campaign accordingly. By then, *Pride of Teesside* and *Coopers & Lybrand* elected to take the strong tide in their favour that ran inside the island of Ushant, putting them into the leading group of boats, but once past that, all the boats had to cross the Bay of Biscay, notorious for storms and big seas. The reputation of being treacherous arose in the days of the tall ships which, unlike our boats, could not go to windward and were often fatally embayed on a lee shore by westerlies. With our more weatherly boats the passage could be uncomfortable but not perilous.

As it was, the fleet did not evade bad weather and, as an area of low pressure skirted by them, the winds and seas built rapidly. This was the proper baptism of the crews: in up to 57 knots of south-westerly head winds and the chilling passage of a cold front, people struggled with sails on pitching, wet decks, and got a taste of helming in heavy weather in close competition. It said much for the solid design of our upwind boats compared to the less durable characteristics of downwind designs that seven of the fourteen entries retired from the Vendée Globe Challenge solo circumnavigation race, which passed through the area at that time.

For the first time in the race seasickness set in for many people. Before the start Gary Ashton, who crewed on *Group 4*, remarked that he considered one of the biggest potential problems to be seasickness. There is no way of knowing whether you are likely to suffer or not before you take up sailing, and plenty of people found that they were vulnerable to it, even if they took tablets. From *Heath Insured*, Adrian Rayson commented: "Crew were sick in the Bay – and some in the heads, one in the cabin, a couple in the companionway and several in a strategically placed bucket which appeared at the doghouse hatch."

A day later, on 29 September, the winds quietened, and almost all had acquired their sea legs, but while the gale lasted, there were quite a few people who were reminded of training in rough seas in the Western Approaches, as well as the adage that seasickness begins with the feeling that you're dying, and ends up with the wish that you were dead! At that point, I think there were some who believed, albeit briefly, that they'd made a grave mistake.

Sail changes in rough weather, when seas constantly deluged the foredeck, made life difficult in other ways. Everyone got a taste of what the Southern Ocean might be like, as they struggled acrobatically on pitching foredecks and got thoroughly soaked. So powerful was the force of waves crashing over the bow, that *Hofbräu Lager*'s jockey pole, used to hold the genoa out when sailing downwind, got washed away.

As the winds lessened to the north-west of Finisterre, the fleet was becalmed with the same abruptness that it had found itself in the teeth of a gale. As you head south, first you pass through the Portuguese Trades, then at about 38°N, you begin to enter the area of possible north-east trade winds in October, but they are not as reliable as most people expect and the courses of the yachts began to divide, according to where their skippers thought the odds of consistent winds to be best.

Hofbräu Lager and *Pride of Teesside* had been engaged in close battle since they rounded Ushant, and their strategies had pushed them to the front of the fleet. Now a canny game of tactics ensued. *Pride of Teesside* had pushed to the front by standing out to the west, for Ian MacGillivray, like Pete Goss on *Hofbräu Lager* and Will Sutherland on *Commercial Union*, hoped that a small depression to the west would bring them wind first. In fact, it did not, for the area of low pressure collapsed and that left the listless calms of the Azores High, a huge area of constantly fluctuating high pressure, out to the west. This was to play a crucial role in the fortunes of the boats.

Meanwhile, in the early hours of 23 September, *British Steel II*, also close to these combatants, began working her way to the west in the knowledge that the two others would see her navigation lights and alter course to cover her. They did so, and a few hours later, Richard Tudor ordered the lights to be switched off and the course altered to the south. By doing so, he committed the other boats to a more westerly route in the hope that it would lead them into lighter winds. He was right. From then on, *British Steel II* broke free to take on *InterSpray*, while *Hofbräu Lager* and *Pride of Teesside* continued their epic contest as far as the doldrums.

Off the Portuguese coast, *InterSpray* and *Coopers & Lybrand* caught a better breeze and *InterSpray* took the lead in style, going from tenth to first place in one day. By 5 October, however, they had lost it again. As the boats progressed south towards the island of Madeira, Vivien Cherry and the crew of *Coopers & Lybrand* were carried along by a 20-knot wind which swept them past *InterSpray*, whose skipper asserted that they were sticking to longer-term tactics, not transitory winds. The boats swapped places within sight of each other in the early hours of the morning, and Vivien Cherry did not pass up the chance of calling up Paul Jeffes on the VHF radio, saying that she was taking over the yellow jersey. As *Coopers &*

Lybrand's white stern light receded ahead of them, Paul responded with mock gallantry, declaring a temporary case of "ladies first".

Coopers & Lybrand had almost matched *InterSpray* in terms of being catapulted to the front, having moved from ninth to first place in one go. It was not to last long for them either though, and as they sailed south through the archipelago of the Canary Islands, they ran straight into a calm, where they floundered as other boats sailed by further to the east and to the west. Within a few days of their brief lead, Vivien Cherry and her crew found themselves at the back of the fleet once again. Quite unaware of the situation on *Commercial Union*, Ann de Boer commented: "The only boat that seems to have got it more wrong than we have is *CU*."

Traditional wisdom suggested to some of the skippers that it would be best to keep west of the Canary Islands and the Cape Verde Islands, but the Azores High was moving west early in October and gradually the fleet divided into two groups. *Rhône-Poulenc, Hofbräu Lager, Nuclear Electric, Group 4* and *Commercial Union* stayed out west, whereas *InterSpray, British Steel II* and *Heath Insured* kept closer to the coast of Africa, laying the foundations of a lead which they carried well into the north-east trade winds south of the equator. *Coopers & Lybrand* and *Pride of Teesside*, meanwhile, had dodged between the Canary Islands and lost the wind behind the high mountains of the islands and they saw the other boats stretch out clear leads.

Matters on *Commercial Union* were worsening. The fracas at the start worried me intensely, especially because I had already been aware of communication difficulties aboard. After the Fastnet/Ushant race, I had met with Will's unhappy crew in London and had gone over an exercise I hoped would help them begin to work out their problems. Everyone had worked hard after that to help. I believe that, unlike in the days of Captain Bligh, £15,000 buys you a seat at the table and that the crew are entitled to voice an opinion, so I told Will and the crew that if it did not work out, he would be offered a chance to resign in Rio. Bearing in mind the mistake that was highlighted when Alec Honey had to resign, I took the precaution this time of going through the list of skippers that had applied and marking one possibility.

Things did not get better, and one night while Will was asleep "Boosie", alias Sue Tight, send me a secret message. The situation we had discussed was as bad as ever, she wrote, and the crew of *Commercial Union* wanted me to honour the promise I had made to them in London. It was not too difficult a decision for me. I could see from the results *Commercial Union*'s alarming lack of progress. The crew were obviously demoralised; they were settling down to apathy – or worse. There had to be a change as soon as they reached Rio.

While the skippers and navigators tried to divine the best winds, other considerations were weighing on the mind of Michael Martin, who sailed aboard *British Steel II*. When he left to go on the race he left behind his girlfriend, Carol McBean. A few days out, he decided, with a little incitement from fellow crewmembers, to make a link call to Carol and ask her to marry him. As he called her on the ship's radio, in the most public of conversations, his question met with an enthusiastic response, but one yes was not enough. The occasion had to be filmed for the record, and Mike had to propose to Carol in numerous takes. Carol, too, was filmed by the BBC at home and had to consent to marry Mike over and over again.

Maybe Mike knew exactly what he was doing, because from then on Carol had to take on the complicated bureaucratic procedures of organising a marriage in Brazil – she even had to buy the ring. One of her first thoughts was to call up and ask me to give her away in Rio in a ceremony aboard *British Steel II*. I was delighted to be asked and gladly accepted, but told her I couldn't understand why she didn't want to spend her honeymoon on the boat . . .

With positions in the race changing day by day, one issue that would not go away was that of the weatherfaxes. We had installed these on the boats so that they could get pictures of weather patterns which are transmitted from various shore stations, but since the start only the one aboard *Coopers & Lybrand* had functioned. Everyone on the Challenge team in England had worked hard to try to solve the problems, and telexes filled with technical questions and answers had been sent back and forth from each of the yachts almost daily. Despite our best attempts, however, the equipment never properly worked and sponsors were getting edgy, because several believed they were being unduly disadvantaged.

On *Group 4*, Simon Clarke took a dim view of the equipment, writing: "For sale: one weatherfax, hardly used, perfect working order. Wanted: women's dress size 12, suitable for all occasions, particularly King Neptune's party. No Velcro please. Also for sale: one set of Hood sails, nearly new. Genuine reason for sale – no wind."

By the middle of October, the boats began crossing the area known as the doldrums. One of the characteristics of the doldrums, or the Inter-Tropical Convergence Zone (ITCZ) as they tend to be called by sailors these days, is that the wind dies where the two established and contrary winds of the northern and southern hemispheres meet. This band of light and variable winds moves to its northerly limit, north of the equator, in August and by October it is tracking south to reach the most southerly limit, the calms interspersed unpredictably with powerful electrical storms and vicious squalls. Yet the actual position of the doldrums can vary considerably from day to day, as can the width of the band of calms. Although in general the width can be between 200–300 miles, sometimes the trade winds to the north or south can burst through and reduce it to a very narrow strip, and this area was where the skippers' skill in reading weather patterns and their research could pay enormous dividends.

Hitting the doldrums at a narrow point would make sure that a boat would burst through into the south-east trade winds on the other side comparatively quickly, putting that crew firmly in the leading pack. It was essential, therefore, to combine skill with good fortune in being at the right place at the right time, because once you run out of wind, you are totally committed; there's no way of moving to the east or the west to look for better pastures. At the beginning of the race, Mike Smith, a British Steel employee who sailed the first leg, asked his skipper if the outcome of the route through the doldrums was critical to winning the leg. Richard Tudor's reply echoed many of the other skippers' feelings then: "No," he said, "it is critical to winning the race."

By the second week of October, all ten boats had experienced calms, some with more devastating severity than others. *Rhône-Poulenc* had been sailing at 8 knots when she reached the calms, and John O'Driscoll recounted that it was "like running into a brick wall". As the fleet got nearer to the equator, the heat steadily increased. The sun beat down on the stainless steel decks, so that they became hot to walk on, and any shade cast by the spars and sails was at a premium. Down below, the heat would build up during the day and, although the boats are well insulated, it inevitably became torrid in the cabins. When we designed the boats, it was important not to have too many or too big openings in the deck. The more there were, the greater the possibility that they might leak, so we kept the hatches ventilating the cabins quite small. There are dorade vents as well that will funnel air down below and work in heavy weather, when the hatches have to be closed and in designing these we complied with Department of Transport regulations. All the same, the crews found that air tended to circulate mainly beneath these fittings, and the bunks themselves remained stifling. To make matters worse, some of the crews blocked up the vents with hats or sunglasses; some even stopped the circulation of air entirely by putting speakers in them so they could listen to music on deck.

In the daytime the sail locker in the forepeak was a popular place to sleep, provided there were no sail repairs in progress at the time. Aboard *British Steel II*, Mike Martin came in for ribbing for his eccentric way of coping with the heat. Mike's theory was that, if you wore all your thermal clothes in bed – long-sleeved vest as well as long johns – they would transfer the heat and perspiration from your body and you would stay cool. On some boats people snoozed on deck, while on others all the off-watch crew were confined below decks, despite the heat. Richard Tudor, for example, had a rule that the off-watch crew could not sleep on deck so that they wouldn't get in the way of the crew on watch, and he had fitted a small fan above each bunk to help move the stifling air of the cabins.

For a week or two, the boats went through incredibly spectacular electrical storms. Fork and sheet lightning flashed across the sky at night, etching the pitch black with vivid whites and purples. The boats all had lightning conductors, so there was little need to worry that all the electrical equipment would be shorted out if they were hit, but from time to time the crack of thunder was frighteningly close and some skippers turned off all the electrical gear as a precaution.

In the middle of a huge electrical storm, standing in the pouring rain, barefoot and in shorts, you know that if you get struck by lightning you'll probably end up like a prune. But I find it extraordinary how seldom people on yachts do get hit. However, the reports that came back to race headquarters reminded me of an incident in the second Whitbread Race. *Great Britain II* was sailing up the eastern seaboard of America when lightning hit her mast. One of the fare-paying crew was standing at the mast when it was hit and the charge that came down from the mast head knocked him out. Rob James dragged him below and gave him first aid and then called me on the radio to report to me.

"Did I do the right thing?" he asked.

"No, Rob," I replied, "what you should have done was to take him below, put his hands on the batteries and recharged them!"

In scenes as gothic as a Hammer horror film, storms swept furiously from the horizon while the Challenge boats were often becalmed. Even as storms approached, some crews reported no wind and an oily sea, their sails slatting noisily as the boat rolled on the swell. Once the wind caught up, sudden squalls of perhaps 40 knots would arrive, with torrential rain, thunder and lightning. The crews had to prepare for the squall and anticipate the direction it would come from, as well as the reduced sail combination that would be needed. Once they'd got that right, they could hitch a ride to take them away from a rival snapping at their heels, or make up some of the miles between them and boats ahead. These storms were a welcome relief from the sweltering heat, bringing a cooling breeze and plenty of fresh water. During one thunderstorm that passed over *Coopers & Lybrand*, all the crew came on deck in the downpour carrying soap and shampoo and while the rain lasted, they showered on deck beneath the boom, where water poured from the shelf of the mainsail.

Despite these breaks, the heat and lack of wind took their toll on all the crews. This was perhaps less so on the leaders, *British Steel II*, *InterSpray* and *Heath Insured*, which all crossed through quite a narrow band, but the boats further west experienced longer periods of calms. There were temperatures of up to 38°C and more to contend with, the incessant slap of the lifeless sails and the frustration of knowing other boats were making much better progress, yet being utterly unable to do anything about it. All these factors combined to cause tempers to flare up and frustrations to grow. As Mike Golding aptly remarked: "Considering it's such low-stress weather, it's a high-stress race."

"One thing that might be starting to sink in," wrote Adrian Rayson, "is that sixty-seven feet is a very small environment in which to spend several weeks with thirteen other people. Arthur [Haynes] mentioned walking to the pub for a pint before dinner this evening and it seemed a very, very good idea." On *British Steel II*, respect for individual privacy was starting to create tension. In Rio, Steve West told of how the over-powering smell of sweaty feet had been bravely ignored by everyone in his cabin until ill-feeling threatened to add to the poisonous atmosphere. But before any ugly showdown could occur, a sudden lurch of the boat dislodged a forgotten cabbage from its place beneath one of the bunks and the suppurating culprit rolled across the cabin. Aboard *Hofbräu Lager* Mike Kay finally gave in to pressure from his crewmates to remove a pair of canvas shoes he kept down below. Once wet, they filled the cabin with a pungent odour and, after much leg-pulling, he threw them over the side. "Immediately, and to the mirth of the crew," Pete Goss said, "a huge shoal of flying fish leapt out of the sea."

David Cowan tried to observe life on board objectively: "There's one aspect of the relationships between crewmembers which I would love to hear analysed by a perceptive psychologist, and that's our non-stop joki-ness. We spend a lot of time laughing, sometimes quite hysterically, which is a great bonus, and I can see that it is perhaps a means of defusing irritations before they become dangerous."

Aboard *Coopers & Lybrand*, there was a sense of humour failure board, and Ann de Boer reported that the highest scorer of the leg had been David Turner, who snarled when she committed what is one of sailing's cardinal social errors – waking someone for a watch by mistake. There was also the Cooper Blooper Book, in which all the ludicrous sayings and inadvertent double entendres were recorded for posterity. On *Nuclear Electric*, whose crew were generally quieter than that of most of the other boats, a baby's dummy mounted on a piece of cardboard and stuck to the saloon bulkhead carried the title The Talk-Too-Much Award.

While the fleet moved through the tropics, daily living was enriched by the sighting of all kinds of marine life. *Hofbräu Lager* reported having found a six-inch squid on deck and there followed jokes throughout the fleet about the strange flying squid in their vicinity. Other boats saw turtles and pilot whales; *InterSpray* even reported that they had seen a killer whale. Nigel Bray claimed that he had been splashed by the tail of a whale while he was helming *British Steel II*, and *Commercial Union* said they had been followed by a shark. Simon Clarke recorded this tale of *Group 4*'s close encounter with a whale: "We nearly donked one on the head while it slept. Skilful helming by Nick Jubert in light conditions led to the near collision in an otherwise empty ocean. Unfortunately, Simon Littlejohn was too busy playing with his f-stops and lenses, and only succeeded in getting a slightly underexposed photo of his left foot as evidence of the encounter. Keep up the good work, boys!"

Rhône-Poulenc, meanwhile, were not observing so much as catching, and when they were pursued by a shoal of tuna, they put out a line and caught some for dinner. All the boats had a taste of fish, for as they went south to the tropics, they got rained on by flying fish. These launch themselves out of the water when pursued and can glide incredible distances, but they also launch themselves on deck and have a habit of landing in the cockpit or, worse, flying through open hatches to land in the cabins beneath. You can fry them and eat them, and they are a delicacy in some parts of the Caribbean, but they only taste good when you are expecting to eat fish, as Andrew Hindley found out on *Hofbräu Lager*. "Andrew had the shock of his life last night," Pete Goss telexed. "While he was eating on deck, a flying fish landed in his custard!"

Hundreds of miles out from land, *Group 4* also had the odd experience of finding a willow warbler on deck, which hopped about and refused all offers of food. Before departing, it flew into the doghouse and perched on Mike Golding's head. *Pride of Teesside* had a strange experience, too. "During the night of 12 October," Ian MacGillivray wrote, "we must have hit something, as the pulpit now has a slight bend on the port side at the after end. There is no damage to the hull, so whatever it was must have been fairly soft but quite heavy. We did have a school of porpoises around performing acrobatics during the night, although I have never known one collide with a boat. I suppose there has to be a first time!"

Top right The crews of the ten boats at Ocean Village, Southampton, the week before the start. On board (from front to back): *Pride of Teesside*, *Nuclear Electric* and *Coopers & Lybrand*. On the pontoon (from front to back): *British Steel II*, *Commercial Union*, *Hofbräu Lager*, *InterSpray*, *Group 4*, *Rhône-Poulenc* and *Heath Insured*. MP
Right Hundreds of spectator boats and over 2,000 spectators watched the start. *Pride of Teesside* was first through both the gates, marked by sail training ships. Here, she leads from *Nuclear Electric*, *British Steel II*, *Hofbräu Lager* and *Coopers & Lybrand*. MP

Above left Richard Tudor (foreground) spent much time training his crew. MP
Above right Hofbräu Lager during the training. Their skipper, Pete Goss, is top left. MP

Above Group 4 was the only all male boat. MP
Left Coopers & Lybrand led out past the Needles, after a neat spinnaker drop and headsail hoist. DB

Above left Rhône-Poulenc had only an average start, trailing the leaders out of the Solent. MP
Above right Commercial Union had real problems on leg one after a disastrous start. PRB

Above John Chittenden was the only skipper to have raced round the world before. MP
Right Storming downwind on the Fastnet training race. MP

Heath Insured was a very competitive boat, and skipper Adrian Donovan, a Master Mariner, brought to the team solid training in seamanship. CR

Ian MacGillivray's crew chant "Four grand, four grand!" to supporters after taking both prizes at the start of the race. BP

David Spratley checks for wear on the spinnaker guy aboard *Heath Insured*. Often the sail was up for days on end and chafe was a potential problem. AR

Heath Insured get their first sight of Rio and the silhouette of the Sugar Loaf mountain as they make their way towards the finishing line on 26 October. H

Chay Blyth giving the first Infolink Trophy for winning an individual leg to
Richard Tudor of *British Steel II* at the Rio yacht club. MP

Now three weeks into the race, *Commerical Union*'s crew were beginning to wonder if they would even reach Brazil by Christmas. Their position as the furthest west of the fleet left them marooned for almost two weeks in a stationary area of high pressure, compared to the twenty-four hours it took *British Steel II* to cross the calmest part of the doldrums. They knew from the daily chat show that other boats were getting wind, so equally they knew in which direction they should sail to get it themselves, but the difficulty was an impossible vicious circle: without wind they couldn't possibly sail to an area where there was wind. So, day in, day out, the crew of *Commercial Union* woke to hear the crack of the empty sails, knowing that, yet again, they were going nowhere. "We still wait hopefully for a bit of wind to speed up our progress to Rio," reported Andrew Stevenson Hamilton, Peter Coop and Roger Boyd on 13 October. "Please send an albatross."

Even so, irrepressible good humour held everyone on *Commercial Union* together. All the crew had a chance to swim over the side of the boat, attached on by a line or a harness. Peter Coop organised keep fit classes for everyone aboard, with Jane Fonda making a special appearance in the guise of Alison McKichan. Endless games of "I spy" were played and the items spied became more and more zany. There was also the distraction of telexing reports to the press office in Petersfield, which we had asked all the boats to do. *Commercial Union* responded enthusiastically with what they named "chatty" reports. They told us of odd incidents that had kept everyone amused. "Ali (Alison McKichan) is minus a torch after giving us a tennis lesson," Andrew, Peter and Roger reported. "In the absence of the favoured equipment, she chose to demonstrate her serve with a piece of paper and a cabin torch. Style was impeccable, but sadly she missed the ball and let go of the racket."

Writing of their unfortunate circumstances, they relayed this scientific philosophy: "Just remember, if we were to draw a line parallel to the rhumb line, add on 50 fathoms, multiply it by the first number that comes to mind and take into account the last few paragraphs of the *Wall Street Journal* on a Thursday, we would be winning . . ."

Although the problems on *Commercial Union* were a special case, all the skippers and crews had to work hard to find constructive diversions from the boredom. On *Rhône-Poulenc*, there were regular quiz nights when teams such as The A-Team, The Goatherds and The Coiled Springs vied for supremacy. On *British Steel II*, B watch held a dance party in the cockpit for A watch and they twirled and waltzed enthusiastically in a temperature of 38°C. The calmer weather also provided time for high-minded pursuits, as Kevin Dufficy remarked: "This boat is turning into a language school. Steve West is brushing up on his French (expletives a speciality), Pat Quinn has just started an Italian Linguaphone course and the whole crew are now getting daily instructions in the Welsh vocabulary. Richard puts a new word or saying, in Welsh, on the saloon wall each day for the crew to learn. At present, we are still on the normal, everyday sayings, but we are hoping to move on to sailing terms shortly. This is so we can discuss tactics in the bars of Rio without being understood by the other crews.''

Just as the crew on *Commercial Union* had done, most people went for a swim when their skippers felt it was safe to do so. On *Coopers & Lybrand*, there was a chance to try high diving as they sailed under spinnaker. Anyone who wanted to have a go was tied on by a rope and walked along the spinnaker pole to the end, where there the rope was released so that they could jump the fifteen feet or so into the water.

Life was not so genial on board *Rhône-Poulenc*, however. John O'Driscoll was not used to leading a team of people who questioned orders before they obeyed them, nor had he been used to a team that comprised women. It called for a lot of skill, but John had that. What it also called for was some enjoyment of the challenges involved, and John was not enjoying the race. *Rhône-Poulenc* was also having problems with her spinnakers. As these were going to be some of the most crucial sails for the downwind stretches ahead, this was a serious problem. The masthead spinnakers on the boats are a vast amount of sail area to handle, and the crew on *Rhône-Poulenc* found the heavyweight spinnaker so daunting that they nicknamed it "Lazarus". Without it, though, they would have had to resign themselves to finishing well down the fleet. So, when their brand new spinnaker exploded a few minutes after it was first hoisted, the crew had no choice but to repair a hundred-foot laceration by hand. For five days, all thirteen crew spent every available moment hand-stitching the sail.

The crew reported the incident thus: "The task seemed impossible. We worked round the clock in shifts, frequently by torchlight on a heaving deck. Who is responsible for this miracle? A skipper, a mate and twelve crewmembers who decided not to ditch the sail. The task was huge, but simple. The ship's company became a human sewing machine: one watch zigged, and another zagged. The fleet's doctor, Campbell Mackenzie, put in more stitches in five days than a hospital sees in five years. Everyone learnt to sew fast: a lieutenant commander, a carpenter, a prison officer, a sales manager, a solicitor, a broker, an airport manager and a barrister – they all sewed as if their lives depended on it. What's more, they sewed well, because all stitches had to pass muster with Valerie Elliott, a primary school teacher from Hampshire whom we dubbed 'Mistress Quickly'.''

Everyone held their breath as the sail was hoisted again and as it filled with wind a modest cheer broke out. For the rest of the leg, the sail was subjected to nervous scrutiny, and while the crew's days of laborious stitching were by no means over, the sail held to take them into the Atlantic trade winds and set them once again in the middle of the fleet.

As *Rhône-Poulenc* fought to catch up and *Commercial Union* was languishing in last place to the north and west of them, *British Steel II* was crossing the equator. Richard Tudor's crew had all the while been edging closer to the African coast, hoping to get a local sea breeze from the land, as well as hitting the ITCZ at its thinnest point. Richard reckoned from his routeing research, allied with any weather information he could get from the erratic weatherfax, that it would be best to cross the equator at a longitude of 20°W. Not only was there likely to be a slimmer area of calms here, he thought, but when they did reach the south-east trade winds in the southern hemisphere they would have a faster wind angle, sending them towards the South American coast on a broad reach rather than a run.

InterSpray, *Hofbräu Lager* and *Heath Insured* likewise drew east, but not so far as *British Steel II*, and they aimed to cross the equator somewhere around 25°W. By then, the ITCZ was moving south and this route carried the possible disadvantage of the doldrums moving further and further away from the boats. Fortunately for them, this did not happen, but it was interesting for all of us watching back on dry land to see, only a day or two later, *Pride of Teesside* suffer badly at the same point *InterSpray* had crossed.

Maintaining a high average boatspeed was always a priority, and *British Steel II* was fortunate to have winds that never quite died, and only twenty-four hours of relatively light airs. In spite of the concentration of the helmsman and sail trimmer, however, crossing the equator was an occasion that had to be celebrated. Traditionally, the equator is where mariners pay homage to Neptune so that he won't then claim them for his watery locker. It is also the proper and messy baptism for first-timers. All the boats had to have a representative King Neptune, boss man of the deep. On *British Steel II*, Richard Tudor led the proceedings, carrying a trident and wearing skimpy shorts, a welder's face mask and a blonde wig. He was joined by Kevin Dufficy, also in a wig, and Pat Quinn, who had covered his entire head with shaving foam. But it was Marcus Gladwell who stole the show, appearing from the companionway in nothing but deck shoes and strategically placed blobs of shaving foam.

InterSpray was the second of the fleet to cross the equator, just fifteen hours later and did so in style: in late evening moonlight, doing 9 knots and celebrating with a champagne party given by Paul Jeffes. Their King

Neptune was Jeff Plummer, who had prepared an evil-looking concoction with which to baptise the rest of the crew. Ricky Scott toted the trident, even though he was supposed to be Blackbeard. The star of the *InterSpray* show, however, was a stunning blonde-haired inflatable doll.

Further back, all except *Coopers & Lybrand* chose to sail the traditional route to windward of the Cape Verde Islands, and Vivien Cherry and her crew benefited from the move. *Nuclear Electric*, *Hofbräu Lager*, *Rhône-Poulenc* and *Group 4* fought it out daily in the middle of the fleet, while *Commercial Union* wallowed helplessly in a void, still irredeemably in last place. They had missed out on the same weather pattern the others had got and experienced lighter winds, where their difficulties were compounded. The further back they fell, the less wind they seemed to get. All the time, the doldrums stretched that little bit further away from them and, on top of that, the crew's morale got lower and lower, making it even more difficult to coax the boat along.

Once south of the equator, the three leaders picked up the 20–25-knot south-east trade winds and they could sail more or less along the rhumb line route to Rio. Separated at that point by over 200 miles, the leaders nevertheless still played a tense game of cat-and-mouse. *British Steel II* and *InterSpray*, in particular, watched each other's progress carefully and worked out each gain or loss at every position report.

As *British Steel II* was edging out of the narrow belt of the doldrums they had positioned themselves in, something happened to remind everyone of the power of even a little wind on these big boats. The boat was running downwind under spinnaker for the third consecutive day, moving steadily along in an easy 15 knots of wind. There was a pattern to the weather with which the crew had grown familiar over the last couple of days: at dawn the breeze would die and they would hoist the lightweight spinnaker; then in the middle of the morning the wind would pick up, and the lightweight sail would be replaced by the heavyweight spinnaker.

Each time the change was made it called for a complicated spinnaker peel. On this morning, the manoeuvre had just been finished and Marcus Gladwell had come down from the end of the spinnaker pole where he had tied a trip line. He was about to fasten the other end to the toerail so it could be used later, when Rob Haine offered to do it for him. Rob was making the first loop of the knot when the spinnaker guy holding the pole in place was accidentally released and the pole shot forward. The thin cord pulled taut as it came under load and the loop he was making closed in a split second, while his thumb was still inside it.

"It whipped off my thumb extremely efficiently, just like a pair of scissors," he recalled. "About half an inch was taken off from the base of the cuticle, straight over to the other side. It was very painful, but although I remember the pain, what I remember most about the next two or three minutes was anger. Anger flashed through my brain because of the consequences of the accident. What was going to happen to me for the rest of the leg? How difficult was treatment going to be? And what about the next leg, round Cape Horn? And what about my job as a semi-professional photographer: how was I going to focus manual lenses?

"Dave Arthur straightaway comforted me and held me. Everybody came up on deck from the off watch and Steve West took his shirt off and put it under my head, which annoyed me at the time, because I was thinking: 'It's my thumb that hurts, not my head!' Richard Tudor was distraught, but reacted in a fantastic way and for the remainder of the leg, he wouldn't hear of me doing anything."

British Steel II's two medical officers, Marcus Gladwell and Yvonne Flatman took Rob down below and opened all the medical chests. While Marcus got out a hypodermic needle and gave Rob two local anaesthetic injections, Giles Trollope called all the other boats to ask for medical advice and telexed race headquarters in England. Within hours Rob's parents had been told about the accident. The tip of his thumb was later discovered in the scuppers where it had fallen. The crew swaddled it in cotton wool and placed it in a box, which they gave to Rob with the recommendation that he bury it at sea.

By Rio, the pain had subsided and the healing process was well underway, but it took four more months for the stump to heal completely and for Rob to get used to using a left hand with only half a thumb. So early into the first leg, it was a tremendous blow to him, and to the crew, who had effectively lost the services of one person. Yet aboard *British Steel II*, as on the other boats, the incident not only reminded people to be cautious about the smallest things, but it also let them see how quickly advice and help could come from their friends on other yachts as well as from race headquarters.

As a footnote to this story, Rob got compensation from his injury in Hobart; like most of the crews, he had taken out personal accident cover of £25,000 with the Heath Group before the start of the race. The underwriters worked out that the loss was worth twenty per cent of the sum, or £5,000. Because the cut was above the second joint, they calculated that a quarter had been lost, or £1,250 worth of thumb.

As the boats rolled downwind under spinnaker to Rio, the trade winds freshened steadily, backed gradually from east to south-east. For two weeks, the wind remained constant, bowling all the boats before it at average speeds of up to 11 knots. It was little compared to the speeds most of the lightweight downwind flyers of other ocean races can achieve, but it was comfortable and exhilarating nonetheless for the helmsmen and crew. Futhermore, as *British Steel II*, *InterSpray* and *Heath Insured* vied for first place, it provided all of us following the race at home with some intense and close racing.

With high hopes of catching their rivals, *Heath Insured* played every wind shift and change of windspeed along a direct route to Rio. "We know precisely how much ground we need to make up on the leaders," Adrian Donovan reported, "and all our energy is being directed to doing just that." With increasing trade winds, though, *Heath Insured's* crew suffered several misfortunes only a week from making landfall. First, their promotional spinnaker, which featured a huge circular logo, blew out across that circular pattern, making it virtually impossible for them to repair the sail in time for it to be of use. Inattentive helming caused another to rip the length of the foot and all the way up the luff. Just when they needed all the downwind sail area they could carry to draw precious miles from their competitors' leads, they had no appropriate sail to hoist.

Then, seven days out from Rio, Carol Randall fell backwards into one of the cabins and badly injured her neck. She recorded in her log: "The result was one large bump, a serious pain in the neck – literally – and tingling in my left hand and foot." That tingling was enough to warn Adrian how serious the injury might be, and he spoke to the medical officers on the other boats, including the fleet doctor Campbell Mackenzie, aboard *Rhône-Poulenc*. The assumption was a neck fracture, so Carol was taken off watch duty and confined to her bunk. A Portuguese doctor in Rio was briefed to take Carol to hospital when *Heath Insured* arrived, and the British Ambassador was also alerted.

Now *Heath Insured* was losing miles against the leaders every day, while in front *British Steel II* and *InterSpray* duelled for first place. However *British Steel II* gradually expanded their lead to 100 miles, and they sailed into sight of Copacabana Beach on 25 October, crossing the line at 1343. Her crew had sailed over 5,300 miles in 29 days, 2 hours and 38 minutes. Champagne was passed on board, and a delighted Mike Martin embraced his fiancée, Carol McBean. The forthcoming wedding between them would be a double celebration.

Only ten hours behind, Paul Jeffes brought *InterSpray* over the line in the early hours of the following morning. Their lead on the following boats was plenty to celebrate, but it was impossible for his crew not to reflect on what might have been had they not twice run into voids of light winds on the run down to Rio.

Right Marcus Gladwell of *British Steel II* goes out to the end of the pole
to reeve a lightweight spinnaker sheet.

Late the next day, *Heath Insured* finished to a tremendous reception from the crews of the other two boats. Carol Randall, who had good reason to be elated at the sight of land, said: "It's marvellous to see land again and it's really true that you can smell it after so many days at sea. It was really frustrating this last week, wallowing around at times in a breathless ocean, knowing that with good winds you could be in a hot bath, sipping a gin and tonic and looking forward to a good meal!"

We had not imagined what drama there would be when the next group of boats finished. *British Steel II*, *InterSpray* and *Heath Insured* had taught us that, once the boats came within sight of the high land around Rio, they gradually lost the wind, and drifted languidly towards the finishing line. This was to be so with *Group 4*, *Hofbräu Lager* and *Pride of Teesside*, which had been racing closely all the way down the Brazilian coast. *Group 4* was the first to appear on the horizon, but no sooner had she done so than the wind died. Behind her, Ian MacGillivray and Pete Goss trimmed and coaxed furiously, for this was a chance to reduce the gap in elapsed time at the finish. As Ian and his crew slowly closed the last hurdle, the fairway buoy off Copacabana Beach, they were becalmed. All the while *Pride of Teesside* was closing quickly, borne by a stronger wind, and with yards to go to the finish they took the lead. *Hofbräu Lager*, too, had been closing and for a while it looked as if she would also pass *Group 4*. As it was, *Pride of Teesside* scraped into fourth place by only 2 minutes 51 seconds. *Group 4* followed, as a torrential downpour belatedly whisked a breeze over the calm, murky water and she finished only fifty-two seconds ahead of *Hofbräu Lager*.

It was scarcely credible, therefore, when the same thing happened thirteen hours later. I was staying in a hotel that overlooks Copacabana Beach and had a room on the twenty-first floor. I got up that morning knowing that I was likely to see *Nuclear Electric* finishing. I looked out of my window and, sure enough, I could seem her, not sailing though, but bobbing to her anchor on a windless sea. As I looked to the horizon, I could see two other boats closing in fast. But on the twenty-first floor I could see a lot further than John Chittenden could from sea level, and I knew he had no idea *Rhône-Poulenc* and *Coopers & Lybrand* were so close. Although I was excited by the prospect of another close finish, I wanted to tell John how near his rivals were and couldn't. It wouldn't have made any difference because the wind picked up only as *Rhône-Poulenc* and *Coopers & Lybrand* sailed into the bay. In an even closer finish than the boats ahead, *Nuclear Electric* beat *Rhône-Poulenc* and *Coopers & Lybrand* by a mere twelve minutes. Even more astonishing was the finish between *Rhône-Poulenc* and *Coopers & Lybrand*. As the crews tweaked and trimmed their sails, the two crossed the line within eight minutes of each other.

Meanwhile, *Commerical Union* was only then pulling south into the trade winds and if any crew fitted the description of "limping in", they did, a full nine days behind *British Steel II*. As crewmember Alison McKichan explained: "It was frustrating, mind-blowing. And the worst thing was that while we were out there, we didn't see a single other yacht from The Challenge. We saw no land . . . it's very difficult to keep up a racing mentality when you've absolutely no idea what you are racing against. We all think now that if we hear the crack of the main again, we'll develop a twitch. It was *dreadful*, like a form of mental torture. We all thought we were going completely batty. We're all united in our complaints (about Will). It was a difficult leg. I want to do this more than anything else, but I want to have fun and get a lot out of it. I don't want to feel demoralised and I couldn't carry on if our situation doesn't change. I mean, you look to your skipper all the time, don't you?"

Rio had diversions enough for everyone to forget about sailing for a few weeks. But as I soon discovered, political squabbles were about to erupt and fear of what lay ahead threatened to get the better of some.

Arrival Times
Race Leg: **1 – Southampton to Rio de Janeiro**

Yacht Name	Status	Arrival Time GMT	Leg Time DDD HH MM SS	Placing
01: *British Steel II*	Finished	25 OCT 13:43:26	029 02 38 26	1st
02: *InterSpray*	Finished	25 OCT 23:32:25	029 12 27 25	2nd
03: *Heath Insured*	Finished	26 OCT 20:59:20	030 09 54 20	3rd
04: *Pride of Teesside*	Finished	27 OCT 19:06:04	031 08 01 04	4th
05: *Hofbräu Lager*	Finished	27 OCT 19:08:55	031 08 03 55	5th
06: *Group 4*	Finished	27 OCT 19:07:03	031 08 32 03	6th★
07: *Nuclear Electric*	Finished	28 OCT 08:45:26	031 21 40 26	7th
08: *Rhône Poulenc*	Finished	28 OCT 08:57:03	031 21 52 03	8th
09: *Coopers & Lybrand*	Finished	28 OCT 09:05:55	031 22 00 55	9th
10: *Commercial Union*	Finished	03 NOV 04:58:45	037 19 53 45	10th★

DDD HH MM SS – Leg time expressed in: days, hours, minutes and seconds.
★ – Leg time modified by protest committee.

Additional Information:
The protest committee at Rio penalised the following yachts for infringements at the start of the Race: *Group 4* by 30 minutes; *Commercial Union* by 2 hours. Times given are corrected for these penalties.

BT Race Results System Data. © British Telecommunications plc, 1992/93.

CHAPTER FOUR

LEG 2:
RIO TO THE HORN

It was the wrangling in Rio that gave the first public indication of how the crews' attitudes to the race had altered. All the way from the Solent to Rio, every change of position, each gain and loss, had been keenly monitored by every single person in the race. No matter how philosophical people had been beforehand, they had to come to terms with the fact that they wanted to win. Part of that may have been predetermined by the kind of people who were attracted to the race in the first place. I've always maintained that the crews are high achievers by their very nature and no natural winner really wants to give an inch to other competitors.

There was another big difference. David Cowan, a crewmember on *Group 4*, recalls how his family's attitude had changed: "I think they were really knocked out by the magnitude of the venture," he remembers. All of a sudden the dream was real to family and friends. You couldn't just say you were dropping out any more without disappointment or loss of face. People who had no knowledge of sailing were suddenly very interested; up to 2,000 people a day called the British Telecom fax service for positions and plots. The pressure of family and friends' desire for people to do well, added to their own ambitions, had made it impossible not to strive for the glory of being first across the line.

Yet business and family demands caught up with some of the crew. One was John Gibson, a fifty-three year-old director of an engineering company in Newcastle-upon-Tyne. The recession was then having a profound effect on businesses and when John's wife Pat came out to Rio, she had bad news for her husband. "John had only been gone from Southampton a week when we lost our second biggest customer," she told me. "We actually moved the plant and it was a big blow to me and to the workforce. It was just the economic situation but the employees felt it was because John had left. John had had the company for seventeen years, so it was very hard for me to come out to Rio and tell him this news. I

Left After *Rhône Poulenc*'s three-day unscheduled visit to the Falklands, Suzanne Emerson has an announcement to make.

wasn't sure if he would want to continue with the race, and for about two days it was touch and go until he decided to continue."

During the week in Rio emotions shifted towards apprehension. There was hardly a person in the fleet who didn't feel some degree of fear about what lay ahead. Cape Horn was the great landmark of the race because it represented the point where the boats turned into the might of the wind and struck out across 4,000 miles of freezing, desolate ocean. Once they left the coast of Chile behind, there would be no respite and no shelter. They simply had to go on, no matter what the weather threw at them.

A few days before the start, I spoke about the next leg to Carol Randall from *Heath Insured*. During the stopover she wore a neck brace, but was declared fit to continue by the restart. She summed up the feelings of so many when told me: "How do I feel? I wish I knew. I think this is the most excited I have ever felt, the most exhilarated and the most scared. I am so nervous, I keep being sick. The hardest thing for me on this most fearsome and most feared of legs, is leaving my husband. We've only been married for a year and yet I'm going to be leaving him for nearly a quarter of that time. He will fly out tonight and I'll drift back to the boat and try psychologically to prepare myself. I feel like going with him! Yet, in a perverse sort of way, Cape Horn and the Southern Ocean is what we've come here for. I have put my faith in you completely, Chay, because you've always said that if one man can do it in a 59-foot boat, then it shouldn't be a problem for fourteen people in a purpose-built 67-footer. Commonsense tells me that is true. Commonsense, unfortunately, doesn't always rule the heart, and that is the difficult part."

Carol was right, I'd often remarked that commonsense ought to reassure everyone about the voyage across the Southern Ocean, but I didn't disguise the fact that it would be difficult. It is one thing to go round Cape Horn with the wind, but an entirely different thing to go round against the wind and current. From the Horn, the swell builds up uninterrupted all the way round the world, rolling over and over until eventually it thunders back to the tip of South America. When the swell reaches Cape Horn once more it is forced on to a shelving seabed for 200 miles around, where the seas are compressed and the wave patterns can become frighteningly disturbed. There could be huge, sharp seas ahead. I have rounded Cape Horn four times, once along the same route the British Steel Challenge fleet was about to take, and three times in the opposite direction, so I knew the conditions they were about to face.

There was the tense navigation of the Le Maire Strait off the eastern tip of Argentina to be faced even before Cape Horn could be reached, and the possibility of trouble thrilled one journalist so much that he stated the boats should not pass through there from the east to the west. Cape Horn earned its fearsome reputation in the days of square-rigged sailing ships, which could not sail nearly as close to the direction the wind was blowing from as can modern yachts. Square-rigged sailing ships could get hemmed in to the coastline if they hadn't left enough sea room between themselves and the land. Once they were backed into a corner they could not drive themselves clear to windward and lay a course for the safety of deep water; their sure fate was shipwreck. In today's yachts, whose Bermudan rigs allow them to sail so much closer to the wind, Cape Horn does not present the same perils and I knew from my own experience that it is no longer foolhardy to sail past from east to west.

Over two years of training most of the crews had soaked up books about pioneering voyages and they had read a lot about Cape Horn. But there were so few people who had rounded it from east to west in modern days that it was impossible for them to know, and so to anticipate, what lay in store. In short, Cape Horn was the spot which symbolised weather so awful they couldn't possibly imagine it. It would be as much a metaphorical as a literal turning point. For me, too, the Cape marked the point of trepidation. There was no knowing what might happen after that. All I could do was take comfort from the knowledge that the crew were prepared and trained for the worst and that the boats were as seaworthy and strong as any yachts had ever been.

In the meantime, there were the perils of Rio itself, infinitely more immediate. The yacht club was all opulence: a thirty-acre haven from the mad rush of the city, the miles of squalid shanty towns and shockingly visible poverty. Everyone was warned not to carry money and not to walk along Copacabana Beach after dark, but after five weeks at sea it was hard to resist the temptation to take Rio on trust.

Yvonne Flatman, a watch leader on *British Steel II*, was walking along the beach at night with a friend of Richard Tudor's, her skipper. As they did so, two men appeared suddenly beside them, one of them with a towel over his arm to suggest that he might have a knife or a gun underneath it. Yvonne had already heeded warnings about pickpockets, and in this situation neither she nor John were going to argue. "It was all very relaxed and polite," she said afterwards, with mild surprise. "They took some money out of my pocket, although I didn't have much on me. They ripped a pocket from John's clothes and then started to go through mine, feeling all around me. I had the money in my bra, so I pulled out the money I had in my pocket and gave it to them."

We had our own difficulties in Rio, the most pressing of which were to find two new skippers. Will Sutherland had failed to lead his crew as they – and we – had hoped and he was given a chance to retire from the race. I did not actually dismiss him and, despite reports, it certainly wasn't true that he was sacked because he had made tactical mistakes. Will had indeed made some errors, and they had cost *Commercial Union* so dearly as to deny them any realistic chance of winning overall, but I've made many such mistakes myself and I know that when you are at the back of the fleet, errors are invariably compounded. It always seems to be the front-runners who get the better weather first. So, we invited him to resign, which to Will's credit he did very gracefully, putting it on record that he wished the crew of *Commercial Union* and the new skipper well for the hard legs ahead.

When I had received that surreptitious message from Sue "Boosie" Tight on *Commerical Union* early in October, I had contacted twenty-six-year-old Richard Merriweather, an extremely able and determined young man who had recently been the skipper of the training boat *Spirit of Scotland*, in which he had taken charge of crews of underprivileged young people. We had been very impressed with Richard when he joined the prototype boat in our tour of Britain, but his youth bothered us. How well would he cope with leading a crew who would be older than he was, how well could he engender and command their respect we asked ourselves. We did not select him then and it was our loss.

Richard's time had now come. He is a very resolute and decisive person with a flair for leadership and he had an aggressive style of sailing that I believed would suit *Commercial Union's* demoralised and disillusioned crew. One of their prinicipal complaints after the first leg was that they had been given no proper areas of responsibility and they did not feel they knew how to race their boat. Richard was to change this, and from the first meetings with the crew he began to repair their self-confidence. He decided to assume, quite sensibly, that the crew knew relatively little and went sailing most days in Rio to teach them much more advanced helming and sail-trimming skills, and concentrated also on developing competent seamanship in the crew. He told them they were responsible for everything below decks, from allocating the ship's money to organising provisions for the next leg, while he took charge of everything above deck. He knew that the crew had an axe to grind and he set out to drive the boat and crew very hard. The sponsors would want that, the crew certainly wanted to do well after the dreadful frustration of the last leg, and we hoped that Richard would do all parties proud.

Just when I thought we had quelled a potential mutiny on *Commercial Union*, John O'Driscoll came to me and said he intended to resign as skipper of *Rhône-Poulenc*. As a Naval officer, John was used to commanding a team of men who obeyed his orders without question, but the British Steel Challenge crews had to be handled differently. On each boat there were thirteen highly motivated and intelligent people, used to exercising their own initiative and familiar with a working environment in which they could question decisions. It could not be the same on a boat, which effectively has one boss and three foremen in the form of watchleaders. Besides, commanding women was totally new to John, and he found it difficult and troublesome to deal with what he saw as a clique of women that grew up on board the boat. When he announced his decision to me, he explained: "I've enjoyed the trip and the crew are really quite good, but it's not what I want to do. It's not the discipline I know and I don't get on with some of them."

I was flabbergasted. First there had been the difficulty of replacing Alec Honey, now John, who I expected would do the entire race, was also resigning. I had absolutely no complaints about his seamanship, his ability to lead the crew or his skills as skipper, so I entreated him to stay on. Unfortunately, my persuasion made absolutely no difference. How was I going to approach the sponsors? What would they say when I told them we were going to have to appoint yet another skipper?

When I told Phillip Malpass of Rhône-Poulenc, he nearly died a thousand deaths. He couldn't believe that after only one leg, we had had to change skippers twice. I could see that at the back of his mind he was considering recommending the company withdraw their sponsorship. He thought it over and said: "Unless we can get some sort of guarantee that this isn't going to happen again, we'll pull out. We need someone who will stay with the boat for the rest of the race." So we took a look at the skippers I had put on standby. I wasn't sure if we had anyone tough enough for the task. Finally, it was Helen who sparked the idea of a man I had known for many years, someone who could drive the crew as hard as they wanted to be driven – Peter Phillips.

We looked at Peter's impressive CV. He was fifty-six, a big, burly man, renowned for his no-nonsense approach. He had been in the Royal Navy, then the police service, and had a history of ocean racing. In 1981, he arranged the funding for a 60-foot trimaran, then the biggest ever built in Britain, and organised the construction of it. The list of events he had taken part in was phenomenal and included the Fastnet Race, the Round Britain and Ireland Race, the Two-Handed Transatlantic Race, the Round Europe Race and the Single-Handed Transatlantic Race. He had done more ocean racing than any of the other skippers, he was tough, he had survived trimarans capsizing, and was one of the most colourful characters you'd ever be likely to meet. Peter always had a tale to tell or a yarn to spin. He is gregarious, fun to be with and a highly experienced sailor.

So we asked Peter to join the race and flew him to Rio where he made it pretty plain to Phillip Malpass that the crew could leave, but he definitely would not. The next day, he met with his crew and offered them two choices: either they followed his rules or they left by the next plane. No-one left. "They are a fine bunch of people," he reminisced after the finish of the race. "They sailed well and they all did their jobs well, but at the time I told them: 'We've got to make sure we do as well as possible in this race. There's a requirement to get on as well as possible, but you don't have a requirement to like me!'"

With his experience of sailing, Peter was one of the least anxious about what lay ahead. "None of it worries me in the true sense of the word," he told me. "There are some advantages to having been in a boat that turned upside-down in the Atlantic, having to be hauled out by the scruff of the neck and then being run down by a second container ship when the first one is trying to rescue you!"

As well as the difficulties of finding replacement skippers, tremendous rows had brewed over the issue of the weatherfaxes. The arguments had become intensely political. Some of the sponsors were up in arms at the thought that their boat might be disadvantaged, so much so that Teesside Development Corporation, whose chief executive was a lawyer, threatened legal action against us. Although we knew that some boats had been getting better pictures of weather patterns than others, and some had not been able to get any pictures at all, it was difficult to work out just how poor each boat's equipment had been. The argument, which turned out to be completely wrong, ran that the leading boats had been those with the best weather pictures. In fact, *British Steel II*'s weatherfax had not worked for much of the leg and *InterSpray*'s had such poor reception its value was dubious. However, no-one wanted to lose out on any redress that might be given, so each skipper reckoned it would be better to say the weatherfax hadn't worked.

IBM generously replaced all ten computers, even though the computer equipment obviously wasn't at fault and we got each of the skippers to sign a declaration to acknowledge that all the boats' computers and software were identical. The company that provided the satellite pictures checked that each boat could receive the same pictures and we asked the skippers to declare that they accepted this. Quite frankly, I didn't regard weatherfaxes as especially vital equipment, and if the skippers weren't happy after every attempt had been made to rectify the problems, then we were going to remove it from all the boats and let them rely on information broadcast by radio from the Met Office in Bracknell.

Three hours before the start of the second leg, a meeting with the skippers revealed that two weatherfaxes still weren't working. *Commercial Union*'s high frequency radio, linked to the weatherfax, wasn't receiving the necessary signals and *Group 4*'s weatherfax also wasn't working. Here we were, a few hours before the start, with all the assembled supporters and journalists getting ready for the off, and the second leg already looked destined to become stormy on shore. To his credit, Richard Merriweather agreed to sign the form and accept weather information from Bracknell, provided he could ask for extra information. It was an enormously generous gesture by him, bearing in mind he had just arrived, and was taking on people with little experience who would be expecting to rely on regular weather information. Mike Golding was still testing his equipment and begged a little more time. It was a knife-edge moment. Would I have to recall all the weatherfaxes in public?

We were just preparing to delay the start of the race for two hours to do that when fate intervened in our favour. My hand-held VHF radio crackled. It was one of Mike's crew on board *Group 4* who had been fiddling with the weatherfax. "We've found the connection," he reported. "We've corrected the fault now and we're getting perfect pictures." Mike was as amazed as I was. Was this a last-minute reprieve? I hurried someone to check before something else went wrong. The message came back that the weather picture was fine, Mike signed the form and we all breathed a colossal sigh of relief.

There were perfect conditions for a boisterous start: over 20 knots of wind, sunshine and a fetch out of the bay. This time the start was more practised, less nervous and although many people from the yacht club in Rio went out to see the fleet off, there was not the hazard of hundreds of spectators' boats nor the distractions of thousands of friends and relatives. Even so, *InterSpray* crossed the line early and *Heath Insured* collided with *Nuclear Electric*, putting a dent in her hull. *InterSpray*'s time penalty for the early start, which the rules called for, was later dismissed because the starting committee, from the Iate Club do Rio de Janeiro, hadn't used the proper recall procedure, but *Heath Insured*'s infringement meant that two hours would be added on to her overall elapsed time.

I watched the boats jostling for position and couldn't help but reflect that the first leg had been the easy one. This leg was a matter of make or break, and the success of the Challenge rested or fell on it. I did not worry about the minor incidents of the start; they were fairly insignificant. As the fleet headed south, though, and I flew back to England, my anxiety began to get the better of me and I went into the race office first thing every morning to hear how everyone was doing. Scrutinising the positions and weather conditions became like a disease for me, as it did for the families and a lot of the sponsors' employees. I had no interest in the print-out of the yachts' progress that the race officers gave me; I wanted to see the most up-to-date information on the computer screen – something might have altered in the time it had taken the printer to issue the latest results.

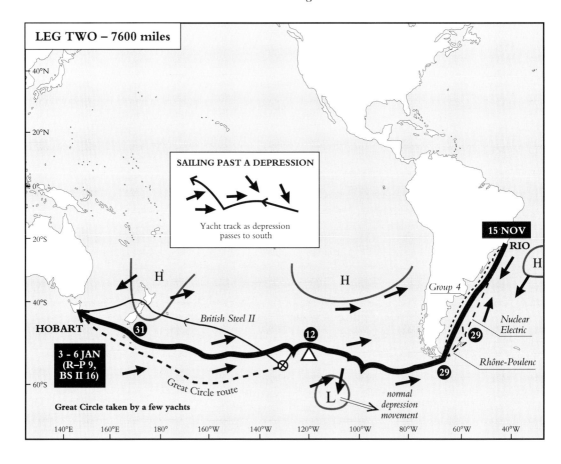

For the first week, the weather was clement. The stretch from Rio as far as the Falkland Islands was at that time dependent on a series of weak areas of low pressure that were reforming again after the effects of the Andes. The predominating wind direction was from the south-west, but the wind was stronger offshore, and the lows themselves were separated by light and variable winds. It meant that the progress of the fleet was slow – only 5 or 6 knots on average – and the temptation was to venture away from the land to avoid the vagaries of the wind and escape the grasp of the counter-current. John Chittenden took *Nuclear Electric* offshore and was followed by *Cooper & Lybrand*, decisions that gained them increasing leads over the rest of the fleet from the first week. As they headed south to Cape Horn and the longed-for appointment with that most evocative of land-marks, they were a full two days ahead. Meanwhile Paul Jeffes took the inshore route, where *InterSpray* encountered lighter winds, often from ahead, and fared particularly badly.

As they sailed south, off the coast of Argentina, I was relieved that conditions were still favourable. You can get savage winds there, as I did in the yacht *British Steel*. The Pampero winds that brew up with surprising force in the area near the River Plate had struck in 1970 with such might that *British Steel* had been laid over on her beam ends and the tiller bent. Oddly, they battered me a second time so hard that it bent back again!

At a quarter to midnight on 17 November, there was the start of a distressing and, for us, desperately worrying series of gear failures. *Group 4* had been making good progress, sailing in 30 knots of wind with two reefs in the mainsail and a No 2 yankee and staysail. It was a dark night, with a large swell, and *Heath Insured* was chasing hard, only two miles astern. "We had earlier fallen off a couple of waves with a sickening crash," Mike Golding reported, "but everything was fairly calm when mayhem broke out. There was a crack and then the deafening flapping associated with a major problem."

The first sign of the problem was evident from the No 2 yankee which was badly ripped. Simon Clarke went on to the foredeck and when the crew called all hands on deck, Mike, who had been off watch, took stock of the situation and immediately commanded the helmsman, Nick Jubert, to take the boat off the wind. What was certain was that the forestay had somehow parted, for the mast was flexing alarmingly. By taking the boat off the wind, the strain would be transferred from the forestay to the intact shrouds and backstay. This quick thinking probably saved damage to *Group 4*'s mast.

Then Simon Littlejohn and Mike O'Regan took the two spinnaker halyards to the stemhead to act as a jury forestay and, when that had been done, the job of retrieving the parted forestay and ripped sail began. In gale-force winds and with the boat heaving madly downwind with the swell, it took five people to tussle with the whipping sail, which had twisted round the shrouds and was threatening to take out a spreader, and lash it to the deck. "Breaking waves swept us bodily down the deck to the mast," Mike said afterwards, "and to make matters worse, our automatic lifejackets inflated as we were buried under the water."

Two hours later, *Group 4* was under control, but they were minus the forestay fitting and Mike Golding judged that heading past Cape Horn would be reckless. The crew were exhausted, drained and bereft. They were going to have to turn back and head for port to make repairs. Essential spare parts would have to be sent out quickly, so the chosen port had to have good air connections. The Brazilian port of Florianopolis was chosen, a day's distance to the north-west, and Tony Hill telexed headquarters to let us know that this plan had been decided on.

Back in Hampshire an operation had be be mounted to put *Group 4* back in the race as soon as possible. Knowing that part of Group 4 Securitas's business is to transport all sorts of items across the world at speed, our press officer contacted them and outlined the enormous logistical problems we were going to have. *Group 4* needed a replacement bottlescrew but the fitting was manufactured in two parts, one made in Retford, Nottinghamshire, and the other at Southampton. Both would have to be collected and sent to Florianopolis with all haste.

To everyone's admiration, Group 4 Securitas rose to this challenge with tremendous resourcefulness and energy. Two vehicles were sent to collect the parts, while Group 4 International Airborne Services called up someone who spoke Portuguese to take the parts to Brazil. Less than twelve hours later, Derek Jones and the new rigging screws were on board a flight to São Paulo and the old one was on its way back to Britain to be analysed by British Steel metallurgists. Less than two days after *Group 4*'s forestay had parted, Derek arrived in Florianopolis on a connecting flight.

On board the boat, repairs to the staysail were being made, but it was beyond the skills of the crew to repair the yankee and the nearest sail loft was North Sails' branch in São Paulo. So, off went Nick Jubert and John Carter by plane to São Paulo. The plan had been to catch a flight back later that day, but North Sails knew they were going to have to do serious surgery to put the sail back together and that would mean missing the last flight of the day. The only alternative for Nick and John was a twelve-hour bus ride. Every minute that *Group 4* was not making progress towards Hobart penalised them for the entire race and it seemed then as if the quest for a quick turnaround had failed.

Having put this new difficulty to Group 4, however, the company again took a look at what they might be able to do. One of their South American associates, Prosegur, was contacted. Could they help put the boat back in the race, they were asked. Yes, was the reply, they could charter a private Lear jet to fly back to Florianopolis. An hour-and-a-half after the last stitches had been put into the yankee, John, Nick and the sail were back in town. Early the next day, 20 November, *Group 4* left port with the crew determined to eat away at the 150-mile deficit they had on the ninth-placed boat, *InterSpray*, and reduce *Nuclear Electric*'s 400-mile lead. Always one of the boats on which good trimming and helming created the best boatspeed, *Group 4* overtook *InterSpray* just five days later. What we did not know then, though, was that the crew of *Group 4* had not fitted all the spares sent out to them. They didn't replace the toggle on the forestay, and that was subsequently to cause further major rigging problems.

Happy though we were that *Group 4* were back in the race, Andrew Roberts and I had a gnawing concern. Since all the boats were the same, it was a reasonable assumption that the same failure would happen on other yachts. We talked it over, and recalled an incident before the start in Rio, when Andrew expressed his concern to the crew of *Group 4*, on seeing them using a long bar to apply excessive force to a rigging screw that tightened the rig. Mike Golding was not aboard at the time. We wondered if that might have been the cause.

The security of the rigs had always been a major concern, right from the first concepts of the design and we had spent considerable time researching historical data and talking to suppliers and subcontractors. However, there was no definitive information on what loads might be imposed on the rigs over long periods in conditions such as the boats were now experiencing, and until we got the analysis of the failed bottlescrew, we couldn't know for sure why it had happened. Anyway, there was nothing now that we could do about it.

A new concern lay ahead and we put the fleet on the alert for ice. Icebergs had been reported in the area off the River Plate and the skippers knew they might have to initiate a lookout rota. Almost 150 miles ahead of their nearest rivals, *Nuclear Electric* had reached that point off the River Plate where ice had been reported. On 12 November we warned the skippers of an unusually large berg that had drifted north and grounded off the coast of Argentina at about 42°S. It was one of the biggest icebergs ever reported and was reputed to be the size of the Isle of Wight. Two-thirds of it was under the water, reaching to a depth of over 600 feet. This had broken up and smaller icebergs had torn away. The smaller ones were reported to be up to 100 feet in height, but there were also many fragments, or "growlers" between that position and the Falkland Islands.

As *Nuclear Electric* reached 43°S, just at the northern fringe of the Roaring Forties, where gale-force winds are encountered much of the time, they reported to us that they had sighted an enormous berg – approximately 300 feet high and half a mile wide. An iceberg as big as that was no worry: there was no difficulty seeing it and it would give a good signal on the radar. As we all watched the daily plots anxiously in England, it was the small icebergs we fretted about, fragments calved from the ice shelves of Antarctica or, indeed, from this rogue iceberg. There might be so little above the surface that they would not be seen until the very last minute and would not give an echo on a radar.

Despite that, they could well be an enormous size beneath the water. Such growlers were potentially lethal, even to our steel boats, which had strong ice-collision bulkheads abaft the bow.

So a lookout would be essential. Some say that there is a peculiar, choppy sea in the vicinity of an iceberg. Others swear that the smell of the fresh water of a berg is borne perceptibly on an otherwise saline wind, and in general the sea and air temperature drop by a few degrees.

On 27 November, just over a week after *Group 4* had made her repairs in Florianopolis, ill-fortune claimed another victim. A vigorous depression was passing to the south of Cape Horn, bringing with it gale-force winds from the north–west. Between 400 and 500 miles away from the Cape, the boats were speeding along under spinnaker at an exhilarating 10 knots. *Rhône-Poulenc* was sailing fast under the new assymetrical spinnaker added to the boats' sail wardrobes in Rio, when she was hit by a gust of 50 knots. Broaching madly under the pressure of the wind, she was knocked down and stayed lying on her side for several minutes until the spinnaker sheet was released. All hell broke loose on the boat as she swung back upright and was caught again by the full force of the wind. The mainsail and spinnaker flogged furiously: 3,500 square feet of cloth flailing in the wind and it was not easy for the crew to drop the sails, recover control and begin to take stock of the damage.

What they found immediately was a bent spinnaker pole and a torn spinnaker. But once *Rhône-Poulenc* was back on course and Peter checked the boat's rigging, he discoverd that the cap shrouds had slacked off. He knew that this would not put the rig in any danger, but in view of the fact that they were rapidly passing the point where any help could be had, Peter started the engine and began to motor south-eastwards towards the Falkland Islands. He contacted us for advice about the rigging and we spoke to Proctor Masts who had made the spar. After more telexes back and forth, we arrived at the conclusion that the masthead tang bolt had been bent and that there was likely to be damage to the spreader. Then we turned to the RAF to see if they could help transport the replacement parts to Port Stanley. Very kindly, they consented.

Rhône-Poulenc's three-day sojourn in Port Stanley was one of the oddest stories of the race. They had no detailed charts of the islands to enable them to make a safe landfall, since we hadn't exactly envisaged the Falkland Islands being a port of call, so when *Rhône-Poulenc* neared Port Stanley, a launch came out to guide them in. I could picture the scene well as I too had called in for repairs on the way from New York to San Francisco with Eric Blunn. I had also been suffering from an extremely painful foot. I could hardly put any weight on it and I was half convinced I had broken my ankle. We were met by the Governor, Rex Hunt, and his wife and, without delay, I was sent to the local hospital where, after some examination, the doctor proclaimed that I had gout which Eric greeted with peals of uncontrollable laughter.

The spares for *Rhône Poulenc* duly arrived and repairs to the damage, which was not as bad as expected, were made good by Simon Walker and Jerry Walsingham. The masthead tang was replaced, but the spreaders turned out to be undamaged, something that was a heartening illustration of how strong the rig was. Meanwhile, the spinnaker pole was taken ashore and straightened. All the while, the officers and crew of HMS Dumbarton Castle, stationed off Port Stanley, were exceptionally helpful. But it was not all arduous work for *Rhône-Poulenc*'s crew. While they awaited the spares, they met with the Governor, David Tatham, and dined out with some of the islanders. Paul Egan went off to have a round of golf at the Stanley Golf Club and Angus Mackenzie put in a memorable performance to snatch the HMS Dumbarton Castle record for the "scuttle run". As a telex to race headquarters explained, it was "a curious game of diving from one escape hatch, across the deck and back through another escape hatch while drinking half a pint of beer – all against the clock!"

Refreshed by this unexpected stop, the crew of *Rhône-Poulenc* set off again at 0300 GMT on 2 December, "raring to get back into the fray", they confessed. They rejoined in tenth position and were firmly in everyone else's wake, but if it bothered the crew terribly, they and their skipper were determined not to let it show. In Hobart, all the crew recounted it as a great adventure and appeared proudly wearing T-shirts that proclaimed: "When the going gets tough, the tough go to Port Stanley."

After almost a fortnight at sea, those who had experienced seasickness had recovered. The only exception was Phil Jones, a steel worker from South Wales and a keen dinghy sailor who had joined for one leg. He had been enthusiastic about doing this, of all legs, as it was the one everyone believed would be the highlight of the circumnavigation. Phil was still unable to keep down any food, and occasionally not even water. He was utterly incapacitated. All medicines and remedies both modern, old and rumoured were tried, but none worked. After only two weeks of this, Phil had to be excused all watches for a day to recover his strength, but once in this weakened state, he became very ill and the crew of *Coopers & Lybrand* ministered to him and tried to keep his spirits high throughout the seven weeks at sea.

As the fleet drew south towards Cape Horn, the air and sea temperature dropped. Day by day, the number of thermal clothes and oilskins that were needed on deck increased. Many of the boats were in sight of each other, closely following each other's tacks and monitoring their progress. The temptation, as always, was not to let a rival behind take a tack or make a course alteration that might take her into different winds and so get a lead. *Coopers & Lybrand* and *Commercial Union*, for example, were engaged in just such tactics. On 23 November, *Commercial Union* overtook *Coopers & Lybrand*. With only a boatlength separating them, the two crews roared and cheered, and Viv's crew tried everything they could to make the boat sail higher and faster. *Commercial Union*, however, was pointing closer to the wind. Some hours later, the wind eased, and *Coopers & Lybrand* edged back, slowly passing *Commercial Union*, to more cheering. Two days later, *Commercial Union* got their own back, overtaking their foes and stretching a lead that Viv's crew were not to break again on this leg.

On 29 November, *Nuclear Electric* became the first of the fleet to round Cape Horn. Like many other friends and well-wishers, I sent them a message congratulating them and wishing them Godspeed. Extraordinarily, for a place where gale force winds blow seventy per cent of the time, John Chittenden and his crew sailed past easily in daylight, under full plain sail.

"The crew are elated," John wrote back to me. "A school of dolphins, two seals, a whale, two penguins, as well as a whole flock of seabirds and pink fish celebrated our approach. The joy was tinged with irony as the wind died and we lay for three hours one mile off the Cape, waiting for a puff of wind. It was a perfect, sunny day and the sea was glassy calm. At dinner time, we celebrated with special chocolates reserved for the occasion and a bottle of whisky to share between the watches. By the early evening, the wind slowly picked up and, having had ample opportunity to take in the Horn from all angles, we began to move west. We are delighted (for once) to follow Chay's instructions and are now smoking west. The only slight niggle to the day is that five sausages have disappeared from the galley. The inquiry goes on . . ."

At the same time, *Commercial Union* was heading the rest of the fleet into the Le Maire Strait. There is a strong tidal effect here that can either greatly help by shooting a boat through the Channel or effectively shut a boat out with a contrary current. Both *Commercial Union* and *Coopers & Lybrand* had been trapped in fickle winds while, behind them, others boats closed the gap quickly, but once they entered the Strait, a strong north-westerly and favourable tidal stream hauled them away again.

Mid-evening local time on 30 December, *Commercial Union* rounded Cape Horn in 5 knots of wind, the second boat to "turn the corner" in uncharacteristically kind conditions. Less than six hours later, *Coopers & Lybrand* followed them round. Ann de Boer wrote: "We rounded at 0130 local time, with the sky showing early signs of dawn. When we first realised that we would go round in the dark, we were all slightly disappointed but, as it was, the dark added to the occasion and the sight of silhouetted rock left some of the mystery surrounding the notorious landmark.

"We rounded doing 10 knots, accompanied by a school of dolphins which, I've been told, is a good omen. The sunrise was one of the most impressive we've seen so far, with flaming red clouds and the sky displaying every colour. There was even a rainbow, which appeared in the west on our port bow and finished over the rugged Chilean coastline. In a way, it was nearly too easy to be true and a big disappointment for the crew who had been looking forward to the rough seas and howling winds we had all expected."

In the late afternoon, *Heath Insured* rounded Cape Horn and the crew broke open champagne and chocolates. Like *Coopers & Lybrand*, they passed on a close reach, doing 10 knots. Adrian Donovan still says he regards that as "the best sailing I've ever done. It was so emotive – and Cape Horn was everything you think it should be." David Spratley, the boat's rigger, was so exuberant that he took off all his clothes and streaked round the deck.

Only three miles after they had passed Cape Horn, *Group 4* struck the ocean swell, took off on the back of a wave and clocked up the fleet's highest recorded speed. "We were hit by a huge wave and a 50-knot gust simultaneously," Michael O'Regan recalled. "We were literally picked up and catapulted through the water. As we accelerated through a tunnel of spray we all started screaming and shouting and the boat hit 21 knots. Unbelievable!" A few days later, the sponsors issued a challenge and a prize to any boat that could better that boatspeed, but none ever achieved it.

From Cape Horn the fleet entered largely unknown territory. When we planned the route and the season the race would pass through the Southern Ocean, we had discussed at great length what course the skippers might take. Most boats making a circumnavigation turn north to pass through the romantic Pacific Islands in the tropics, just as the sailing ships of old had done. No yachts had ever raced this way before, so the information we had was relatively sparse. The Roaring Forties that the boats would pass through is primarily a belt of strong westerly winds, along which track series of depressions. As they rotate clockwise in the southern hemisphere, they upset the pattern of weather, so that there can be easterly winds to the south of depressions and winds of 60 to 70 knots to the north. Racing in the opposite direction, Whitbread fleets learnt that there could well be headwinds to the south, and we knew that even further south there would likely be lighter and more variable winds.

The shortest route to Hobart for the British Steel Challenge yachts was along the Great Circle route, further south than that historically taken by Whitbread yachts. An extreme southerly route might be attractive to the skippers, not just because it was shorter, but because there would be a good chance of some favourable winds. However, there were other factors they would consider. For one thing, it would be much colder down there, with freezing winds being whipped off the ice shelves of Antarctica. For another, there was the peril of icebergs, in particular those

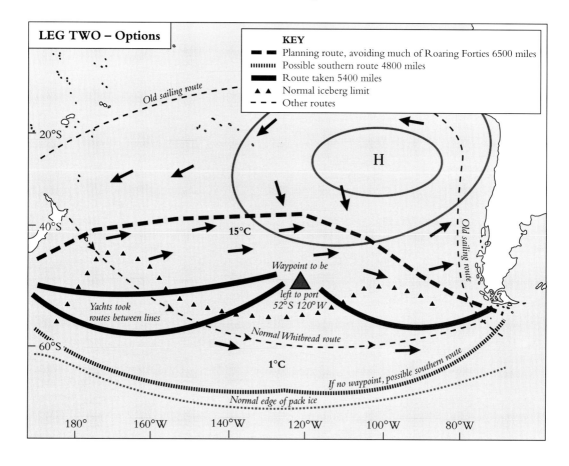

lethal "growlers" to be considered, where collision might result in damage at a point where there were no safe havens, and no rescue facilities. So, we decided to create an imaginary waypoint, a co-ordinate in the Southern Ocean. Nothing was there, no land to be seen nor anything visible to round, but it would force the yachts to put some northing in their course after Cape Horn. The course we had planned would add miles to the route, but the requirement to round the position of 52°S 120°W would, we hoped, keep them out of the areas of likely ice. The idea was not new, as both the Whitbread and the Vendée Globe Challenge races impose similar routeing rules.

We wanted a fairly speedy passage, too, because it would give us time for the planned maintenance work in Hobart. As the boats would then have raced hard halfway round the world, the last 7,000 through very difficult heavy weather conditions, refit work was planned, and that would take time. Along this route, an estimated time of arrival of 16 January, or a week either side, could be relied on. As it turned out, we needed all the time in Hobart we could get.

CHAPTER FIVE

LEG 2:
CAPE HORN TO
HOBART

After rounding Cape Horn, John Chittenden and his crew on *Nuclear Electric* had little choice but to head west, following a course of 250° magnetic. As they turned the corner into the Southern Ocean, they met the predicted long ocean swell and headwinds, and that heading was all they could fetch. They could have tacked, but had they done so, they would have been forced to go up the south-west coast of Chile and confront much more unpredictable weather conditions. Instead *Nuclear Electric* traced the curve of the Great Circle route towards the way-point and made a remarkable average of almost 8 knots. In their wake, each of the following skippers chose the same course. Even *Rhône-Poulenc*, 800 miles astern, chased along the same line.

Out in the uninterrupted might of wind and waves, eastbound depressions, some close by and others far afield, swept through the yachts in succession. North-westerly airstreams whistled by and typically vigorous fronts whipped up winds of as much as 70 knots. Depressions and high winds passed quickly, but there would be little respite before another stormed out of the west. Only a week past Cape Horn a huge storm with winds of up to 80 knots pressed most of the fleet. "We are totally at the mercy of the elements," wrote John Carter aboard *Group 4*. "The seascape is awesome. We reckon the waves are fifty-five feet, with some up to eighty feet."

Conditions aboard were difficult and wearying. For those who have never experienced a gale at sea, the effort of daily tasks, let alone pushing a boat as fast as it would go, is almost unimaginable. Having been in such conditions time and time again, I could identify all too easy with David Wallbank, who sent us this vivid account of life aboard *Pride of Teesside*:

"'Wake up. Wake up!' It was 3.30 in the morning and I was being called for my next watch. I had only just fallen asleep. Sleep is so difficult. I'd finished my previous watch at 11.30pm. By the time I had brushed my teeth and taken off the layers of protective clothing, it was midnight. I'd lain in my bunk exhausted but with my head spinning. The storm we were in was throwing the boat around like a toy. You could feel her lifting up and up on the gigantic waves and hovering weightless for those few breathless seconds before crashing down. The noise was deafening.

"We couldn't lie still in our bunks. There was constant and often violent movement, and everything was shaking. When I climbed into the bunk, which involves risking life and limb in a desperate jump, I reached into my side netting for a clean T-shirt. They were all damp. I'd worn the present one for a week and was beginning to smell a little. No-one had washed for two weeks and the best we could manage was a Baby Wipe bed bath.

"So, I'd put the T-shirt on and lay for a while trying hard to stop thinking. It's difficult, because twenty-four hours earlier I was just going on watch and had to be wide awake. That's the problem with a watch system, there's no routine for sleeping. People tend to be dozy all the time or, like me, have great problems getting enough sleep. Yet, eventually I must have slept, maybe for forty-five minutes or so, and now I had to get up again. It was bitterly cold and the thermals felt hard, almost frozen. Shivering, I put them on and tried to ignore the unpleasant sensations. Soon, I reasoned, they would defrost. As we fought to put on our wet oilskins, the watch crew struggled to say hello to each other, but that's about all we could manage as we jostled for a space, or a place to hold on. The world on deck was dramatically different. It was pitch black and the wind was blowing at 35 mph, with higher gusts and rough seas. The howling wind alone would have made communication difficult, but with our protective gear and hats and balaclavas, it was impossible.

"I took the helm and tried to control the boat. Every time the boat hit a wave the spray shot across the deck at me, horizontally. Although I had goggles on, stinging pebbles of icy water hit any exposed part of my face and as the goggles steamed up, I had to take them off. This left me guessing when the next salvo of spray would come across. I didn't always get it right.

"After I'd been on the helm for an hour and a half I handed it over and collapsed into the cockpit, where I lay still for a couple of minutes. The concentration needed for helming the boat is incredible, let alone the sheer physical strength you need to fight this wild and wasteful ocean. Someone offered to make tea, and that's not an easy job. You have to watch the kettle in case it decides to fly across the galley, despite the pan clamps. Cups dance around and, because of the angle of heel, you can only fill them half full and only by making a chain can we hand out the cups without loss. Last night, the elements were against me: a gigantic wave broke down the length of the boat and my cup was left empty.

"A while later, we had to change sail and struggled up to the foredeck to pull down the headsail and hoist the storm staysail. We already had three reefs in the main. Working on the foredeck at night in a storm is unreal – so different from anything you could experience in normal life. You have to hold on with one hand and work with the other. Your legs get washed away so a good handhold is a lifesaver. We always clip on our safety harness, but there are moments when you have to transfer it and take a small act of faith.

"A song keeps going through my head. Goodness knows why. It's the Eurythmic's song, which goes:

> Sweet dreams are made of this,
> Who am I to disagree,
> I've travelled the world and the Seven Seas,
> Everybody's looking for something.

"It's amazing how many songs are about the seas, oceans and sailing. I suppose the open sea conjures up images of space, freedom and new beginnings. But what we are experiencing now is not the stuff of sweet dreams. I wonder if each one of us will find what we are looking for . . ."

On 14 December, *Pride of Teesside*'s radar broke down. Now there was no way that they could safely watch for icebergs at night and Ian faced a dilemma, which was later compounded by the discovery of a small, leaking crack to the skeg, the structure aft of the keel which supports and protects the rudder blade. In Hobart, we found the crack along a weld, but the exact cause remained a mystery and we came to the conclusion that it had been caused by a grounding during the summer. Ian and his crew knew the shortest route to Hobart would take them directly into likely areas of ice. He thought it over – not for long – and took the decision of a true seaman by turning north. I agreed whole-heartedly with him, but felt for the situation he was in; nothing was worth the possible cost of chasing south – certainly not the 400 or so extra miles that the safer route would add. "It's disappointing," he telexed back, "but I feel this is necessary for the safety of the crew and the yacht."

We had long discussions with Raytheon, the manufacturers of the radar, to try to find out how to get *Pride of Teesside*'s unit working again, and as with the forestay failures, a list of diagnostic questions and answers rallied back and forth between *Pride of Teesside* and race headquarters as we tried to isolate the problem. Two days later, Ian rebooted the unit following the instructions we gave him and got it working. Still the problem with the skeg remained and, although she now dipped further south, *Pride of Teesside*'s was one of the most northerly courses.

On 6 December, a report from Viv told us that *Coopers & Lybrand* had suffered a forestay failure. The forestay bottlescrew had also sheared and, in so doing, had transferred the tension to the luff of the yankee, which ripped badly. It sounded like an exact repeat performance of *Group 4*'s rigging screw failure and sail damage. Quick reactions by the helmsman of *Coopers & Lybrand* saved the sail and possibly the rig, as the boat was turned quickly off the wind and the pressure taken from the forestay to the backstay and shrouds. Viv and her crew thought carefully about solutions, some way of reinforcing the broken bottlescrew so that it would hold and came up with a clever solution, using part of the strong Spectra spinnaker halyard wrapped round the bottlescrew again and again.

The same day, *Group 4*'s second forestay bottlescrew failed. For Mike it was more than worrying; it was truly soul-destroying to have had the same thing happen once again. Meanwhile, we were horrified and worried in equal proportions. We had been wrong in assuming that this was a one-off failure. Now, it looked like the same problem was going to sweep through the fleet. Already people following the race back in Britain were speculating about when a disaster might happen – an accident or a dismasting – and frankly we shared that fear.

The report that had come back from *Group 4*'s first forestay showed that it had sheared across the stainless steel threaded part because of tensile overload – in other words, shock loads that somehow exceeded the loads it had been designed to take. We understood that it had gone because of an exceptional load in extreme conditions, which was momentarily in excess of the yield strength of the bottlescrew. However, the threaded part just above the fork end had also stretched, and the manufacturers, Norseman-Gibb concluded that stress corrosion and fatigue might also have played a part. All of this was puzzling. The prototype boat, equipped in exactly the same way, had sailed over 28,000 miles, many of them in conditions just as bad, and had not had any similar damage. Why was it happening now, and why on three of the boats?

While we were asking these questions, Andrew immediately set about trying to ensure such damage didn't happen on other boats, or occur again on *Group 4* or *Coopers & Lybrand*. As the boats slammed repeatedly into waves and fell into the troughs, putting incalculable shock loads on their forestays, it would be the forestay rigging screws that would bear the strain. Andrew therefore consulted with rigging experts and advised all of the skippers to transfer their forestay rigging screws to one of the aft lowers and put on a webbing strop as soon as the weather permitted. The reasoning was straightforward: fatigue was almost certainly a factor and the loads on the aft lowers were slightly less, with much lower fatigue loads. Support by the webbing strops would give no extra strength, but it would limit the damage to sails and rigging alike if a rigging screw were to fail.

Pete Goss transferred the rigging screws as advised, yet several days later, he reported that the weakened one had failed at the aft lower shroud.

He had contained the damage and was continuing, but the anxieties for everyone involved intensified. Those worries seemed justified when, a few days later, the forestay bottlescrew broke on board *Heath Insured*, whose skipper, Adrian Donovan, had likewise been careful to reinforce the fitting. At least his foresail was not badly damaged, however, as he had also prudently fitted a strop to the tack of the sail in case the fitting failed. It seemed only a matter of time before the rigging problems claimed yet more victims. John Chittenden later commented that the worst part of the Southern Ocean leg was waiting for something to break, and I knew exactly how he felt. The whole fleet was vulnerable and the danger in losing a mast was that someone could be injured. Even if no-one was, a long, desolate ocean would separate fourteen people and their disabled yacht from help. They would have to get up to weather to head for New Zealand or else run all the way back to Cape Horn. The nearest place downwind that they could get help would be Port Stanley, and there weren't many facilities there. The coast of South America was another possibility on a downwind route, but that, too, had few facilities. Besides, to go so far back would put any yacht out of the running: they would certainly miss the start from Hobart. It would be a disaster and a crushing disappointment for everyone.

British Steel II, meanwhile, was closing on the leaders and by 14 December were in third place. The rigging screw failures on *Heath Insured* and *Coopers & Lybrand* allowed them to leap from fifth place in a matter of days but, even so, they were looking strong. Behind them, *Group 4* was reducing the distance behind the others, day by day.

The leading boats were now closing fast on the mid-Pacific waypoint. For John Chittenden, protecting *Nuclear Electric*'s lead was of paramount importance, and that buffer from the following boats allowed him to heave-to for heavy-weather sail changes. This, he knew, was a safer practice, making it easier for the foredeck crew struggling on a pitching, wet deck with water cascading over them. It also helped preserve his sails, on which every fraction of boatspeed was dependent.

Commercial Union and *British Steel II* were chasing hard and could afford few manoeuvres that lost them time or miles. "The wind patterns here are so predictable and constant," wrote Giles Trollope on *British Steel II*, "that it is difficult to make a significant breakthrough in a one-design fleet. Three other yachts have been within thirty miles of us since the Horn – 1,500 miles back."

Each day, I watched the fleet's progress anxiously, knowing the dangers of the weakened rigging screws. Yet despite these problems, the skippers and crews were racing and did not stop pushing their boats hard and racing fast. We were amazed and proud that in spite of all the difficulties they were encountering they were making 8 knots through the water to windward even in heavy weather. With careful study of the wind direction, the boats worked tactically to windward, so that they usually steered within 30° of their desired track. Between Cape Horn and the mid-Pacific waypoint, all the yachts maintained an average speed of 6 knots.

In the three days before the leading half of the fleet reached the waypoint, there was a full gale, with winds of 50 and 60 knots and waves up to fifty feet high. Ann de Boer on *Coopers & Lybrand* wrote this report: "Winds gusted up to Force 12 and we were hit with lashing rain and whipping spray. The waves were bigger than we had ever seen, some rising up to forty feet, which in Admiralty pilot books would be described as 'phenomenal'. It was extremely cold and unpleasant, but at the same time quite exciting. As soon as it was light, Vivien decided it was time for the trysail to be hoisted – a tricky operation in rough conditions and one which resulted in Matt Steel-Jessop falling on his lower back on to the mast winch, hitting Vivien in the face on the way down. This was only the second time we had put this particular storm sail up; the first time was in the Solent in a gentle swell and a mild south-easterly breeze.

"Not long afterwards we had to take the staysail down; it had been flogging for far too long. We replaced it with the storm staysail and reassessed the damage. Nearly all the hanks looked like they had seen better days and along the leech were many ripped seams. It looked like we had our work cut out for us stitching the sail for the next day or so.

"As the day progressed, the wind eased slightly. The sea, however, was still huge, with mountainous waves. Big walls of water confronted us, which the boat climbed and descended with relative ease. Fun park rides will certainly seem tame after this! Everyone's tired, though we're pretty excited: this is what we all expected to see and experience. There are still a good number of big icebergs around and they make the bergs we saw at the start of the leg in the Atlantic seem like growlers. One chunk was particularly enormous and the spray of the waves we saw crashing over it must have been swept as high as 150 feet. Magical!"

On the approach to the waypoint, we saw the average speeds of the boats drop to 5 knots, as they tacked and worked their way to windward to round the imaginary mark. The rounding of the waypoint was momentous for many, even though there should have been nothing to see

Top right Fresh winds gave a boisterous start to leg two off Copacabana Beach in Rio. Here, *Nuclear Electric* gets past *Coopers & Lybrand* after her collision at the start line. BP
Right Rhône-Poulenc had a new skipper to come to terms with. Peter Phillips had made it plain how he would run his ship and spent the last week of the stopover training the crew. BP

Pride of Teesside trim their yankee to gain a little extra boatspeed and give chase
at the Rio start. AC

Above The elaborate web on the frame forward of the wheel prevented *Heath Insured*
helmsmen being swept through by breaking waves in the Southern Ocean. AR
Right A crewman on *Group 4* is hoisted to the clew of the yankee to make sail repairs. SL

Above A crash helmet for braving the wet and pitching deck to reef the mainsail. RH
Right Taking in a reef in heavy weather needed several people. SE

Life at an angle for weeks on end meant some of the *InterSpray* crew found it easier to lie on the cockpit sole than to sit on the seats. PB

Above British Steel II prepare to step their jury mast in heavy seas. The boom, lying fore and aft along the port sidedeck, became the 'new' mast once it had been hauled upright. RH

Right Mast work as *Pride of Teesside* crashes through the waves. AC

other than the co-ordinates 52°S 120°W illuminated on the GPS display. As it was, there was a huge iceberg there, and a lot of jokes winged their way back to us from the boats claiming that we were responsible for putting it there in lieu of a tall ship.

Conditions were still rough. *Heath Insured* sent us back this telex in a shorthand version in response to a request from their sponsors that they keep the costs of communications to a minimum, although at first we mistook it for an indication of how difficult the uncomfortable conditions were making keying in messages: "At 0259 GMT on 13 December, *Heath Insured* passed the Southern Ocean waypoint. *Hofbräu Lager* were one mile astern at the time. We had been sailing towards this position, some 1,800 miles from Cape Horn, for ten days and it was smthng of a watershed. Althgh thr are still 3,800 miles of windwrd sailing to Hobart, we're allwng rslvs to think it is all downhill frm here . . .

"The roundng was a fillip for us. We'd struggld with unchctrstclly lght winds fr the previous 48 hours. Boat spds of 0.5 to 2 kn in 3 kn of wind in the mddle of the Sthrn Ocean. Mist n fog compltd the scene, which was made worse whn we discovrd at the evening chat show that other boats had been movng steadily. Ten days of chippng away at the leading boats gone, and the chasing pack around and past us. *Pride of Teesside* passd the waypoint 2 miles ahead of us. The mood did lighten as we approached the w/p, marked as it was by 'a minefield of bergy-bits and growlers' to quote one. The skipper reveald his dilemma: 'It's a mark of the course but there's nothing to hit,' he said, bemused."

By the middle of December, they had all rounded the waypoint, but oddly enough, the position we expected would take the fleet away from most of the icebergs seemed to be a magnet for every berg in the area. Most of them were visible on the radar, but the threat of growlers prompted the skippers once again to post lookouts. Richard Tudor took the view that "maximum vigilance" was needed, and put three crew on deck and two below at the navigation table on every watch. Each time an iceberg was spotted, the position was carefully noted and relayed to the other boats at the next position report.

In those rough conditions, injury to the crew was, if anything, likelier than damage to the boats. People were thrown around on deck, hurled against the wheel when a wave cascaded down the boat, and sometimes sent down the foredeck in cartwheels when they were changing sails on

Top left Sailing past icebergs was one of the wonders of the Southern Ocean legs, but the crews always had to be vigilant for lethal 'growler' icebergs just below the surface of the water. NS

Left One of the sights that make a race like this so remarkable. A huge iceberg left in *Hofbräu Lager's* wake in the long Antarctic twilight. HL

the foredeck. Everywhere on the boat was a potential hazard, something which was brought home to the crews of *Coopers & Lybrand* and *Group 4* in particular. "At times we were suspended in space, with our boots just two or three feet off the deck. At other times, the water swept us down the deck until either the safety line stopped us or we collided with a piece of deck equipment. Believe it or not, we loved it!"

The worst incident on *Group 4* came when Gary Ashton was sent hurtling down the deck by a breaking wave and slammed into a dorade vent guard. Briefly, he was knocked unconscious and came round to find that he had bitten through his lower lip, broken two teeth and was deeply bruised across his back and down his leg. Mike Golding and his medics kept alert for possible concussion, but there was none. Serious bruising was so common on the boat anyway that it merited little attention. Part of the trials of sailing in the Southern Ocean in these conditions, as I knew only too well, is to keep going however tired, sick and sore you may be.

On *Coopers & Lybrand*, where Phil Jones was still badly seasick, Vivien was suffering from a swollen knee after a cartilage injury which had caused her discomfort on the first leg and now began to give her serious pain. It could have caused another skipper drama. She could easily have dropped out in Rio, but didn't. In fact, she forfeited an operation in Rio and had it done in Hobart instead. It showed incredible tenacity, particularly on the occasions when she could barely move, yet still had to come on deck to issue instructions and sail the boat. I was very impressed by the courage she demonstrated in keeping going.

There were other injuries, too. "One of the many hull-vibrating waves made Geraint Lewis's leecloth give way," wrote Ann de Boer on 15 December, "and threw him out of his top bunk, complete with sleeping bag. John Kirk heard him hit the floor and immediately called Viv, Brian Bird and Samantha Wood for a quick assessment. After consulting the "proper" doctors in the fleet on the SSB radio for advice on what to do, Brian concluded that Geraint had probably fractured his collar bone. It was extremely painful and uncomfortable. Paul Titchener also took a nasty tumble or two and badly bruised his rib cage, which means he won't be able to do any serious sailing. Now injuries and seasickness have affected the watch system. To cope with the work load and give the "sickies" time to recuperate, Vivien divided the crew into two watches, run by Matt Steel-Jessop and Neil Skinner, with Vivien floating between. Robert Faulds and Paul Titchener are the back-up down below. Geraint and Phil (who was seasick) have to stay in their bunks.

"As a result of the bad weather, our course has been awful: we were either going north or south. Again, we lost ground to *Heath Insured* and are in sixth place. During the night, *Nuclear Electric* lost the lead to

Commercial Union and *British Steel II* for the first time since the start of the second leg. I am sure they are frustrated and will be trying with all their might to get back in front again."

While *Nuclear Electric* was trying to regain the leading position and *Commercial Union* and *British Steel II* fought it out, disaster struck on 16 December. Giles Trollope describes the events of that night:

"At 1900 GMT on 15 December we were in a very strong position, lying 2nd to *Commercial Union* by just thirty miles and with our nearest rivals, *Heath Insured*, 150 miles behind. We had made a decision to sail conservatively after the *Group 4's* second bottlescrew failure and because we had such a good overall position to protect. Just to be sure, we had put a sacrificial strop of Kevlar rope on the tack of the storm jib so that if the forestay did fail, damage would be minimised.

"On the morning 16 December, we shook out a reef in the main and were tramping along at 8 knots, not overpressed. Mike Sherwood and Steve West were with me in the cockpit. At the moment when I was looking forward to coming off watch and having a cocoa, the boat came off a wave with a huge bang. We often did that without harm, and nothing seemed to have changed with the handling of the boat. It was dark, and we couldn't see the rigging, but decided to check the forestay anyway.

"Mike went forward with a torch, looking first at the suspect bottle-screw. Horror of horrors, what he found was that the windward half of the lower shroud, also reinforced with a light tape webbing strop, had failed and the webbing preventer was now taking the strain. But before he could warn us of what had happened, the strop slowly parted and the mast collapsed."

From the view in *British Steel II's* cockpit, the events ran as if in slow motion. First, the mast moved sideways, tearing away at the partners, and when it had slid to leeward as far as the guardrails, the huge column rotated clockwise and snapped at the gooseneck. Rigging and ripped sails lashed the side of the boat so that each crewman had to find a corner of the cockpit in which to shield himself from flailing wire and cloth. Everyone was safe, but without a mast *British Steel II* was out of the leg. Worse still, her predicament left her no chance now of winning the race overall. As all the crew came on deck in panic and confusion, it was one of their first thoughts.

In the dark and freezing cold and with heavy seas pitching the now unbalanced hull horribly, Richard Tudor and his crew worked to cut away the remaining rigging, which kept the mast alongside the boat and threatened at any moment to pierce the hull. With every breaking wave the crew clung on desperately and pulled to the ends of their harness safety lines as the force of the rigging beneath threatened to drag them over the side. Using bolt-croppers to sever the wire, they worked frantically to disentangle the rig, trying to salvage whatever they could of the mast and stays. Later, they knew, these would be needed to build a jury rig, for when the shock receded the realisation struck that they were over 2,500 miles from any land. *British Steel II*, like all the other boats, had sufficient food and water to last sixty-five days, as long as they would have needed to make a port in any direction, and they had enough power to provide an electrical supply for at least the same time, but to go downwind to Chile or to reach to Tahiti would put them out of the race, while to shape a course upwind towards New Zealand would soon exhaust their fuel. They were adrift, precariously, in the depths of the Southern Ocean, at the furthest possible point from civilisation anywhere on the globe.

In the very early hours of daylight near the equinox of the southern high latitudes, Richard Tudor and his crew tried to piece together what had happened. The rigging screw had clearly failed, shearing right across just above the forks. Fortunately, the INMARSAT telex was not dependent on the mast for transmission or reception, which allowed Richard to telex race headquarters with the news and later discuss the problem. At just the time his crew were struggling to salvage all they could of their mast, sails and rigging, I was at the Royal Ocean Racing Club in London, getting ready to go into a committee meeting and we had been discussing the consequences of a rigging failure. Just as we were about to sit down, I was told that there was an urgent telephone message for me and left to take it. The worst times to get phone calls are early in the morning and late at night, because you know that no-one calls you then except if it's a bit of an emergency. So a mid-morning call did not make me feel particularly anxious. All the same, I remember looking at my watch and noting that it was 1021.

The message about *British Steel II*'s dismasting was devastating. You can imagine how I felt when I heard that the very worst case scenario we had dreamed up before the race began – a boat being disabled halfway between Cape Horn and New Zealand – had actually happened. For a minute or two, I just couldn't believe it, especially since we had got such fantastic reports from the boats only a couple of days before, when morale had been high and they had been doing 10 knots to windward in a Force 8 gale. I asked when it had happened and was told that the mast had come down exactly twelve minutes before. Modern technology had been remarkable in relaying the information rapidly, and the speed of the report also proved that Richard must have had all his wits about him. I was impressed. Yet out in the Southern Ocean, *British Steel II*'s crew were on their own, and we were powerless to help them. The implications for the rest of the crews were also terrifying: one by one rigging screws were snapping like matchsticks, even when they had been transferred from the forestay. How many more were going to fail before the fleet reached Tasmania?

I went upstairs and relayed the message to the RORC committee. The meeting that followed was tense. I had to think about how to limit possible damage and about fixing the problems once and for all in Hobart, and the committee had to ask whether it was worth the risk of sending the boats on the planned southerly route past the Kerguelen Islands on the next leg. We also had to examine the precedent set by every race in the past. In all of these a plight such as *British Steel II* faced could mean disqualification. The rules laid down that a disabled yacht might motor into port, get repaired with outside assistance, leave the port again and then once bound south of the port, resume the race – provided there is no gain. This is what happened with *Group 4* when they went back to Florianopolis, and what happened with *Rhône Poulenc*, when they mo-tored to the Falkland Islands. The rules of previous races also say that if the yacht gains an advantage thereby, the race committee is entitled to penalise her.

Group 4 obviously hadn't gained any advantage, because sailing to Florianopolis meant having to turn back. The question over *Rhône-Pou-lenc* was slightly different because when she left the Falklands, she was a little nearer Cape Horn than when she started motoring. After considering this, the race committee later agreed that she hadn't gained on the other yachts; on the contrary, her damage had lost her two days.

The problem arose in judging *British Steel II*'s position now. There was no nearby port, so we prepared to put to the committee the argument that, as the dismasting had happened in mid-ocean, and Hobart was not only the finish port but also the only realistic port she could be repaired in, her time of arrival there could be considered as her elapsed time for the leg. We felt the rule could be interpreted this way because *British Steel II* would surely lose days, if not weeks, because of the dismasting. But only an international committee could decide this, and they would have to meet in Hobart at the end of the leg. In the meantime, *British Steel II* had little choice but to carry on towards Hobart as quickly as possible in the hope that they could either protest or would be reinstated. However, neither they nor we yet knew if it would be possible.

Out at sea, only practical assistance could help Richard and his crew. As soon as they heard the news, other skippers offered help. Among them, Adrian Donovan and Mike Golding, both of whom were in the same area, decided to go and give any help they could. *Heath Insured* was nearer and Adrian and his crew tracked across the 140 miles separating them to give *British Steel II* some extra fuel. With more diesel and supplies, Richard could make progress north-westwards, out of the worst weather of the southerly latitudes, and gain more favourable winds. Here, too, they might rendezvous with a commercial ship for fuel.

Heath Insured reached *British Steel II* just after midnight local time on 18 December. Carol Randall wrote: "Not a word was spoken in respectful silence for *British Steel II*'s plight as we came alongside in the darkness. She was a terrible, sad sight, being tossed about like an oversized canoe. It struck us how small and vulnerable she seemed." They passed over fourteen five-gallon jerry cans of diesel. In the dark and with *British Steel II* pitching and rolling furiously without the steadying effect of a mast and rigging, it was a most difficult operation to pass the cans of fuel over on a heaving line and retrieve them along another, and it demanded total concentration from the crew and impressive seamanship and boathandling skills from the skippers. "The skippers had to manoeuvre the yachts to keep a constant distance of no greater than thirty metres in those heavy seas at the dead of a moonless night. There were all hands on deck on both yachts for this exercise, everyone giving up valuable sleep."

"We were deeply moved," Carol reported. "The silence was broken when a *British Steel II* crewmember asked Arthur Haynes if he knew any good jokes. A lot of banter then started, with good wishes exchanged between the crews. The ultimate gesture came when *British Steel II* sent a parcel of goodies across to us, including sweets and two CDs. It was pretty tear-jerking coming from a crew which faced thousands of miles' motoring to a port of call before they could restock." The operation took over an hour to complete and afterwards *Heath Insured* turned again and resumed the race.

By then, Mike Golding and the crew of *Group 4* had appeared over the horizon and the same exacting procedure was followed, with the skippers keeping their boats parallel and the crews ferrying jerry cans to and fro along a heaving line. Again, there was good-spirited banter between the crews, as Giles Trollope and Kevin Dufficy wrote: "Christmas goody bags were exchanged, containing booze, cigarettes, chocolate, etc. This whole exercise and the offers of help from other yachts truly reflected the spirit and camaraderie that the Challenge has engendered in all the crews. We are tremendously grateful, for without their help our plight would have been serious indeed. We now have the remaining five feet of mast, the boom, which is intact, and two spinnaker poles and are creating a jury rig. This is being designed by our resident leg-two crewmember Grenville Davies. It has to be capable of withstanding the Southern Ocean's fierce winds. Even as we write, a gale Force 8 is forecast within twenty-four hours."

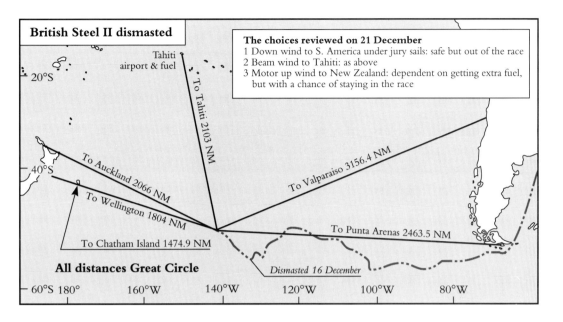

British Steel II dismasted

The choices reviewed on 21 December
1 Down wind to S. America under jury sails: safe but out of the race
2 Beam wind to Tahiti: as above
3 Motor up wind to New Zealand: dependent on getting extra fuel, but with a chance of staying in the race

Tahiti
airport & fuel

20°S

To Tahiti 2103 NM

To Valparaiso 3156.4 NM

40°S

To Auckland 2066 NM

To Wellington 1804 NM

To Punta Arenas 2463.5 NM

To Chatham Island 1474.9 NM

All distances Great Circle

Dismasted 16 December

60°S 180°   160°W   140°W   120°W   100°W   80°W

News of the dismasting had broken back in the UK the day it had happened and people began speculating about what had occurred and why. It certainly did not make our jobs any easier. We issued an immediate press release which stated: "*British Steel II . . .* has been dismasted in very heavy conditions in the Southern Ocean. There are no injuries to any crewmembers. The team is currently assessing the situation and the possibilities of erecting a jury rig. The crew are heading north, away from the iceberg belt, and will then reassess the situation before deciding which port in New Zealand to head for. The yacht has plenty of food on board for the completion of this voyage, estimated to take three to four weeks, and with full engine power as well, water making will not be a problem."

Naturally, most of the yachting journalists were interested principally in how it had happened and where the blame might lie. Speculation began enthusiastically; I think there were a few who had been waiting for something to go wrong in an event that dared to allow "amateurs" to do what had previously been the domain of professionals. Others felt it was in the public interest to comment on the implications of the event. *The Guardian* carried the most swingeing report: "The risks associated with the British Steel Challenge were well-known: this was the race in which the amateurs could screw up so badly that lives might be lost. But once the fog which still hangs over the shambolic second leg clears, it is not the amateurs who will be called into account; it will be the professionals who must explain how and why they failed the amateurs so badly."

I was amazed that the article was so negative, and took the trouble to write to the sports editor, the first time in my life that I have ever done so. He replied that his reporter had asked for an interview, a request I never received, and he had got comment from a top helmsman who described our boats as underspecified. It was infuriating. The man didn't know anything about the specifications of our boats.

In a more measured, investigative report, *Yachting World* reported: "What seems to have happened . . . is that the 14mm Dyform (forestay) wire has been selected for its high strength, but the equivalent pin for a 14mm wire is below the required breaking load . . . In other words, it appears that the rigging screw is not as strong as the wire. Although this would not necessarily cause the failure, it gives a guide to the possible weak link." This allegation was later repeated when it appeared in the *Daily Telegraph*.

It was too early to draw conclusions and we were irritated and dismayed by these reports. To be honest, we felt hard done by, for failures and structural damage are by no means uncommon among racing boats and we felt we were getting an especially unsympathetic press. After all, on leg one we had passed safely by the Vendée Globe Challenge fleet, half of which had had to retire after serious construction faults. I remembered, too, the second Whitbread Race in which *Flyer* suffered structural damage to her hull after a short period of heavy weather sailing to windward in the Southern Ocean, and she had been exceptionally well-prepared beforehand. Granted that ours were one-designs, with the inherent risk that a problem with one would be a problem with all, but we could not have prepared them more thoroughly or consulted any more exhaustively with designers and engineers. It was not just we who felt disappointed. When we met them in Hobart many of the crew confessed they, too, felt let down by the aspersions, for these had taken away from the seamanship and initiative they had shown.

All the while, Andrew Roberts was investigating the possible causes far more vigorously than anyone else could have done, and he issued this report:

"Bureau Veritas approved the structural elements of the design and subsequently inspected the construction of each yacht. During each stage of the project, input was received from manufacturers and suppliers as to individual components' strengths. On the basis of this information, together with experience and historical facts, decisions were made. Bureau Veritas did not have any part in approving the rig. Rigging decisions came as a result of discussions with the manufacturers and historical data.

"The standing rigging came under particularly close scrutiny, with both visual inspection and electronic testing being employed. Our experience with *British Steel Challenge* and formal surveys after she had sailed 28,000 miles, reinforced the conviction by all concerned that the construction, fit-out and equipment had proved extremely strong and durable and was entirely suitable for what was always considered the toughest yacht race.

"The failure of the first and subsequent rigging screws came as a shock to all concerned. Lots of conclusions have been jumped to by pundits but a large number of inconsistencies cloud the true picture . . .

1 *British Steel Challenge* has sailed over 30,000 miles with no deterioration by the time the problems were beginning.
2 *Rhône-Poulenc's*, the tightest rig in Southampton and Rio, had not failed after 17,000 miles.
3 The second tightest rig failed after 13,000 miles.
4 *Group 4's* second rigging screw failed after about 2,000 miles.
5 The slackest rig has not failed after 17,000 miles.
6 Visual inspections carried out on the failed and other rigging screw components at sea have not detected a reduction of the thread count or any other signs of threads stretching.
7 Each yacht's rig was set up by her skipper and crew and each was set up with slightly different rake, prebend and rigging tension.
8 Varying but small amounts of corrosion of the faces of the rigging screws were reported on all but *Group 4's* second unit.
9 Opinion from the yachts tends to indicate fatigue as a factor."

Andrew asked Norseman–Gibb to carry out some previously untried tests on the top of the range 14mm stainless steel and bronze units of identical specification to those used on the yachts. They found that one person tightening the rigging screw with an 18 inch adjustable spanner could apply a load of 4.5 tonnes, and that a load of 9 tonnes could be applied by just one person with a four foot bar. The yield point of the thread, or point at which it starts to stretch, was found to be 8.5 tonnes. They also discovered that the rigging screw failed at just under its calculated strength of 16.5 tonnes, but in a different manner to the way the ones had gone on our yachts. They were also different from a previous test conducted several years ago, in which failure occurred at over 18 tonnes.

The only honest conclusion was that we could draw no conclusions until all the boats reached Hobart. In the meantime, the message went out to the fleet to sail as conservatively as they could in the circumstances, and to reinforce the weakened parts. While we went back to Norseman–Gibb and asked them to design new rigging screws which would be twenty-five per cent stronger and made of a higher tensile material, less susceptible to fatigue. Journalists quickly leapt to the conclusion that we needed to up the specification but the point was that we had to make decisions while the boats were still at sea, without knowing exactly what the causes of the failures were. Not until the fleet arrived in Hobart could we possibly tell what new fittings would be needed for the next leg and ten custom-made rigging screws couldn't be produced overnight.

While we waited anxiously for news from the fleet about their progress, rigging failures were not the only worries they were having to contend with. Accidents are virtually impossible to prevent in the Southern Ocean. Falling from the full height of sheer waves caught crews below decks unaware for, unlike their colleagues on deck, they couldn't anticipate what sudden, unpredictable lurch the boat might make. Whoever was on galley duty had to be very careful. A large pot of boiling water swayed back and forth on the gimballed cooker, but a violent pitch or roll might fling it off. In the heads, too, there was scope for injury to the unwary. Seated occupants would be lifted into mid-air as the boat plummeted from the crest of a wave to the trough beneath, and at the constant acute angle of heel all sorts of weirdly nimble stances had to be adopted for the daily wash. Such matters tended to be discussed bawdily on board the yachts; there was no other way to treat "the daily constitutional" in a situation where there was little room for dignity and even less for privacy.

After the waypoint, all but *British Steel II* and *Pride of Teesside* turned south, deep into the latitudes of the Furious Fifties and a few as far as 60°S – the Screaming Sixties. Here the fleet divided in a choice between the stronger winds and ice of the deep southern latitudes along the Great Circle route, and the direct rhumb line course. *Coopers & Lybrand* and *Commercial Union* were among those that elected to go into the bitter cold of the Screaming Sixties, while *Nuclear Electric*, *Hofbräu Lager* and *Heath Insured* stayed in the pack that took the middle ground. Further north was *InterSpray*, with *Pride of Teesside* and *Rhône-Poulenc* following roughly along the latitude of 50°S.

From the boats furthest south there were many reports of ice. These were not usually the peaked bergs of the Arctic, but those high-sided cliff faces of ice, that have been calved sharply from the ice shelves of the Antarctic. "One of the beauties that I remember most distinctly on the entire leg was the icebergs," Eric Gustavson from *Commercial Union* recalled. "These came in a variety of shapes and sizes and, although one thought of them in one's initial ignorance as white, they are in fact the most lovely eggshell blue. At one stage we had three relatively close to us and we sailed between them, quite overawed. It became a game to recognise shapes in them. One closely resembled a Fox's glacier mint, complete with a polar bear on top; another an old barn with a bent roof.

We saw one iceberg with towering cliffs and a flat top that we measured on the radar as five-and-a-half kilometres in length.

"Of more worry were the growlers. You can only keep your eyes open and hope that you see them before you come near, but at night it really is pot luck. I will never forget the sight of one on a day when we were changing headsails and everyone's attention was focused on what was happening on the foredeck. I suddenly turned and there, on our beam forty feet away was a lump of ice the size of a house. It was bobbing like a cork in the waves, one minute disappearing totally under the water and the next rising suddenly above it."

Back in England, we had been working hard on finding a way of getting more fuel to *British Steel II*. Each boats' fuel capacity was 425 gallons, adequate for motoring approximately 600 miles and as much as most long-range cruising boats carry, but over 3,000 miles it was insignificantly small. Even bolstered by some extra diesel from *Heath Insured* and *Group 4*, the crew had a pitifully small amount for such a distance, particularly considering it was to push the boat against the prevailing winds and seas. Another source had to be found and by 18 December we believed we had the solution. Further north than the fleet's course was a container ship route and if we could persuade such a vessel to rendezvous with *British Steel II* to drop them off fuel, motoring at low revs most of the way to a port in New Zealand might be possible.

By 19 December, we were able to confirm to Richard that a rendezvous in mid-ocean to transfer 1,000 litres of diesel would indeed be possible. Giles Trollope and Kevin Dufficy wrote: "This would be sufficient for us to make New Zealand or the nearby Chatham Islands. But bad luck continues today however, with the news that she has engine trouble and will not be able to put to sea for at least four more days. Another contact of ours, a New Zealand radio ham, tells us that the chief engineer is privately admitting a departure after Christmas.

"We have decided to motor at 1,000 revs only, giving us three knots headway into building winds and seas. With our estimated fuel load, this gives us a range of about 500 miles and 1,800 miles of grey, threatening Southern Ocean separates us from New Zealand. Crew frustrations are surfacing, mainly in connection with the uncertainty of knowing when and where landfall will occur, so as to make arrangements with families."

Grenville Davies and others of the crew had been working hard on designing and constructing a jury rig from what was left after the dismasting. The mast had snapped at two places: at deck level and just above the gooseneck. The part between had been salvaged before the rest had been cut away for safety. From this and the intact boom a new mast was made. What remained of the mast was laid flat on the deck so that one of the halyard winches fitted through the aperture in the deck where it had previously been stepped. Once that was done, a line was taken from the halyard winch on the other side of the mast, down through two spinnaker blocks at the mast step down below and winched tight to give the base stability.

After that, the boom was hoisted perpendicular to the mast, using the jockey pole to create leverage, so that the full length of the boom could act as a mast from which to set sails. Richard and his crew fitted a bridle to the top of the boom so that they could attach stays to the new rig and set up two shrouds and two backstays. The boom vang, too, gave the jury rig lateral support. Once it was complete, they set the trysail from the new mast, attached upside down so that the leech became the luff. Then they began slowly to make progress.

On 21 December, we got more bad news – *Coopers & Lybrand* had suffered another setback as their Kevlar rope lashing on to the unbroken body of the rigging screw had chafed through, and the stay broke loose with a sickening, familiar bang. Fortunately, this time they were prepared and the wire attached from above the bottlescrew to the tack of the yankee prevented the stay, and thus the sail, from being dragged into the water. Within a few hours, the forestay had been jury rigged again and the boat was back on course.

As if to balance out that misfortune, the following day *British Steel II* got the heartening news that the container ship, *New Zealand Pacific's* engine troubles had been fixed, and that she was leaving to keep her appointment with them. Richard continued working his way to the north-west. Extraordinarily, the rendezvous took place on Christmas Day. Giles and Kevin wrote: "In the middle of the South Pacific in winds of Force 6 and in high seas, we have just witnessed a great spectacle of seamanship. At 0815 the container ship *New Zealand Pacific*, 43,000 tons, came into view on the horizon. At 21 knots she bore down on us in no time at all. Communication via VHF radio was established between Richard Tudor and the ship's master, Captain David Watt.

"Already briefed, the crew of *British Steel II* took up their allotted positions above and below deck. The ship turned north to give us some protection from the high seas and slowed to two knots. Gradually, we came alongside and a line was set up between the two vessels. This was the danger point, as Richard had to ensure that our yacht was not dragged into the side of the ship yet be close enough to allow one hundred cans of diesel to come across one by one on a pulley. The operation went very smoothly and in less than an hour the fuel was safely stowed on board. The best Christmas present we could have hoped for: enough fuel to get us to the Chatham Islands, 1,000 miles away.

"The *New Zealand Pacific* also sent across several small crates of Christmas goodies, including fresh vegetables, beer, books, a Christmas tree, wine and whisky. Earlier, all the crew had spoken to their families back in the UK, a present from British Telecom. These gestures are typical of the terrific support we have received since being dismasted nine days ago. Good will to all men has certainly been evident this last week or two."

It was a strange feeling for people to be so far away from their loved ones, which made celebrating Christmas Day in festive style all the more important. On *Group 4*, Donald Deakin had prepared well in advance. Food rations were doubled for the day. They didn't have a turkey, but as a substitute they had tinned ham and boil-in-the-bag Christmas pudding with reconstituted custard. Christmas presents were distributed and for Tony Marsden, whose hand had been injured and who suffered particularly from the cold, there was a charcoal hand-warmer to use when he was helming.

Nick Jubert produced a bottle of home-made sloe gin to warm the crew of *Group 4* for the day, but no sooner had he taken it out of its stowage and settled down to his lunch than he was called on deck to attend to a batten that had chafed its way through the mainsail. "To say my Christmas Day was different from the usual would be an understatement," Nick later commented. "Instead of enjoying the Christmas pudding, I found myself with a needle and thread, sewing up the ripped sail. When I finally made it down below, most of the gin had gone!"

On *Coopers & Lybrand*, Brian Bird produced a Christmas service with hymns that were sung by all the crew after they had opened their presents. The crew of *British Steel II*, whose spirits were now high in spite of their circumstances, treated the occasion more cynically. Giles Trollope wrote: "If you want to know what life is like on board a yacht in this race, then play the following game this Christmas. Before beginning play players should:

1 Not sleep for 24 hours to get suitably tired.
2 Fill up three saucepans and the bath with cold water.
3 Sell your house and give up your job.
4 Attach a rope to a tree in the garden.
5 The temperature must be under 5°C.
6 Each player should write out a list of the food they do not like.
7 Each player sends a cheque for £14,850 to pay for a berth.

How to play:
1 Each player puts into the bath the following clothes: socks, hat, trousers, jacket, tracksuit, raincoat and wellington boots.

2 Each player takes it in turns to get their clothes out of the bath, stand on a skateboard and get dressed.

3 Every four hours the player goes into the garden and pulls on the rope.

4 When back inside the house they are served with food from their list, then they sleep on the floor for two hours, are woken up and sent back into the garden for 30 minutes.

The winner:

The person who, at the end of the game, can most enthusiastically say what fun that was and how it has changed their life.''

Ever since that memorable meeting with the Royal Ocean Racing Club when I heard that *British Steel II* had been dismasted, we had been discussing an alternative route for the third leg, which made the French Kerguelen Islands the waypoint that had to be passed to port. The RORC had understandable misgivings about the plan of sending the boats again into those fierce latitudes and we drew up another route, using the more northerly Amsterdam Island as the waypoint. However, I decided to leave the final decision to the crews. They were out there; who better to judge whether or not the original route or a more merciful one would be appropriate to their challenge?

We sent a message to each of the skippers and gave them the two options. The replies were unbelievable: with few exceptions, the crews wanted us to keep an open policy and said that they would prefer to go to Cape Town via the Kerguelen Islands. This was the challenge they had signed up for, this was what they had prepared for and this was what they wanted. Those answers were quite a thrill for me. In the worst ocean in the world, hammering into the sea, with rigging screws failing and one

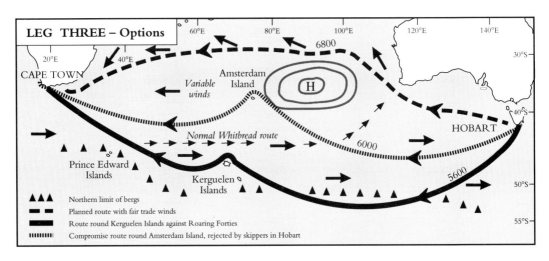

boat dismasted, they still didn't want us to alter the route. In a bizarre way, I experienced a certain swelling of the chest with pride for their determination.

That didn't mean to say that the crews were enjoying life on board, or that the weariness, cold, boredom, monotony and frustrations were in any way easy to tolerate. Carol Randall wrote in her diary of the race: "People don't understand that the social deprivations are really the worst thing. It isn't just the fear of the storms, but also the difficult conditions in which you have to live. I think the big challenge for me is living with these people, trying to understand my crewmates. You have to try to be as decent as possible. A Christian attitude is the best way to get the best out of all of us, because we have to go on even when we're feeling really quite poorly and run down and so tired we can hardly stand up."

"Off watch and in your bunk, you can lose your whereabouts," wrote Liz Macdonald, a *Nuclear Electric* employee sailing that leg of the race. "You have to work to avoid the claustrophobic feeling of the boat and the agoraphobic feeling of the ocean. The most frustrating and never-ending business on the boat is looking for the matches when you're in the galley. With four smokers on board who can only smoke in the companionway (nicknamed the chimney), they have usually stashed a box in the cubby hole there, put one in the chart table or in their pockets. One thing I don't like is the shouting. It's necessary to be heard with the howl of the wind and the clanging of the rigging during a manoeuvre, but I always associate it with anger."

By the end of December, the cold, wet and dragging constant weariness were also taking their inescapable toll. Adrian Rayson on *Heath Insured* wrote us this report: "To windward in the high southerly latitudes, bashing into gale after gale after gale. It is noise and more noise. Wind howls around the spars, breaking waves hiss on all sides, the rigging creaks and spray driven into the oilskin-clad bodies of crew batters their ears with a strange ripping sound. *Heath Insured* drives forward hard and fast, but bucks and kicks like a mule. Helmsmen grunt and grimace with the effort of steering her. She falls forwards off mountains of water and crashes into the deep valley troughs with an explosion of spray and foam. Terrible noise. For a moment, she is hidden from the full force of the wind. Then, as we rear again, she heels and pushes on. Moving below deck requires patience, as you go from handhold to handhold. The galley watch prepare meals for the other crew while fighting to remain standing. Everything is at a crazy angle. Things fly out of lockers, food slops from saucepans, and mugs empty themselves. In cabins, off watch crew are strapped into their bunks but they lurch about sickeningly, chasing sleep that often does not come."

"Why did I ever think I needed a challenge? Was my former life so boring?" wrote Lisa Wood, also on *Heath Insured*. "I am permanently wet, always cold and the skin on my hands is white, mushy and peeling. Every movement and task in these unpredictable seas is difficult. Getting into bed is as hard as getting out. Weather systems move through here so quickly. In no time, the wind gusts up to sixty knots, howling like a thousand banshees, and the spray feels like it is lacerating your face and then freezing it. The power of the wind and the sea is beyond my vocabulary adequately to describe. I feel exhilarated, desolate and ecstatic in succession; you find yourself laughing and crying in the space of a few minutes. I think when this is over and people ask me what it was like down in the Southern Ocean, I shall have to say that it was sometimes the most magical, beautiful experience and sometimes the most unutterable, intolerable hell."

Hard racing continued relentlessly, as the crews pushed their boats towards Hobart. At the front of the fleet *Commercial Union*'s lead over *Nuclear Electric* was lost as they ran into a surprising area of calm winds for twenty-four hours. It did not affect John and his crew and by the end of that time *Nuclear Electric* had once again taken the lead by a margin of almost seventy miles. The reason was that as the fleet approached the longitude of New Zealand, the southward movement of a high-pressure system disrupted the normal pattern of weather. Throughout the fleet, conditions varied widely: some, like *Commercial Union*, experienced flat calm, others had 10 knots which built rapidly into strong beam winds that sped them along.

All was still not well on *Coopers & Lybrand* and *Hofbräu Lager*, though. The strain rigging failures had put on the masts was beginning to show itself. Pete was the first to discover a serious crack round the base of *Hofbräu Lager*'s mast where it went below the deck. Who knew how many days ago such damage had occurred? Immediately, he had sent a radio message to the others to check their masts, and when Vivien checked *Coopers & Lybrand*'s, she found a similar crack which likewise had been concealed by the gaiter. As it turned out, Vivien's mast had cracked more severely, fracturing around almost eighty per cent of the circumference. Each creak and groan as they progressed on the final part of the leg across the Tasman Sea to Hobart was listened to with apprehension, if not fear. Everyone on deck at any given watch had a place of refuge in mind should the mast fall. For Vivien and Pete I knew that the strain of worry must be huge, for there was no way to prevent the crack

White water on the way aft from a headsail change in
heavy weather aboard *Rhône-Poulenc*.

growing, though they could slow down the process by sailing more slowly, more conservatively. Yet as they chased each other through the Tasman Sea, the desire to push as hard as possible was difficult to resist.

On *Coopers & Lybrand* the problem of Phil Jones's seasickness was becoming acute. Phil had been sick for well over a month. He had lost more than a stone-and-a-half in weight and was in a very weak condition indeed, as he could eat nothing and had reached the stage that even fluids were being brought back up again. Brian Bird, one of the boat's medics, wrote: "I was called to see Phil one morning, as he had been vomiting blood for the last four hours. On examining him, I found that he could not breathe through his mouth or even swallow his saliva; his throat had almost closed up. He was in a lot of pain from his throat and was whispering: 'Oh, Jesus, Jesus, Jesus.' I asked him why he was saying 'Jesus' and he replied: 'He's about the only one who can help me now.' I then asked Phil if he would like me to pray for him and he nodded. I prayed out loud with him, asking God to heal him and at the end of our prayer Phil said: 'I feel really peaceful now. I think I will be able to sleep.' He was fast asleep within thirty seconds and slept for a solid six hours. I stayed for a further hour, praying silently (I didn't fancy fitting him up with an IV drip anyway!). From that day until we arrived in Hobart, Phil slowly improved and was not seasick again."

I knew how both Phil and Brian must have felt. During my solo circumnavigation *British Steel* back in 1970–1and I had struggled together through terrible storms and all I had to set against the fear that the sea would find a weakness in my boat, or that the mast would come down, was faith in God. In the Southern Ocean, I endured storm-force winds for days on end, with gusts of perhaps 90 knots. I had been exhausted and sick, and wondered how much longer I would be able to keep on going. All I could do then was pray. At those time, prayer was immense comfort.

As the boats raced towards Hobart, they encountered headwinds that slowed their progress and put more strain on the cracked masts of *Coopers & Lybrand* and *Hofbräu Lager*. *British Steel II*, meanwhile, had made the Chatham Islands after over two weeks of motor sailing. Local people and fishermen had heard that they were stopping there and gave Richard and his crew as much help as they could. While they were refuelling and taking on more fresh food, a man came along and casually asked Richard if he would like a mast. Amazed, Richard said yes, please. The trail led to a field where the man had been building his own 30-footer some years ago. The project had withered and the boat and plans were abandoned. Somewhere in this field, Richard was told, a mast was buried, and if they could find it, it was his. After some enthusiastic digging the mast was unearthed and taken down to the pier on a truck. Richard's crew then stepped it just forward of the helmsman so that they could use it in the same way as a mizzen.

Before they set off for Wellington, where they intended to stop again to take on some more fuel, Marcus Gladwell was sent to dive below the boat to check that all was well. Under the water, he noticed the carcase of a shark that had been caught in fishermen's nets and cast overboard. He surfaced, then dived again, picked up the dead shark and wrestled it alongside *British Steel II.* When he came up this time, he thrashed the water, gasped, screamed, flailed the water and, as a grand finale, manipulated the jaw of the shark open and stuck his head inside it to the initial horror of *British Steel II*'s crew gathered along the side.

From Chatham Island *British Steel II* motored to Wellington, where they shipped more diesel. Like the boats in front, they encountered headwinds across the Tasman Sea and had to tack back and forth, making only 4 or 5 knots on average.

At the same time, *Nuclear Electric* was holding her lead from *Commercial Union*, rapidly closing on the Tasmanian coast until, on 3 January, she sailed up the Derwent River on the approach to the finishing line off Hobart. It was, in some ways, disappointing that the finish occurred in the middle of night, when fewer Hobartians could applaud the achievement as John and his crew tied up alongside, but the drama of storming across the line in the dead of night was incredible. Tired, weary, unshaven and jubilant, *Nuclear Electric*'s crew took the Infolink Trophy for winning the toughest leg of the race after forty-eight gruelling days at sea.

Little over six hours behind was *Commercial Union*, pursuing as closely as ever. Richard's crew crossed the line the next day, on 4 January. It had been a particularly hard leg for them, for although they all had a point to prove after the humiliation of the first leg, there were the new ways of a new skipper to learn and they had had a steep learning curve. Coming in second gave everyone a tremendous feeling of elation. Spectators and supporters, too, felt the vicarious excitement of their transformation into a hard-driving, competitive crew. Eric Gustavson said of the leg: "We had no serious interpersonal differences, although gradually each person withdrew into himself as he needed more and more mental effort to keep going. We had learned to walk away from any confrontation and to apologise for any short-tempered outbursts immediately and I think this kept us in good spirits."

As they struggled on, *Coopers & Lybrand*'s and *Hofbräu Lager*'s masts were worsening day by day, and the strain of wondering if and when they might be dismasted was showing more and more on Vivien, Pete and their crews. A few days out from Hobart, Pete decided to be cautious. He lowered the mainsail and hoisted the trysail to reduce the stress on the mast and sailed haltingly under this reduced sail plan towards the entrance to the Derwent River and Hobart. Behind him, Vivien and her crew elected not to give up the chase for the sake of caution. They were less than half a day behind then, and I think that they saw Pete's drop in boatspeed and his obvious prudence as an opportunity to go for it. Yet *Hofbräu Lager* was far enough in front and sufficiently well sailed to keep her lead and she sailed across the finishing line just over a day after *Commercial Union*.

Coopers & Lybrand, however, came into Hobart mid-afternoon on 5 January, broad reaching with the promotional spinnaker. No greater strain could have been put on the brittle base of the mast. As I watched the boat appear over the horizon from the vantage point of a spectator boat and saw Vivien hoisting the spinnaker a couple of miles from the finish, I was dumbfounded. In a flash, astonishment turned to anger. Was this bravado or sheer stupidity? I convinced myself it was bravado because, after all, Vivien had got her boat and crew to the finish without losing the mast. Still, it was pushing it a bit too far . . .

The next day, Mike Golding and *Group 4* arrived. It was the end of an extraordinary sail for them after having to go back to Brazil for a spare rigging screw and having turned again to go to the aid of *British Steel II*. So it was no small achievement to have made up those miles against the wind, all the way catching up on the leaders, mostly because of good sail trimming and quick sail changes.

A short distance behind was *Heath Insured*. Like *Group 4* in the last week of the leg she had to contend with steering problems. With the huge seas and strains put on the rudder and steering gear, a steering cable had snapped and they had fought on by steering with the emergency tiller while the cable was replaced. Nevertheless, Adrian's crew had kept the pressure up to finish only three days after *Nuclear Electric*.

Pride of Teesside finished on 6 January after taking the northerly route wisdom had dictated when their skeg began to leak. It was a course that had obviously lost them miles, but that was just the fortune of war. Ian admitted that the decision to stay north had been a hard one for him, and it was ironic that he was to have to make a similar difficult choice on the leg to Cape Town. Though other boats had experienced serious problems, Ian's praise for his was fulsome, and it gave us encouragement as we began the long process of putting the fleet in order for the next leg.

"Just driving her to windward and seeing her staying there was amazing," he told me. "We had 65 knots of wind. I'm not talking about wind over the deck, I'm talking about pure wind speed. I never, ever put my trysail up; I just went down to three reefs and a staysail, and I could still drive to windward. They are brilliant boats, and a brilliant design. I'm one hundred per cent convinced on that.''

InterSpray finished just under a day later, then *Rhône-Poulenc* three days after that, Peter Phillips's crew never having recovered the delay of calling into the Falkland Islands in the first weeks of the leg and he, like Paul Jeffes, had not benefited from taking a relatively northerly route to Hobart. It was interesting to note, though, that the crew of *Rhône-Poulenc* appeared now to have a different attitude, influenced perhaps by Peter's command that everyone should arrive at the dock in Hobart with a grin on their face or leave. The straight talking seemed to have worked.

Only *British Steel II* had not arrived by mid-January, but even so I was delighted, relieved and proud in equal measures to see the fleet in Hobart and all the crew looking safe and sound. I slept a lot easier after that. At the same time, it was the start of a crazy schedule of work for everyone involved and for the next five weeks Andrew Roberts and Alastair Hackett worked unstintingly on repairing, preparing and provisioning the boats. They, along with maintenance engineers Gara Hampton and Chris Winzer, did a fantastic job. The Challenge team also included Greg Bertram and Helen Wybrow, whose hard work here was, as ever, absolutely invaluable. A full maintenance programme had always been envisaged, but not one so extensive or time-consuming as this. We were relieved, at least, that the average boatspeed of 6.5 knots on the leg had brought the fleet in earlier than we expected.

Almost a week later, on 16 January, *British Steel II* made her way towards the Derwent River, after laboriously wrestling with headwinds in the Tasman Sea, against which she could make only sluggish progress with her inefficient jury rig. By then, all nine others had had their masts removed for repairs or examination and were alongside the dock in Hobart, looking small and peculiarly proportioned without them. Mike Golding had removed *Group 4*'s wheel to solve the wheel problems they had had as people bucked and crashed into it under the force of breaking waves. However, every single one of the boats and their crews cast off as *British Steel II* arrived and made their way out downriver to greet Richard's crew. It was really a very moving spectacle to see the fleet together and only *British Steel II* with any sort of mast up at all! The crews cheered and shouted, threw over beer and chocolate and *British Steel II* turned off her motor to sail over the line in Hobart.

As she did so, everyone noticed the protest flags flying from the jury-rigged backstay: Richard was protesting the circumstances of the dismasting. An independent international protest committee, in which we played no part, later decreed that she should be reinstated in the race, the elapsed time she recorded motor-sailing being accepted for her result in the leg. They found that although she had "effectively motored 3,065 miles in 31 days at a speed made good of 4.1 knots, over the same period, all other yachts had a speed made good of about 7 knots". In short, they ruled that *British Steel II* could be reinstated because she had gained no advantage and had been motoring to the port of repair, also the port of call.

The decision caused first amazement, then alarm among some of the other skippers, who believed that, as it had no precedent, it was unfair. Vivien Cherry was one of the more outspoken: "It makes a mockery of the race if they (*British Steel II*) can motor 2,000 miles and not be penalised . . . the rules are quite clear," she told *Yachting World*. Ian Bailey-Willmot, race director of the Whitbread event, was quoted as saying: "I can see no circumstances in which the yacht would have escaped a penalty in the Whitbread Race."

But the entire British Steel Challenge had no precedent anyway, for unlike the Whitbread boats, they were neither specified nor chosen by crew or skippers. It was entirely a different concept. In any case, *British Steel II* could not hope to make up a week of elapsed time on the overall leader, *Nuclear Electric*, so the arguments were rather petty and academic. All races have a learning curve, and it was interesting to remember that in the first Whitbread Race Eric Tabarly had built a boat called *Pen Duick* and used spent uranium in the keel. This was considered to be an exotic material and was therefore disallowed. In theory, Eric's boat couldn't take part, but because there were only two or three glamour boats in the race and it would have detracted from it if Eric had been disqualified, one of the committee members asked me could I please *not* put in a protest. If I protested, they told me, they would have to give him such a severe penalty that *Pen Duick* might have no chance of winning. I agreed, and Eric took no penalty. In any case, I got some amusement from reading a quote from Ian Bailey-Willmot in which he said that the travel agents in Hobart would be busy with arrangements for people who wanted to leave the race. In fact, only two people did.

For going to the assistance of *British Steel II*, *Group 4* was awarded a time allowance of twelve hours, and *Heath Insured* of sixteen hours. Again, there were mutterings from the skippers, some of them under increasing pressure from sponsors to put their boats in the limelight and to perform well. The leg had begun with some wrangling, and it ended in more. But I had to turn to more practical problems.

British Steel II arrives in Hobart under jury rig.

Arrival Times
Race Leg: **2 – Rio de Janeiro to Hobart**

Yacht Name	Status	Arrival Time GMT	Leg Time DDD HH MM SS	Placing
01: *Nuclear Electric*	Finished	03 JAN 14:26:03	048 22 26 03	1st
02: *Commercial Union*	Finished	04 JAN 00:20:21	049 08 20 21	2nd
03: *Hofbräu Lager*	Finished	05 JAN 02:29:55	050 10 29 55	3rd
04: *Coopers & Lybrand*	Finished	05 JAN 08:43:19	050 16 43 19	4th
05: *Group 4*	Finished	05 JAN 20:47:11	050 16 47 11	5th★
06: *Heath Insured*	Finished	06 JAN 05:59:06	050 23 59 06	6th★
07: *Pride of Teesside*	Finished	05 JAN 23:58:20	051 01 58 20	7th★
08: *InterSpray*	Finished	06 JAN 20:44:30	052 04 44 30	8th
09: *Rhône Poulenc*	Finished	09 JAN 22:58:40	055 06 58 40	9th
10: *British Steel II*	Finished	16 JAN 06:15:00	061 14 15 00	10th

DDD HH MM SS – Leg time expressed in: days, hours, minutes and seconds.

★ – Leg time modified by protest committee.

Additional Information:

The Hobart protest committee made the following decisions which are incorporated. Infringement at start: *Heath Insured*, 2 hour penalty. Redress; *Heath Insured*, 16 hours; *Group 4*, 12 hours and *Pride of Teesside*, 6 hours. *British Steel II* re-instated, her finish time being the time when she actually crossed the finish line.

BT Race Results System Data. © British Telecommunications plc, 1992/93.

CHAPTER SIX
LEG 3: HOBART TO CAPE TOWN

There was much more repair work to be done in Hobart than we had anticipated. The maintenance schedule we had planned for included inspections, repairs and hauling the boats out and originally a relatively small amount of spare rigging equipment was consigned for Hobart in containers. We were to need a lot more. Our spare mast was destined for *British Steel II* and freighted out in two sections, and we decided to replace two lower mast sections on *Hofbräu Lager* and *Coopers & Lybrand*. The so-called "Proctor Doctor", Dave Fremantle from Proctor Masts, was set to be frantically busy for the entire five-week stopover.

We needed to replace the forestay rigging screws, too, and had ordered them on 12 December, while the boats were still at sea. We would have much preferred to wait until we had some hard and fast information about why they had failed but decisions had to be made early. Norseman-Gibb had manufactured a stronger replacement, with a diameter of 16mm, from information largely based on *Coopers & Lybrand*'s experience with the broken strand at the top of the stay soon after Cape Horn. We meanwhile had had time to become concerned that there might be seriously under-strength wire on top of all the rigging screw problems.

Andrew Cawley, a representative of Norseman-Gibb, came out to Hobart to look after his company's interests, as did John Messenger, a yachtsman and surveyor from Sydney, instructed by the underwriters to inspect the rigs and make sure there was no underlying defect in design or specification. For the underwriters had read the newspaper and magazine articles and were concerned about the speculation. While Andrew observed all the proceedings with keen interest and assisted when asked to, he was able to stand back while they took over the inspections. With 120 rigging screws to inspect and 300 Norseman terminals, the process took several days, but it soon became apparent that the failure of the rigging

Left Mark Hodge using two adjustable spanners to tighten *Commercial Union*'s port shrouds in Rio.

121

screws had been caused by the toggle, or universal joint, at the lower end of the forestay and rigging screw not being able to articulate properly. As on many other yachts, the jib tack shackles were pressing against the forestay toggle and the lower forks of the rigging screws. Each time the forestay sagged, however slightly, the shackle at the tack of the sail worked against the toggle. The harsh conditions and merciless pounding to windward the boats had endured showed how a previously unseen, relatively small, restriction in movement could have very serious consequences. And it was not only the boats that had suffered rigging screw failures that were affected: an identical problem was evident on *Commercial Union*.

Hood Sailmakers were likewise set to work hard. The team in Hobart worked all day every day for five weeks, inspecting and, where necessary, repairing 200,000 square feet of sail. They had anticipated repairs on all ten boats and were set up to do them, but some quick thinking was required to build a new mainsail for *British Steel II*. We had spares but decided, as we had time, that Richard's crew should continue to use as much of the original as was salvageable. Seven of the twenty-eight panels could be incorporated in the new sail. Hood's loft in England did not have the capacity to build it, so they cut the panels and sent them to be sewn together in Sydney in good time for the Hobart restart. What no-one had reckoned on, though, was a cargo handlers' strike, which meant that the vital cloth was trapped in the airport for weeks, and cleared just in time for the new mainsail to be made with only a few days to spare.

We had shipped new mainsails out to Hobart and offered them to all the skippers. But by a majority they turned them down, choosing to sail on with the same ones and thus remain true to the ethos of the Challenge and the ideals of good husbandry and seamanship. What they did largely agree on, though, was that they needed another sail to cover the wind range of the Southern Ocean and a gap they believed existed between the No 2 yankee and the storm staysail. We asked Hood to come up with a No 3 yankee and the solution we agreed on was to replace the existing No 2s with identical new ones and cut down the originals to make the smaller No 3s. There had been some problems with the piston hanks of the sails chafing through on the forestay, so they were replaced with stronger ones. Hood Sailmakers faced an odd problem with *British Steel II*'s new No 3, though. Since this was to be a cut-down version of the larger sail, the orientation of the panels was technically wrong. With *British Steel II*'s sail, though, they would be starting afresh and to ensure that Richard and his crew gained no advantage from a different cut of sail, they made full panels, as if for a No 2 and then cut them down to the shape of the No 3 to make certain that they had the identical "wrong" panel orientation. For Hood, it must have been one of their most unusual orders.

What we didn't know until the inspection was that *Nuclear Electric* would also need a new mast section. Weeks back, John Chittenden had found that the bottlescrew at the base of the lower shrouds had unwound. He did not know how the seizing had loosened to allow this to happened or even if, for some inexplicable reason, the rigging screw had not been seized. In any case, the rigging screw was immediately wound on again and the shroud re-tensioned.

The kink in his mast was as much a shock to John as to us, not least when we found out that nothing could be done to straighten it. So, back we went to Proctor Masts and asked them to build us a new upper section. That they could do, but again it left us with the problem of how to get it and the others out to Hobart in time. We looked into the possibility of air freighting it, and faced the problem of how to get a mast that size on a plane. We know now that it would have been easier to have a mast in three sections, but that was part of our learning curve, and the fact remained that it was made in two sections. One of the airlines we contacted quoted a reasonable rate for transporting *Nuclear Electric*'s, *Hofbräu Lager*'s and *Coopers & Lybrand*'s mast sections, but it turned out that they were all just two feet too long to fit in their cargo hold. Another carrier was prepared to freight it for us, but they were asking for a quarter of a million pounds! This was exactly the problem we had had when looking at the possibility of getting a new mast for *British Steel II* to Wellington or Auckland, and why in the end the only realistic repair port had been Hobart, where we could have all the new sections we needed shipped.

Once all the masts had been unstepped, we prepared to haul the fleet out for inspection. What we saw beneath was, on the face of it, dramatic. The boats, in particular those that had gone furthest south on the last leg, had had the steel plating hammered against the frames by their continual pounding against waves. The effect was like ribbing, as the steel beneath the waterlines of the boats had indented most noticeably between the stringers they were built upon and the shell plating. For good reason, this effect is known as the "hungry dog" look, a term which conveys it perfectly. Although it looked alarming, this had no structural consequence for the boats and we were not worried. The term "hungry dog" is usually applied to Naval frigates, where one can almost always see some settling of the steel plates against the frames. The Bureau Veritas inspector who examined the boats agreed: it was nothing to be concerned about and would not in any way affect the integrity of the boats, he reported, so we were satisfied.

A few days later, when *Nuclear Electric* was hauled out of the water for routine maintenance work, we got another shock. From top to bottom of the keel, there was evidence of an enormous crack. John could think of nothing that might have caused it, but he did remember a mysterious incident in Rio. On a blisteringly hot day, while he and his crew were doing some jobs around the boat, he heard a very loud bang which he described as being like a gun shot. John's cautious first assumption was that it had not come from on shore, but somewhere aboard the boat, and he began checking. First, he looked closely at the rigging, but there was no damage and nothing that could explain the noise. On deck and down below there was likewise nothing out of order. He reported it to Andrew, who also could find nothing, and the next day we sent a diver down to inspect the boat underwater. However, the water in Rio is peaty with filth and he too could not see anything to explain the crack, only feel around the boat to check if anything serious was amiss. He reported nothing wrong. We were baffled and had to accept that the bang must have carried across the water from somewhere on shore.

The inspection in Hobart proved that the noise had, indeed, come from *Nuclear Electric*. It seemed that the heat had exacerbated a fault caused by internal stress during the casting of the lead keel. This had neatly split the keel in two along a perpendicular line. We discovered later that the chance of this happening is about five million to one. *Nuclear Electric* had sailed across the Southern Ocean with this serious problem and, amazingly, had come in first. There was no time to have a new keel casting made, so we took local advice as Nuclear Electric had a good relationship with the Tasmanian company Hydro Electric who sent down an expert to examine the keel. Bureau Veritas sent their expert too. For our part, we sent faxes to the designer, David Thomas, with details to help him draw up a repair that would make as little detrimental impact on boatspeed as possible. Thankfully, there was no movement from the two halves of the keel and no structural damage to the boat. So, the decision was made to bolt on a long brace on each side to hold the keel together. The Bureau Veritas inspector was satisfied that the result was strong. One difficulty remained: not only was the keel now heavier because of the bracing straps, but they jutted out rudely from the smooth hydrodynamic surface of the boat. So, our painters faired and filled around it, smoothing the surface.

We knew all about the crack in *Pride of Teesside*'s skeg and had her hauled out promptly in Hobart. The problem wasn't immediately obvious as the crack was relatively small and Andrew had to chip away at the filler on the hull to get a good look. What he found was an inch-long crack along a weld, which wasn't as bad as we had anticipated. So, worrying though any leak is, *Pride of Teesside* had been in no peril: the steel skeg is extremely strong and there was never any possibility of it falling off. Again, Bureau Veritas, among others, was consulted and we had a repair done that satisfied all the experts.

By the time all the boats had been inspected, we found the decks had suffered such a pounding that they had been breaking the sail room pillars, bolted in fittings that keep the decks from lifting. Andrew, along with our maintenance engineers Gara Hampton and Chris Winzer, replaced three sets of pillars and discovered that the failures had been caused by babystay tension. Despite these unforeseen problems, the boats were generally in exceptionally good condition and a tribute to the skippers and crew, as much as to the builders. After all, each of the boats had sailed nearly 200,000 miles since the launch in April the previous year and had come through the Southern Ocean.

For the skippers and crews themselves an extremely thorough schedule of maintenance, repair work and general preparations had to be followed and, just as all the British Steel Challenge employees worked exceptionally hard to make sure everything was right for the leg ahead, so too did the crews. Adrian Arnold, on board *Heath Insured*, wrote: "The boats were lifted from the water for hull inspection, cleaning and anti-fouling. The standing rigging was replaced or strengthened where necessary and all running rigging, sheets and lines checked for chafe. The lines most used, for example spinnaker sheets, halyards and headsail sheets, were replaced. All sails – seven tons of sailcloth in total (three-quarters of a ton each) – were inspected panel by panel, seam by seam. Below decks, all cabins, the saloon and galley were cleaned out. Hatches which leaked were resealed. The engine, watermaker, electronic navigation equipment, communication systems and safety gear were overhauled. Then, in the final days before departure, refuelling and provisioning began."

When I looked around the boats a few days before the start of leg three, I was impressed. Here were all these people working knowledgeably and competently, yet eighty per cent of them had never sailed before in their lives before joining the British Steel Challenge. Even those injured on the earlier legs, like Carol Randall on *Heath Insured*, or Steve Rigby from *Hofbräu Lager*, who had hurt his leg after falling through the wheel, were all bravely getting ready to set off on a leg that had every promise of being tougher than the last.

One of the jobs that needed to be done was to buy fresh food. Alastair Hackett had done a terrific job of organising dehydrated food for all the boats in advance and getting it shipped out to all the ports, but other fresh foods needed to be bought by the crews to supplement this. Buying things to supplement the dried foods was something of a contentious task, as Adrian Arnold recalled:

"The routine of sailing the boat is punctuated only by sleeping and mealtimes, so it's no surprise that what and how we eat plays a significant part in shaping morale and tempers on board. For those whose job it is to organise the feeding of fourteen people three times a day for up to seven weeks when preparation and cooking facilities are limited and there is no refrigeration, provisioning requires imagination and creativity. Add limited storage, weight restrictions and the fact that all the crew, skilled culinary artistes or not, are expected to take their turn in the galley, and you'll begin to grasp the situation. Our staple ingredients are dehydrated foods which, before you add water, all bear a remarkable resemblance to a mean sand and cement mix. They are transformed into beef madras curry or chicken supreme or apple crumble. Some are excellent; others manage to retain the texture and flavour of wet cardboard, no matter how many spices or cunningly devised sauces are added."

On top of this, the contention surrounding *British Steel II*'s reinstatement still seethed, fanned by media comment. Some skippers and crews had been, in my view, unduly worried about the threat of *British Steel II*; I think they felt that Richard was some sort of a racing genius and was still likely to win the race overall. He had won the Fastnet/Ushant race, he'd won the first leg and he'd been creeping to the front of the fleet when the boat had been dismasted. It did not seem to allay people's fears that *British Steel II* now effectively had a twelve-day penalty and not the slightest chance of making that up. There was so much controversy that the protest committee was asked to consider that if *British Steel II* was to be be reinstated it should be with the proviso that she could not take the overall prize if she ended up coming first. But the protest committee decreed that she was to be reinstated and that there was no reason why she should not compete for the overall prize.

If all the controversy about *British Steel II* and the unstinting work everyone did gives the impression that Hobart was a fraught stopover, that would be completely wrong. Of all the ports of call, Hobart was by far the most popular with us all. The fleet was received with incredible enthusiasm by Hobartians – indeed Tasmanians as a whole. Crews were invited to dinners and barbecues, they were welcomed into people's homes, and the help and support we got was phenomenal. I don't think I have ever been involved in a race stopover where everyone was so hospitable. Adrian Arnold summed up all our feelings when he wrote: "For us, after thousands of miles of harsh Southern Ocean sailing, it was a case of need being met by an open-hearted generosity which was both lavish and unexpected. Put simply, the crews, their supporters and the townspeople came together in one of those rare instances of harmony and mutual respect which great sporting events can sometimes foster."

The Challenge had its own celebrations, too, which will long be remembered. I had been moaning that the stopover was making me miss

Burns Night and Helen Wybrow had the bright idea of importing it to Tasmania. She decided to have a self-funding haggis party at Muir's fish restaurant next to the fish dock and only a few hundred yards from where the boats were berthed. All the Scots rallied round, as did some Tasmanians. Duggie Gillespie from *InterSpray* was the piper and we commanded that all present must wear tartan. Suzanne Emerson from *Rhône-Poulenc* turned up in very short tartan boxer shorts and Nick Fenner from the same crew wore what can only have been a hand towel, wrapped around him in the thinnest kilt I have seen in my life. We appointed Campbell Mackenzie, likewise from *Rhône-Poulenc*, as chairman for the evening and he made a great job of it. My role was to address the haggis and various others had to recite some of Mr Burns's poems. The evening was hilarious, partly because most of the recitals were given by people with English accents, gamely striving to burrr their r's, achieve the right guttural pitch for the "och ayes" and remember to say "noo" instead of "now". But the highlight of the night was a recital by Alison McKichan of *Commercial Union* of a poem she and her sister Sue from *Pride of Teesside* had written together. It celebrated at some length an intrepid wooing and began:

> Donald McGaul was four foot tall
> and he loved a big lassie called Bella.
> But being six feet, it wasni' a treat
> to be seen wi' such a small fella.

Its recitation was one of the great memories of the stopover. As for the meal that night, it demanded a lot of resourcefulness from the chef who had never heard of a haggis in all his highly qualified years. But he had done some homework on this mysterious dish and when it appeared it was unmistakably the cousin of the Scottish haggis, though with meat like a smooth pâté laid out on the plate in the style of nouvelle cuisine, with a tiny bit of haggis and a small arrangement of mashed neeps.

During those five weeks, few of us got time off. Andrew, Alastair, Gara and Chris were not able to leave Hobart but luckily I was able to go riding up in "Man from Snowy River" terrain for four days, through forests and rocky paths, completely alone in a place where no-one knew me from Adam. That was a fantastic break, one I'm sure that saved my sanity. For the rest of the time, though, the hard work was a strain, especially for those who were bearing the brunt of the repairs. The workload was horrendous, and they just had to laugh when people back home phoned and asked if they were enjoying themselves.

When the race restarted on Saturday 13 February, people turned up in their hundreds to see the fleet off. The Derwent River was full of boats

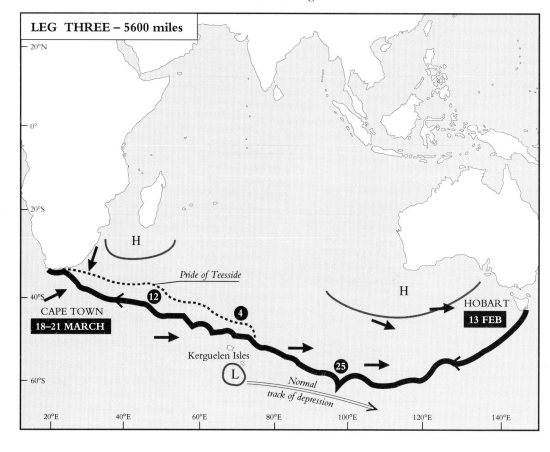

LEG THREE – 5600 miles

20°N

0°

20°S

H

Pride of Teesside

40°S

(12)

(4)

H

HOBART

13 FEB

CAPE TOWN

18–21 MARCH

Kerguelen Isles

(25)

L

Normal track of depression

60°S

20°E   40°E   60°E   80°E   100°E   120°E   140°E

cheering the crews on, and the local newspaper ran a cartoon that typified the relationship we had struck up: it showed the Challenge fleet with their anchors entangled in Hobart, towing away the island full of local people, one of whom is saying: "Something tells me they liked us!"

Dr David Grieves from British Steel and his wife Muriel had flown out to Hobart to start the race and she was stationed in a shed for officials on the shore end of the start line. Mrs Grieves was given the starting gun but as the race official was calling out the last few seconds of count down, she must have altered the angle of the gun somehow and when she fired the start signal, she also blew part of the roof off the shed.

As the fleet weaved in and out of the flotilla of spectator boats, the field of combat for the next leg was being marked out. Richard Merriweather

Top right Commercial Union at the restart in Hobart, determined to keep up the pressure of the previous leg. But this time they crossed behind Hofbräu Lager (right) as the fleet beat out of the Derwent River. BP
Right A final message to the friends and families of Heath Insured's crew as they leave Tasmania. BP

If it was hard to make oneself heard above the gale, it was often just as difficult to tell which of the crew was which on deck. PB

Above Repairs near a reefing cringle of *Coopers & Lybrand*'s mainsail. The crew could brace themselves in the fold of the reef as they worked and clip on to the boom. NS
Right Stormy weather after Rio resulted in a broach and damage to *Rhône-Poulenc*'s rig. But the freezing Southern Ocean wind had not arrived, hence the crew's shorts. PE

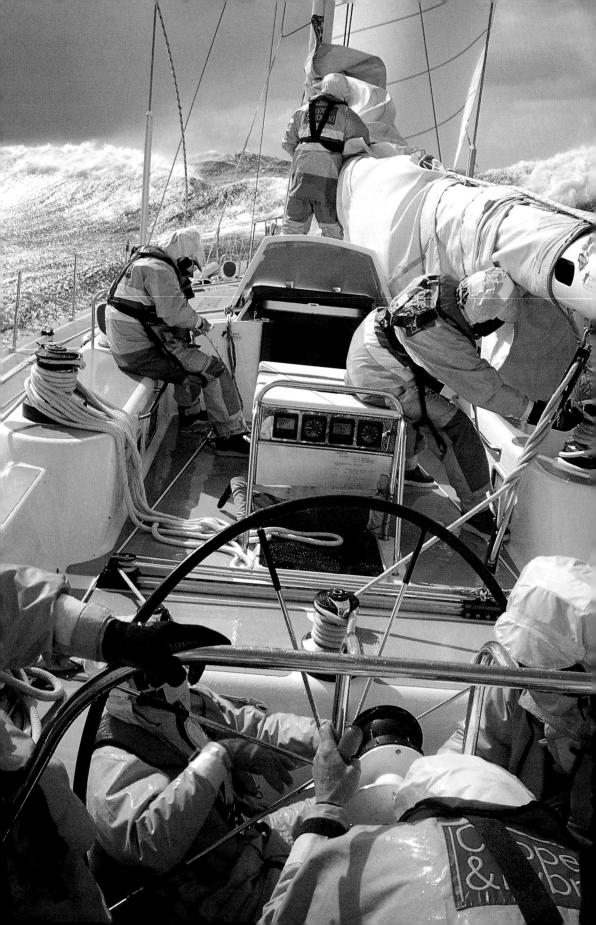

Above left Heavy-weather helming in a fog of freezing water on *InterSpray*. PB
Above right Rhône-Poulenc corkscrews down a wave to come face-to-face with the next. PE

Above Goggles were worn by many during legs two and three to protect the eyes from
piercing spray, driven in high winds at stinging velocity. AC
Left The mainsail is taken down, while four crew take off the wheel to fix *Cooper &*
Lybrand's broken steering cables. NS

Above Everyone learnt to keep hold of a guardrail on deck; it was easy to be washed to the length of one's lifeline by waves breaking over the bow. SE
Left Adjusting the leech line of *British Steel II*'s mainsail to give it optimum shape after putting in a reef. RH

Chay Blyth congratulates Mike Golding on winning the Infolink Trophy for leg three, while crewman Michael O'Regan splashes the victors' champagne. MP edged *Commercial Union* over the line ahead of the others in a start much more cautious than that in Rio. Right behind him were *Group 4* and *Nuclear Electric*. Paul Jeffes on *InterSpray* got off to a tremendous start and kept out of the pack. By doing so, he managed to sail right up to the front of the fleet as they made their way down the Derwent River out into the force of the Roaring Forties. Paul always made excellent starts but couldn't keep up the momentum. He is definitely a round-the-cans man, in my opinion, rather than a long-distance racer. This time, however, *InterSpray* had a penalty to take because they had a new No 1 yankee, as did *British Steel II*, which had a new storm staysail, a new staysail and the best part of a new mainsail. Instead of an arbitrary time penalty, we asked them to sail an extra course distance of seventeen and thirty miles respectively as they left the Derwent River.

As the fleet turned west for Cape Town, they picked up strong, favourable winds almost immediately. Newly restitched spinnakers were hoisted and, within a day, some of the crews were back into the unyielding routine of racing. Aboard *Coopers & Lybrand*, for example, the spinnaker was carried beyond its wind range and tore badly along the foot and leech. It was back to work for everyone as they took turns repairing the tears during their on watch duties.

Nuclear Electric was settling down to some new crew, a couple of them taking part in only one leg. John had been short of one crew a few days before the leg began because the doctor lined up pulled out at the last minute. We thought it would be good if we could get a Tasmanian replacement, so we made an announcement in the press. One of the replies we received was from Bill St Leger, a fireman from Hobart and a qualified medic. The local fire service were enthusiastic and willing to give him time off, and before the start, the whole of the Hobart fire service had turned up with their fire engines to make a deafening fanfare.

Less than twenty-four hours out, *Nuclear Electric*'s heavyweight spinnaker was hoisted and the boat clocked an easy 9 knots in a southerly direction with 35 knots of wind behind them. Just after midnight the day after the start from Hobart, John Chittenden decided that the spinnaker pole needed lowering and Martin Clark and John "Nasher" Nash were sent up to do the job. As a member of the crew doing only one leg, Martin Clark was not entirely sure how to lower the inboard end, so John told him to stand where he could watch. "He lifted the jammer on the cleat fixed to the mast, pulled through the amount of slack needed to lower the pole at the outboard end, but did not lock the jammer in the jammed position," Martin remembered afterwards. "As soon as he pulled on the rope the pole started to move and there was no stopping it. I was standing directly underneath and my head was the first point of contact. It hit me on top of my head with such force that it knocked me out for about forty-five seconds. I remember as I came round hearing Nasher shouting at the top of his voice: 'Get the medic. Get him on deck NOW!'

"Other watchmembers were now relaying the message aft, as they had seen what had happened and were expecting the worst. As I was regaining my senses a lone voice shouted from below: 'The medic is in his bunk. Who wants him?' Someone shouted back: 'Nobby Clark has had an accident. The spinnaker pole has hit his head.' The lone voice answered: 'The medic can't get out of his bunk, he's seasick, but he said to give Nobby some aspirin; it will get rid of his headache no problem.' At this point I had come back to the cockpit and when everybody heard the reply they fell about laughing. I still look back on this incident and find the casual reply very amusing. Incidentally, John Chittenden kept a very close eye on me for twenty-four hours just to make sure I wasn't concussed. As for our medic, "Tassie" Bill, he suffered from seasickness for about a week, which must have been terrible for him."

Six weeks of indulgence took their toll in many other crews until they found their sea legs again. The skippers, meanwhile, had to address tactics once more on an upwind leg where the distances between boats were likely to be quite lean margins. An area of high pressure was sitting over southern Australia and local sailors had suggested that one option might be to sail into the Great Australian Bight to skirt the north of the high pressure. However, the extra miles they would have to sail represented obvious risks and as it turned out everyone took the Great Circle route course towards the waypoint north of the Kerguelen Islands.

By the end of the second day out, the fleet had begun to separate, with *Commercial Union* four miles ahead of *Nuclear Electric*, and *InterSpray* already seemingly committed to a tail-end position, seventy-eight miles behind the leader. By now, too, the sea and air temperatures were dropping perceptibly, by about $1°C$ each day. People came on deck swathed in ever greater layers of clothes. For most of the first week the winds were fair, and 20–25 knots on average swept everyone nearer to the zones where unfavourable winds and poor conditions awaited. For the first time the personal radio beacons the crews wore to enable the boats to pick up automatic transmissions of anyone who fell overboard were a problem. It had been new technology, and the units we had supplied were effectively prototypes of the latest developments in personal safety, but we discovered that a thorough drenching while on the foredeck for a sail change tended either to stop a few of them working or to put out a distress signal on a number of others. In some ways, the equipment was too sensitive. These transmissions, broadcast unwittingly from some of the crews of *Commercial Union* and *Group 4*, were picked up by passing aircraft and relayed to the Australian rescue authorities in Canberra and we had to alert them that they were false alarms. Those incidents did one good thing, though: they concentrated people's minds wonderfully on the uncertain fate they faced if they did go overboard. "We all realised that the chance of rescue is virtually zero," Eric Gustavson, on board *Commercial Union*, recalled somewhat dramatically. "The whole point is to clip on at all times and make sure that the inevitable does not happen."

That first week skippers had to reassess their crews, particularly if they had people on board who lacked the experience others had of the Southern Ocean. "To use the crew's abilities to best advantage for their satisfaction and the boat's sake, skills have to be used as appropriate," John Chittenden wrote. "With four new crew, this takes time and watches cannot be set in stone. Surprises emerge as desk men exhibit astonishing courage and determination by battling knee-deep in freezing water with flogging sails. Almost unbelievably, they really enjoy it and hate applying their agile minds to number-crunching in the comparative comfort below decks. Others used to and expert at man management don't wish to run a watch but will cheerfully cook, wash up and work for hours on deck in miserably wet and cold conditions, while practical, strong people who are natural foredeck men gain immense enjoyment from ponderously number-crunching and using radio communications. The frustrations of all of this are compensated for by a person coming off the foredeck, cold and half-drowned, with a grin as wide as a plate."

The boats passed within a hundred miles of the magnetic South Pole and a week after the start, some skippers remarked that the needle of the yacht's compass pointed dead ahead no matter what heading the boat was on or else rotated lazily through 360°. Down there, the earth's magnetic field has a very small horizontal component and it made the compasses extraordinarily sluggish. Sometimes, the best helmsman and skippers themselves were at a loss to know which direcion to steer and the satellite navigation equipment was the only way of being sure which heading they were on. It made life difficult, because helmsmen had to use the wind instruments for guidance and, as the cold intensified, goggles were needed by the helmsman to protect him or her from piercing cold spray. Often these steamed up, making the job of steering accurately all the more tricky.

By 17 February, four days out from Hobart, the first Antarctic depression began to bring increasing north-westerly winds, which backed to westerlies as the depression passed through. It heralded the deeper, closer spaced depressions of the Southern Ocean, which would whirl past the fleet more and more quickly and predicatably. It was now crucial for the boats to tack strategically as the wind backed or veered, to get all possible advantage. With rougher weather came injuries: on board *Hofbräu Lager*, Steve Rigby's elbow was smashed into the cockpit coaming when he was hurled from the wheel by breaking seas. Pete Goss reported a suspected small fracture and Steve's elbow was put in a sling.

In the middle of that first depression, *Group 4* clawed her way to the head of the fleet. Close behind them, within a space of twenty-five miles, was Peter Phillips and *Rhône-Poulenc*, getting his first taste of being a serious front-runner, *Commercial Union* and *Nuclear Electric*. Further south was *Pride of Teesside*, who were finding that the southerly course was not paying as well as they had hoped. Margins between the boats were still small, as we could plainly see every day from the "distance from Cape Town" column on British Telecom results sheet, but the plotted courses of the boats showed me that already the scene was set for considerable gains and losses. The fleet was spread out across a front of 230 miles, with the leader, *Group 4*, about a hundred miles closer to Cape Town than *InterSpray*. It now meant that they could encounter quite different weather conditions, which potentially could split them up even further.

With the passage of regular depressions, race officer Captain Spencer Drummond could show me very clearly from the comfort of our headquarters in England how boats gained miles from timely tacks and anticipation of the fronts whistling though. Positions changed every day now, although the pattern of depressions made for tiring and sometimes tedious sailing. To occasional observers it might have seemed like the weather the boats were encountering was a carbon copy of the storms of the deep Southern Pacific Ocean, but it wasn't so. There, profound depressions and the accompanying storms had taken longer to build – mostly one or two days – and were trailed by a relatively calm period of a day or so when everyone could recuperate. This time there was no such lull and storms brewed rapidly, producing relentlessly steep seas.

On the second week out, most of the boats experienced their first true storm of the leg. The wind built solidly for three days and seas got higher and higher. Few had seen anything so dramatically violent on the second leg. It seemed as if the finger-waggers had been right: this leg of the race was the one where the crews would really be put to the test by the elements. Reports from on board noted that the waves were massive, with heights of sixty and seventy feet quite common. They were compared to flights of stairs, like the advancing legions of waves I had been so awed by during my solo circumnavigation, and wrote about in *The*

Right A headsail change aboard *InterSpray* on leg three. Heavier hanks had been put on some of the sails in Hobart.

Impossible Voyage. Once again, I felt almost as if I were on board one of the boats, seeing for myself the spume and trails of spindrift being driven across the tops of the waves by the wind.

This series of depressions, phenomenal waves and winds that gusted up to 70 knots took their toll on boatspeed. Captain Drummond was able to show me from the plotted positions and the data supplied by British Telecom that the daily noon-to-noon averages were dropping. One day the average to windward was an amazing 6.1 knots; the next 5.7; then 4.2. Then, as the seas subsided slightly, they rose: 6.4 knots was the average. The addictive disease of watching the fleet's performance had bitten hard again; I was hooked.

During the back-to-back fury of the storms at the end of February, *Commercial Union* started to have sail problems. We knew that their sails were in a worse condition than anyone else's, first because they had been slatting and wearing longer in the windless conditions of the doldrums, and secondly, perhaps, because they had pushed so aggressively in the second leg. Richard had been a keen dinghy sailor and I think he had the dinghy racer's tendency to let the leech of the mainsail flog. It put them in a worrying position as one of the leading boats. Should any major repairs be needed to the mainsail, it would have to been taken off for repairs, and every hour that the boat sailed without that driving force was miles lost to rivals close behind. *Hofbräu Lager* had already had to face the prospect of losing hard-won miles that way during the first week out, when they discovered a small hole in the mainsail, but they had been able to repair it by sending one of the crew up on a halyard, where he swung giddily with a palm and needle. Pete had then reported a circular stain on the sail which he said he believed had been caused in Hobart by acid. Andrew telexed back immediately that such chemicals as could damage a sail would not be kept in a sail loft and that a huge puddle would have been needed to do that damage. In Cape Town we found that the small area of discolouration coincided with an area of chafe.

Commercial Union's problems were potentially more serious. The storm jib blew its hanks and ripped in half, and while the crew were retrieving the pieces they noticed a tear in the reefed tuck of the mainsail, perhaps caused by ripping on an exposed split pin. The first attempt to get the sail off was aborted and Richard hove-to in 60 knots of wind to make it easier. Then they hoisted the very much smaller and less powerful storm trysail to maintain as much boatspeed as possible. Other repairs followed as the wind built. The storm jib blew open its hanks and the No 2 yankee piled into the face of a large wave and blew out as well. It meant another marathon stitching session. Jokes did the round of the boat about Eric Gustavson, a plastic surgeon by profession, spending his time sewing a sail. How much would that cost per stitch everyone wanted to know.

On *Heath Insured*, there was also a complication. The conditions on board made it almost impossible for the crews to wear clean, dry clothes or have proper washes and although they used Baby Wipes and had so-called "bird baths" of fresh water, hygiene left something to be desired. Adrian Donovan ran an orderly boat, and it is hard to say exactly why it should have been so, but a plague of carbuncles began to afflict the crew. For the uninitiated, a carbuncle is a multi-headed boil. Adrian Arnold was terribly tormented by them, sporting several, on his top lip, his bottom lip and his bottom. At mealtimes he had to be given his food in a baby cup with a small spout used by the helmsmen so they could drink while they steered the boat.

Exhaustion came to be a factor on most of the boats. Some of the older members of Ian MacGillivray's crew had trouble sleeping and each successive watch sapped their energy more and more. Once or twice people had to be taken out of the watch system altogether to get some rest, but it was not easy. With *Pride of Teesside* crashing thunderously from waves every few moments, there was simply no silence on board. Ian resorted to issuing sleeping tablets twice and admitted to me later in Cape Town that several of his crew were physically and emotionally drained.

It is difficult to explain what happens in really big waves when a yacht is going to windward. If you can imagine a yacht driving forward hard at 8 or 9 knots and a massive wave doing up to 10 or 15 knots in the opposite direction you may appreciate the forces involved. A boat will crash her way until she rides the crest of a wave and is suddenly left in mid-air as the wave passes through. Then the yacht drops like a lead weight, sometimes as much as ten feet, and lands with an almighty bang and crash. Our boats weigh about forty tonnes, and when they land they displace a great amount of water on either side. After that, the wind picks up the displaced water and flings it straight back in your face.

Worse was to come. On the way to the waypoint north of the Kerguelen Islands, Ian found that *Pride of Teesside* was leaking again from the skeg. About thirty gallons an hour were pouring into the boat and, although the bilge pumps could cope with this and *Pride of Teesside* was not in jeopardy, it was a constant source of concern. How did we know whether the crack would get any larger with the incessant pounding and how could Ian reconcile himself with good seamanship if he were to follow the other boats south into worse seas and worse weather? Around the Kerguelen Islands is shallower water, where the shelving seabed kicks up short, vicious seas. Ian knew that because the forces involved in working to windward there might worsen the cracks at the skeg, it had at all costs to be avoided. Not knowing the extent of the problem, he was also concerned that he might lose the rudder and so, very prudently, he stayed north. At least then he made good speeds and it became a fleet joke to refer to Ian's reputation of going extremely fast – but not always in the right direction!

Yet again, telexes went back and forth between Andrew and Ian, trying to tease out facts about the extent of the damage and its cause. We were as worried as he was. *Pride of Teesside* was out in the middle of nowhere, very nearly as far from repair as *British Steel II* had been. The job we had done in Hobart obviously hadn't worked and we faced three possible theories: either the repair had not been done properly, or the advice we had been given about how to do it had been poor, or there was some inherent design or construction defect. The last possibility was the most distressing, but there was no way we could tell why it had happened again until *Pride of Teesside* was hauled out of the water and examined in Cape Town.

Our worries were compounded when the boat's sponsors, Teesside Development Corporation, got the news. Duncan Hall, the chief executive, was, understandably enough, very concerned after the business with the weatherfaxes in Rio, and there were considerable mutterings when the radar failure and skeg crack had been seen to contribute to *Pride of Teesside*'s seventh place during the second leg. How on earth would they react now? We had very good cause for concern, because Duncan Hall started to make ominous noises about his boat not being the same as the rest, and therefore handicapped by being materially disadvantaged. The dispute had to rest until Cape Town, but I felt certain we hadn't heard the last of it.

By the beginning of March, the fleet was approaching the waypoint north of the Kerguelen Islands. These French-owned islands are desolate and virtually uninhabited – apart from scientists. They aren't on any former trading routes or present day cruising routes and few races pass them by. Those that have, have given them a reputation for ferocious weather, as Ian MacGillivray had rightly taken into consideration, for the sea conditions can be dreadful. Of the skippers, only John Chittenden had been there before, when he stopped to make repairs to *Creightons Naturally* during the 1989/90 Whitbread Race.

As the boats neared the Kerguelen Islands they got the worst weather of the entire race. In turn, each had up to 70 knots of wind, biting cold, and waves that towered fantastically above them. Far more awesome than before, the seas piled up and up, until the crest broke over the boat and left the crew facing a giddying drop to the trough. At the time the British Steel Challenge fleet was crossing the Southern Ocean, a British-registered Antarctic survey ship nearby recorded a wave height of twenty-seven metres. On deck or below, the crews were thrown around continually. Tired, unwashed, bruised and worn down by the unrelenting attrition that day upon day of heavy weather racing means, some people appeared to lose motivation. It was never easy for the skippers to motivate all their team or to keep them questing for every possible percentage of speed in conditions when the simplest jobs were difficult and when you never saw your rivals. Yet it had scarcely ever been more important for the skippers to keep their crews driving hard. The leg results, of course, depended on consistent performance but keeping the crews working reasonably harmoniously in adversity was a part of the Challenge, and part of winning.

All I could do was hope that the skippers would be prudent and not go in too close to the islands. I had ferocious weather near there when I was sailing *British Steel* and knew their notorious reputation is well-earned. So I lived on my nerves for that week, jumping every time I heard the phone ring at home and dreading the message that would give form to my fears. As it turned out, all the skippers stayed well clear: a great relief for me. Organising an event like the British Steel Challenge is not for the faint-hearted. When you are responsible for everything, from the race rules to the crews, the boats and the funding, it's a business with many potential pitfalls, complications and possible catastrophes.

New storms came, one hard on the heels of the last, with little respite between them. Most of the boats rounded the waypoint on 4 March, a south-westerly wind allowing nine of the boats to pass north of the Kerguelen Islands. They were all hard on the wind again, in 40–50 knots of wind. Lulls, when they came, lasted only two or three hours and abated only to a relatively calmer 30 knots. It was difficult for everyone – tedious sometimes – and the unrelenting conditions made it difficult to get necessary repairs or maintenance done. *Coopers & Lybrand* was one of six boats bunched tightly behind *Nuclear Electric* and twice in one day they lost their steering. It took all Vivien's strength and stamina to steer the boat by emergency tiller while the wheel-steering cables were being fixed and she graphically recalled life aboard during those storms in this report:

"Bruised and battered, the fourteen new members of the Southern Ocean Club have been well and truly baptised after the last twelve days. Depression after depression followed through with very little or no break between, bringing constant gale force winds. This is what we had all expected from the Southern Ocean: gales on the nose most of the time. A steady 40 knots wind has replaced 35 knots as the commonplace stiff sailing breeze. The latest weather system has topped even that from a steady base of 40 knots the winds are blowing up to 60 knots. So far, we have avoided any damage in this latest storm, but earlier we had a saga of steering faults. The wheel spindle locking pin sheared and the wheel started pulling out from the pedestal. Two hours steering a 67-foot yacht with an emergency tiller, in 40 knots, is certainly an experience I would not want to repeat.

"These constant gales give the crew and yacht a terrible battering. The constant wind-powered spray finds any unprotected skin with a piercing sting. This is enforced by the crashing waves scrubbing the decks clean of detritus (usually human, entangled with ropes) then washing out the cockpit well. The boat recovers, shakes, picks up speed and surges forward trembling with anticipation but you know that with the next awkward wave the cycle starts again. The crew on deck are unrecognisable with faces hidden behind hats, hoods, scarves and goggles. Only in the doghouse do they emerge, red faces glowing with excitement and fear, to tell of the last enormous wave. The maximum gusts of 65 knots have them holding on tight to the helm with their eyes shut waiting for it to end, the lulls at only 45 knots are a gentle rest and almost enjoyable sailing. How relative values have changed; never before have I said that sailing in 45 knots of wind is enjoyable. What madness is this?

"The waves find more and more novel ways of outwitting the helms, and we have taken to giving them names, not all of which are printable, but descriptive enough to reflect the feelings on board. At each of these waves, the helm either shuts his or her eyes to avoid the smarting spray, or ducks behind the wheel knowing full well that the motion would rip the wheel out of your hands, if you hadn't let go first. The cockpit aquabatics team now comprises Matt, Sam, David, Bertie, Arnie and myself all sporting a variety of swellings and bruises. Our showpiece is the inverted wheelspin, a very stylish manoeuvre, but the landings still require practice.

"Back to the naming of the waves: the Take-off and Landing, the Bellyflop, the Mountains, the Galley Growler, the Bunk Bouncer, the Crapper Flapper, the Smoker Soaker, the Stern Whip and the Corkscrew. The Stern Whip breaks upon the quarter and manages to give the helm a full soaking. The Corkscrew has to be the ultimate, as there is no warning and no way out.

"Everything is wet, the sodden sailors drip in the doghouse, the washing up water leaps around the galley, hatches leak and the mast gaiter pours water in. If there is the smallest pinprick, this ocean will find it. All through the gales, we keep sailing our best, gaining a mile or two on our closest rivals and sometimes losing some. Spirits are high, even though people are tired and wet, and if willpower could win this race we would already be in Cape Town.

"The dreams of the tropics get stronger as our track is now slightly northward and the distance to go less than 1,800 miles. There are more depressions rattling round the Roaring Forties, though. This baptism is not over yet."

In all this, Mike Golding's crew drove *Group 4* exceptionally hard, and around the Kerguelen Islands they took a lead that we could see was going to be terribly difficult to break down. In winds of 60 and 70 knots, Mike elected to reef down, change foresails but not to drop the mainsail and sail on the trysail. This strategy worked, allied to constant monitoring of the rapid passage of depressions and the care they took always to find each successive favoured tack as the storms passed through. By the end of the first week of March, *Group 4* had extended their lead by another forty miles. They were now ninety-four miles ahead. As John Chittenden ruefully observed: "*Group 4* seems to have wings attached to their hull."

It was truly astonishing that after the thousands of miles since Hobart, the boats could still be so close. Behind *Nuclear Electric*, *Hofbräu Lager* was catching steadily and was only five miles behind. The next five boats – *Commercial Union*, *Coopers & Lybrand*, *British Steel II*, *Heath Insured* and *Rhône-Poulenc* – were separated by only twenty miles. *InterSpray* lagged further behind and *Pride of Teesside* was some 200 miles to the north. I was amazed at the speed of the boats. The crews were pushing them to tremendous limits now that the gnawing anxiety of rig failure had been removed. In 40 and 50 knots of wind, the boats went fantastically, clocking about 8 or 9 knots through the water and making good almost 6 knots (that is, their speed over the ground, along the rhumb line course). Never before had yachts gone to windward at such incredible, consistent speeds. A grand prix boat could not have endured this.

At about this time, we got a report from Adrian Rayson, which I keep proudly on record: "Of the entire fleet one cannot speak, but from our experiences on *Heath Insured* it would seem the yachts are performing admirably the tasks for which they were built. *Heath Insured* is powerful to windward and we have managed to keep boatspeeds in excess of 9 knots, pretty close-hauled in wind speeds of 30–40 knots. It is interesting to note the boat's upwind performance with different sail plans, with which we can keep her going in a variety of conditions. The boat's performance in the Southern Ocean is a testament to all the hard work put into them by Andrew Roberts and his team."

From the Kerguelen Islands, the boats were somewhat constrained in the tactics they could use by the need to pass north of the tiny Crozet Islands, 800 miles to the west. This they had to do to stay well south of the windless high-pressure belt that lurks off the south coast of South Africa. Should they stray into that, hard won places would almost surely be lost. So all but *Pride of Teesside* stayed on course well to the south and continued tacking into an endless string of westerly gales.

Fatigue continued to be a difficulty, sapping morale and motivation. On *Hofbräu Lager* Pete used a daily pep talk to tell everyone the short-term aims as well as the overall strategy and it was a good way of keeping his team enthusiastic about pushing the boat in trying circumstances. Aboard *Commercial Union* Richard had to call a meeting to fire his crew up, and it was unfortunate that on 8 March, as people were beginning to feel the limits of their endurance, they suffered another blow. As they were sailing at night in confused seas and 50 knots of wind, the on-watch crew gybed accidentally and the mainsail split completely in half and then tore down the luff and another seam. All hands were called and the job of manhandling the heavy sail began. In the darkness and still with massive cross seas, it was tiring work to get the sail off the boom, through the narrow companionway and along the corridor into the fo'c'sle. After that, the crew wrestled with the sail and sorted it out into the correct pieces and panels. The process of restitching over twenty feet of sail took forty-eight laborious hours and the price they paid was to drop from fourth to sixth place.

Gradually, the northing that the boats had to make was taking them out of the path of westerly gales and closer to the fringes of the great area of high pressure. Ahead of *Commercial Union* the diminishing winds reduced the distances between boats and, remarkably, by 10 March only five miles separated *Nuclear Electric*, *Hofbräu Lager*, *Rhône-Poulenc* and *Coopers & Lybrand*. It had never been more exciting to follow the race and, to my delight, positions between second and fifth place changed almost every day. There was intense excitement aboard the boats as well. The skippers reported that daily position checks were listened to more avidly than ever. Slipped places created gloom for the rest of the day; places gained made for euphoria. Either way, the chat shows determined the mood.

Uncertain winds between this high-pressure area and the passing depressions to the south led to frequent sail changes, as every fraction of speed was fought for. Tension replaced the tedium of survival conditions, one form of stress replacing another. *Group 4* was the first to hit light winds and in the last week of the leg, Mike lost a hundred miles in one day to *Nuclear Electric*. His lead was still over a hundred miles and that was a good buffer, but as *Group 4* closed the coast of South Africa I knew he would draw into the influence of the Agulhas Current, which runs down the east coast of South Africa at up to 4 knots and dissipates in an eddy at the tip of the continent. At the point where they were going to join it, our routeing charts indicated half a knot of counter-current, but these indications are only approximations. There might be areas of greater current and even half a knot of current running against you makes a difference of twelve hard-won miles every day.

At the same time that *Group 4*'s lead was ebbing, *Nuclear Electric* and *Hofbräu Lager* were pulling away from the pack. *Rhône-Poulenc* had been snapping at the heels of *Nuclear Electric* for almost a week. They could see each other on the horizon much of the time and the close competition drove each other on. By 10 March, though, *Nuclear Electric* and *Hofbräu Lager* had opened out a gap of a hundred miles over the boats behind. Pete had a battle on his hands and the potential reward would be to jump ahead of *Heath Insured* in the overall results table to third place. That would leave him in an excellent position for the leg home.

At some point further degrees of northing would have to be made, and *Nuclear Electric* and *Hofbräu Lager*, still fighting it out together, made the decision to turn north early. At first this lost them some miles but they knew that sooner or later the others would have to press through the same lighter winds while they, hopefully, would pick up again in firmer ones. *Group 4* still held her lead and gradually closed on the Cape of Good Hope, borne along by a light south-easterly following wind. This was where places could be wrenched away and I well remembered the first Whitbread Round the World Race, when it took us three excruciating days to cover the last 200 miles of the leg. Before you get to the Cape of Good Hope, you come to False Cape, a long bank of shallow water, and to a place known as "the Starting Box". Here, in the shadow of the mountains, you generally get light and flukey winds where you have to fight for every inch. Possibly *Group 4* would suffer there.

Less than a day from the time they were expected to finish, *Group 4* was getting nearer to the Cape of Good Hope. Jørgen Philip-Sørensen, the chairman of Group 4 Securitas, who had been incredibly supportive and enthusiastic about his boat and crew from the start, decided to charter a helicopter and go out to see them round the Cape. He went up, waved and cheered on his crew, took some pictures and returned to greet them in. Soon after, he phoned up to see how far they had progressed. The answer was: "Not much!" More telephone conversations ensued, but each time there was very little more to report. *Group 4* had run into virtually a flat calm and was ghosting up the coast. When she finally crossed the line off Cape Town in the evening of 18 March, taking almost a day to cover the last fifty miles, she received a tumultuous welcome at the Victoria and Alfred Waterfront. Fire engines from the city came out and the local firemen marked the triumph of another fire officer with sirens and flashing blue lights. From all the many waterside bars and restaurants, people came out, stood on the balconies or wharves and cheered. They had won the toughest leg so far – and won it by an impressive margin, as *Nuclear Electric* and *Hofbräu Lager* were not due for almost another twenty-four hours.

That night, *Hofbräu Lager* increased her small lead over *Nuclear Electric*. Pete Goss made the decision to go further north than his rivals and in so doing, gained more wind for a critical few hours. After making their way slowly up the coast, they crossed the line in the middle of 19 March, eighteen hours behind *Group 4* and less than one day behind them overall. *Nuclear Electric*, meanwhile, found the going just as slow but, for the last few moments of the leg, caught a breeze as she came to the finishing line, to be saluted at the pierhead by employees from the local power station and in the dock itself, there was a deafening welcome for the crew that had hung on heroically to their overall lead by eight hours.

The next boat in was *Coopers & Lybrand*, which came in on the evening of the following day. Viv and her crew had sailed a tremendous race. She had had to contend with injury problems – her own and others – and again had a crew who had been weakened by seasickness. Gary Hopkins had not been afflicted as severely as Phil Jones on the last leg, but he was ill for much of the time.

Next were *Rhône-Poulenc* and *Heath Insured*, which finished within three hours of each other on 20 and 21 March. Peter Phillips had earned the reward of driving his crew hard this time, and took fifth place. *Heath Insured* had pushed hard, too, despite a serious accident to one crew member soon after the start. Carol Randall had been helming the boat in about 30 knots of wind when a wave broke over the starboard bow and threw her off the wheel. She fell, twisting her knee severely, and when other crew ran to help her they found her grimacing in agony. Taken below in sickening pain, Carol was helped by Arthur Haynes, who saw the swelling and deduced that she had torn a ligament. Arrangements were made for her to go to hospital as soon as she arrived in Cape Town and Carol knew she faced the devastating prospect of having to pull out of the next leg, the victorious return home.

In the most exciting finish of that leg, *British Steel II*, *Commercial Union*, *InterSpray* and *Pride of Teesside* finished on 21 March within seven hours of each other. The two Richards' crews and, in turn, Paul's and Ian's had had one another in their sights for most of the way up to Cape Town from the Cape of Good Hope. For the last few weeks of the leg, Ian had taken *Pride of Teesside* north and had benefited from a different air stream where he held the miles lost by the diversion he'd made after finding another leak from the skeg. In the end, Ian finished only five miles astern of *InterSpray*.

It was a huge relief to see all the boats in safely again. Plenty of maintenance was scheduled, but I didn't expect it to be anything like as hectic as Hobart. Besides, the Victoria and Alfred Waterfront was proving to be very hospitable, and each boat was introduced to its own sponsor bar or restaurant with mutual enthusiasm. Things seemed to be going well.

Only one immediate cloud on the horizon lurked: Duncan Hall of Tees-side Development Corporation was about to arrive. He was anxious to know how his boat would fare in trying to obtain redress for the skeg problem and the diversion Ian had taken.

Arrival Times

Race Leg: **3 – Hobart to Cape Town**

Yacht Name	Status	Arrival Time	Leg Time	Placing
		GMT	DDD HH NN SS	
01: *Group 4*	Finished	18 MAR 19:06:24	033 17 06 24	1st
02: *Hofbräu Lager*	Finished	19 MAR 12:54:58	034 10 54 58	2nd
03: *Nuclear Electric*	Finished	19 MAR 16:23:02	034 14 23 02	3rd
04: *Coopers & Lybrand*	Finished	20 MAR 19:06:58	035 17 06 58	4th
05: *Rhône Poulenc*	Finished	20 MAR 23:34:48	035 21 34 48	5th
06: *Heath Insured*	Finished	21 MAR 02:46:40	036 00 46 40	6th
07: *British Steel II*	Finished	21 MAR 12:48:09	036 10 48 09	7th
08: *Commercial Union*	Finished	21 MAR 18:44:40	036 16 44 40	8th
09: *InterSpray*	Finished	21 MAR 19:09:12	036 17 09 12	9th
10: *Pride of Teesside*	Finished	21 MAR 19:53:54	036 17 53 54	10th

DDD HH MM SS – Leg time expressed in: days, hours, minutes, seconds

Additional Information:

The arrival times were confirmed by the Cape Town race committee. The request for redress, from *Pride of Teesside*, was not allowed by the Cape Town protest committee.

BT Race Results Systems Data. © British Telecommunications plc 1992/93

CHAPTER SEVEN

LEG 4:
CAPE TOWN TO
SOUTHAMPTON

Twenty-four hours of euphoria followed the fleet's arrival in Cape Town. Everyone had come safely through the appalling conditions of the Southern Ocean and they had done so at amazing speeds. Considering that for much of the time they had been labouring to windward, *Group 4*'s average speed was remarkable: 6.9 knots. Even *Pride of Teesside*, the tenth placed boat, recorded an average boatspeed of 6.3 knots. We had always felt confident the boats would take all that the Southern Ocean meted out but we had no idea that they could get faster, or be pushed harder, in worse weather than they'd had between Cape Horn and Hobart.

The prevailing feeling among the crews was that it was all a straightforward downhill run from here. The next leg would be mostly tactics and thus demanding in a totally different way but everyone knew that sailing back into Southampton would mean a sense of complete achievement, public recognition of their extraordinary feat and the fitting finale to four years' hard work. It also signified the end of an overriding ambition and the return to a job, or job-hunting, to families, friends and, perhaps, uncertainties. Understandably, Cape Town was going to be relished as the final fling.

Cape Town is an exciting port, deservedly called "the tavern of the seas". Overshadowed by Table Mountain, the newly developed Victoria and Alfred Waterfront has preserved the worthy architecture of the old commercial port and mixed it with new shops, bars, and restaurants. Tourism and commercial shipping are also mingled in the harbour in a unique atmosphere. The facilities provided for us by SAF Marine were also first class. Brand new containers with all the gear and supplies each boat needed had been brought right to the dock, and the management could not have been more helpful. Perhaps it was a surprise to some people that the flavour of the place seemed liberal; black and white strolled around the harbour and shopped together, which may have been why the later unrest shocked us all so much.

Left Pete Goss, skipper of *Hofbräu Lager*.

One of our immediate duties was to organise the international committee to hear *Pride of Teesside*'s protest. Duncan Hall of Teesside Development Corporation was very keen to get redress for the skeg problem that had been the cause of Ian's diversion north and had pressed Ian to claim material disadvantage. The basis of the protest was International Yacht Racing Union rule 69, which had also been the substance of *British Steel II*'s claim for redress on the second leg. This has since been amended but then stated: "A yacht that alleges her finishing position has been materially prejudiced through no fault of her own . . . may request redress . . ." After *British Steel II*'s protest, however, we had amplified this rule by a note to the Notice of Race to clarify the race committee's views on the points that arose during that protest. Our notes were as follows:

> 1 Yachts "should" accept the technical advice of the fleet captain but the final decision remains with skipper and crew. (The word "should" was here defined as advisory.
> 2 Failure of a yacht and/or equipment, unless caused by another vessel that was required to keep clear, shall not be grounds for redress.

It was because of this amplification of the rule – which became classified as 69a – that the protest committee ruled out consideration of redress for *Pride of Teesside*. Even had redress been allowed it would have been a complicated procedure to work out by how much she should be compensated, since Ian had, in fact, gained some miles towards the end of the leg because of their northwards diversion.

The episode left a bitter taste in people's mouths. Several of *Pride of Teesside*'s crew felt very sour about the pressure that had been put on them by their sponsors to do well. I interviewed all the crew and discovered that the belief on board was that the sponsors were happy when the boat was up in front but the minute they fell back enthusiasm for the boat and crew waned. It was a great pity that this should happen, particularly as the essence of the Challenge is as much – if not more – about the endeavours of people as about good results. It was also a shame for Ian, who had been put in a difficult position. He naturally felt great loyalty to his crew, but he was employed by me. Yet he was also answerable to Teesside Development Corporation. From my point of view, I never forgot that the TDC was our client. It was all very complicated. I had a chat to Ian about his feelings and he admitted: "I suppose it's a bit like being the meat in the sandwich. Yes, it is incredibly hard. You have to do things that are not necessarily to everyone's liking and you can't keep all the people happy all the time. The hardest part of the race is trying to be a diplomat to three different groups of people because it doesn't always work." At the same time as the Challenge fleet was in Cape Town, Robin Knox-Johnston and Peter Blake limped in to the Royal Cape Yacht Club in their trimaran *ENZA*. They had been taking part in the Jules Verne Trophy, a non-stop race around the world with a prize for the first boat to do it in eighty days or less. Past the Cape of Good Hope and well out into the Southern Ocean, *ENZA* had struck something floating in the water and been holed. Her crew had had no choice but to make emergency repairs, turn before the wind and run for the safety of Cape Town.

ENZA had been modified and renamed but she used to be called *TAG* and owned by Mike Birch. I had sailed with Mike on her a number of years ago and was interested to have a look at this reborn 86-foot racing machine. Andrew Roberts and I went down to the Royal Cape Yacht Club, accompanied by Captain Drummond, Greg Bertram and some of the crews of the yachts. They were enthusing about this incredibly fast boat when I said that I had sailed a similar boat called *Great Britain III*, an 80-footer which had a mast of about the same size – and that I'd sailed her single-handed. They all looked at me, seeing a huge boat on one hand and a golden oldie Scotsman on the other and I could see they were speech-lessly making up their minds whether to believe me or not.

The crews greatly enjoyed meeting Robin, and he was very good to them, mixing well and coming aboard some of the boats to give the crews some hints and tips. It coincided with an evolution that had been happen-ing over the last two legs and was now very obvious: the crews had ceased to be merely eager amateurs who lacked experience. In Hobart, I had seen people change from being nervous and edgy, as they had patently been in Rio, and by Cape Town all the Challenge team agreed that it would have been hard to distinguish them from full-time paid crews. They knew exactly what they were about, knew what work had to be done and where to get the right equipment for the job, and you could see every-one working hard and competently during the day to get their boats ready for the race home. It was an amazing transformation and I was both delighted and very proud of their achievement.

For Simon Littlejohn, who was crewing on *Group 4*, Cape Town was an emotional last stopover. He had signed on for the entire race but had been thrown the length of the boat during rough weather. The impact of his fall had torn all three knee ligaments, confining him to below-deck duties. Once in Cape Town he knew he was due for a major operation to repair the serious damage and the surgeon warned him beforehand that there would be no chance of him being back on board in time for the last leg. This was a devasting decision for him to accept: he would not be able to sail right round the world and *Group 4* was lying such a close second that victory was easily possible. Back home he would follow his boat's progress in each position report, eating and sleeping their fortunes with the same sort of addiction that I had developed.

Carol Randall went into hospital for treatment to her ligament injury and emerged in discomfort, seriously hampered by a full-length leg brace. She, too, faced the possibility that it might not be possible for her to do the full circumnavigation, but after discussing what she might be able to do on board with her skipper, Adrian Donovan, decided that she could do the final leg as "galley queen". Her courage in continuing, though obviously in pain, made a great impression on everyone, especially me as I saw her climb aboard *Heath Insured* in her leg brace the morning of the race to take up a sweaty incarceration below decks.

Over the next few weeks, the Challenge team got very familiar with the Victoria and Alfred Waterfront. With all the facilities there, we were almost cut off from the city and, although there was nothing like the work load we'd had in Hobart, we hardly ever got out of the place. We all managed a trip by cable car to the top of Table Mountain during the one-and-a-half days off we had that month, but I never felt I was really in South Africa. One knew that there were underlying problems there but they never affected us; we were self-contained and somehow distanced from them. So we were unprepared when, about a week from the restart, Cape Town erupted in riots.

A protest rally had been organised in the city and the word was that it might spill over to the Waterfront. I was not particularly worried, until the following day, when I was sitting in a waterside cafe having a cup of coffee. Suddenly the waitress announced that they were closing. "How much do I owe you?" I asked, in no great hurry. Her reply was: "Forget it." With that she was gone. The shops and restaurants and bars closed in seconds and everyone just disappeared.

Jolted, my immediate worry was what might happen to the yachts if the rioters came this way. I looked at the fleet of boats, berthed neatly bows-to the pier, and wondered if we could get enough crew together to get them right out of the area. Were a riot to begin here, it would have been pretty hard to explain to people that this was an event founded on principles quite the opposite of elitism. I didn't think that an argument based on how our crews had given up their jobs back in England and sacrificed all their life savings would cut much ice with someone from the miles of appalling shanty towns outside Cape Town.

I went to our offices and got Andrew and together we mustered as many of the crews as we could. What we would do if the rioters headed our way was to slip the lines and motor all ten yachts out to the edge of the harbour to wait until the unrest had subsided. We managed to get three people for every boat and we all stood by near our charges as we waited for news. By 4 pm we were told that the rioters were beginning to disperse and as the danger receded we left, shaken but relieved. We heard afterwards that although the riots didn't touch us, much of the business district of Cape Town, less than a mile away, had been damaged.

Before the start, we held a final briefing to the crews, as I had done before every other leg. I gave them my three faithful pieces of advice once again: remember that the shortest distance is invariably the fastest; go for speed and not necessarily for course; and that races are won and lost in light winds. The last leg home was going to be the decisive one. If the fleet was winnowed out by the same amount as it had been in the first leg, overall places would change dramatically. Even taking into account the fact that all were now experienced and well-practised yachtsmen, there was a very slender margin between *Nuclear Electric*, *Group 4* and *Hofbräu Lager*, and precious little between them and most of the other boats. It was still anyone's race.

Tactics and knowledge gained from historical data about conditions around the doldrums would create the breaks that made the winner of this next leg, and the overall winner, because the chances were that the overall winner would not necessarily be the first home in Southampton. It was really the first Whitbread Race that changed the ways of long-distance sailing. Before, one would have used the old trading routes from the days of sail, going before the trade winds in the right direction. Nowadays, many boats sail fastest just free of the wind; multihulls, for example, will sometimes sail with sheets just cracked for speed, even if it takes them fifteen or twenty degrees off course. On the first Whitbread Race, sailing from Southampton to Cape Town, Eric Tabarly on *Pen Duick* and I had taken the old-fashioned trading route course, while Les Williams and Peter Blake on *Burton Cutter* and the Royal Navy boat *Adventure* sailed close-hauled to the trade winds and cut straight across the south-east trades to Cape Town. That strategy had paid handsome dividends. Eric and I were well beaten on that leg. From that time on, skippers and navigators on ocean races ceased to worry where the winds came from; generally speaking, they always follow the shortest distance.

It would be so with our crews. Once they had passed over the equator they wouldn't go way out west towards the Azores to gain fair winds; they would hug the coast of Africa and probably sail on the wind towards Britain. The last leg had demonstrated beyond any question that the boats could sail fast to windward and, on a leg where the seas would be nowhere near as destructive, they could make very good speeds.

As it was probably the last advice I would ever give these men and women, I went over what we, as the race organisers, had set out to do and told them that they had already achieved remarkable things. I recalled those interviews with each of them when they applied to take part in the British Steel Challenge and how nervous and worried many of them had been about meeting me and getting a place in the event. The situation had been reversed, I said: the honour of knowing them was mine and I saluted their bravery, determination and incontestable accomplishments. I read them out part of an article by Elaine Thompson in *Yachting World* and one by Keith Wheatley in the *Sunday Times*, both acknowledging the magnitude of the crews' feats.

I also told them for the first time that Roger Peek, who had trained with them and crewed on the previous leg aboard *InterSpray*, had been a spy in the camp. Roger was a treasurer at British Steel and a director of the Challenge Business, watching the money for British Steel and we had been keen for him to join in and be sure that what we were doing was right. Roger had enjoyed the leg from Hobart to Cape Town immensely and had taken part in everything with enthusiasm and now he came to the front of the amphitheatre and gave a speech. He told the audience exactly what British Steel had got out of the project and how rewarding it had been for them. More than that, he conveyed his fervour for the event in a way that blended the feelings of the crews for the race with the evident business interests.

As good as Cape Town was, the time came to leave and on 17 April, the boats left the dock for what should by now have been a slick and well-practised start. Winter weather had arrived early, and a savage storm passed across the southern tip of South Africa at Easter, bringing 200-kilometre per hour winds just a few days from the start. The result was a disturbed ocean swell from the west. In the harbour it was flat calm, with slight winds of about 10 knots, but once the fleet was outside the protection of the breakwater, they encountered a powerful swell. On the start boat, which lay stationary on the line, I, the committee and Brian Moffat, chairman and chief executive of British Steel, accompanied by his wife, Jackie, rolled fiercely on each passing wave.

The start line was wide, and when Mrs Moffat fired the gun to signal the beginning of the final leg, the boats were well spread out. So far were they scattered that, for a moment, I thought some of the skippers must have misread the signals. In some cases, it took three minutes to sail over the line; it was extraordinary that after all the expertise they had gained it was still such a relatively scrappy affair. What we did not know at first was that the fifteen foot ground well, associated with the storm long past, had dragged the first mark out of position and it was difficult to judge where it should have been. The position it ought to have been in was three miles north-east of the committee boat position, but it had dragged almost a mile southwards.

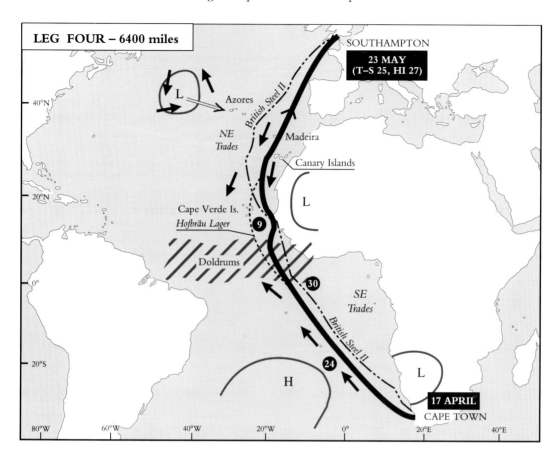

Heath Insured believed they had got a good start, and were neatly on course for the first mark but they were wrong. Most of the others had seen it across the peaks of the waves, but I could tell Adrian was using his GPS and sailing to a computer-generated position. Not until he saw the other boats keeping down to leeward did he realise something was amiss. Immediately he altered course to round the buoy correctly and so avoid a penalty but I knew what was going to happen next. Sure enough, thirty seconds later I saw the protest flag being broken loose from their backstay. It was a claim they were not to win.

Within hours of the start, all the boats were able to hoist their spinnakers and head north-eastwards in good following winds. It was soon apparent that this leg would be completely different from the other three: it was downwind, but the experience of the crew and the stronger winds meant more testing spinnaker work and higher consistent boat-speeds than at almost any other time. In 15–20 knots of wind, the fleet bowled along in the warm air of the daytime and the cool breezes of the night at up to 13 knots. Seasickness for some for the first few days out did not detract from the magical sailing. Had they needed to turn back, though, and shape a course to windward, the apparent wind speed would have increased to 30–35 knots and the wind chill whip away any feeling of balminess: the memories of the Southern Ocean were still vivid enough.

With strong winds, sails blew again. *Commercial Union* blew out their heavy spinnaker on the second night out and took it down to find the sail utterly beyond repair. That was a severe blow, as it would be needed on the run up to the doldrums and again, perhaps, on the critical sprint down-Channel to Southampton. And since the standard of sail repairs had risen so very remarkably throughout the race, it said much about the damage done that it could not be resurrected. By then, though, they were lying first and could effectively set the smaller asymetric spinnaker.

The first fortnight of the leg, sailing up the west coast of Africa, gave more wonderful sailing, the stuff of brochures: balmy days in warmth that crept up day by day, clear starlit nights, dolphins and seabirds and glorious following winds that could be harnessed under spinnaker. At dawn on 22 April, the crew of *Pride of Teesside* were amazed to find what seemed like the scum of an oil spill on deck. Ian MacGillivray reported:

"The foredeck was covered with black streaks, along with the No 1 yankee. The thought of trying to clean the sails of oil and the mess that this would create did not appeal. Gary Bailey collected some multi-purpose cleaner from the galley to start the awesome task, only to find that on contact with water the black substance dissolved. On closer inspection the oil turned out to be a form of plankton that was of such density that it appeared as thick as oil. Exactly what caused the plankton to gather like this I have no idea, although along the coast of Africa recently there has been a large amount of red plankton bloom which, according to reports when we were there, has caused the shellfish to take on a form of toxin."

At the same time *Pride of Teesside*'s crew were cleaning, the crew of *InterSpray* were stitching. The lightweight spinnaker blew and four days and nights of sewing followed to repair 400 feet of ripped cloth. *Group 4*, meanwhile, had blown their heavy spinnaker twenty minutes after its second hoist on the leg and it took almost the same time to sew back the luff and leech tapes of the sail. Unlike on the previous leg, though, Mike Golding was content for crew to spend time out of their watches mending. His comment was: "We must repair at all cost. The additional work load is possibly beneficial to a team that thrived on tough conditions in the Southern Ocean and now find themselves with little to do in the stable conditions of the trade winds."

As the fleet powered along at eight to nine knots, there was a similar incident on *Commercial Union*. Their promotional spinnaker blew out on 26 April. As on *InterSpray* and *Group 4*, they were able to stitch it back to life by chain gang, sewing across most of the luff and about 120 feet of cloth across the girth of the sail. For forty-eight hours, four people put in over 100,000 stitches. The lovely sailing conditions made the labour infinitely more enjoyable than the mainsail repairs on the last leg, but again they took their toll, for *Commercial Union* dropped from first to second place.

Positions changed day by day. It was shaping up to be a very exciting leg; everything we had hoped for. *Hofbräu Lager* had dropped back to the middle of the fleet and it was obvious that Pete would have to plump for a route that balanced risk with reward. He was lying third in the overall placings and had less to lose than *Group 4* and *Nuclear Electric*, both further ahead and looking good as potential overall winners. *Commercial Union* and *British Steel II* had even less to lose by aggressive sailing, because a win on the last leg, a finish that would take them first past the crowds of relatives, friends and supporters would in some measure make up for earlier misfortunes.

Nuclear Electric, however, were still in the impossible situation of having to cover her two nearest rivals, *Group 4* and *Hofbräu Lager*. A week out from the start they came across *Group 4* running inshore on the opposite gybe and *Hofbräu Lager* thirty miles astern, making them the three leading boats. Soon after, Pete Goss began to make his way eastwards, while *Group 4* stayed to the west. John Chittenden elected to chase after *Group 4* but remarked that possible tactical mistakes after almost a year's hard effort from his crew involved "a certain amount of agony". It must have been agony, too, for him to see how *Group 4*'s crew consistently sailed their boat faster. "I am forced to conclude that she is faster than us," he reported. "It is a bitter pill to swallow."

In the days that followed, positions were juggled. Richard Merriweather began to make up the miles and was in exact joint first position with Richard Tudor by 29 April. This was unquestionably one-design racing at its best, seeing how slick – and frequent – sail changes, skilful sail repairs and intelligent and intuitive tactics could mix the fleet over and over again.

The same day that the British Telecom results showed *British Steel II* and *Commercial Union* tied precisely together on distance to Southampton, *Coopers & Lybrand* hit a whale. Whales are not so uncommon in the oceans of the world as most people suppose and ocean racers and cruising yachtsmen alike rarely cross an ocean without a sighting, if not a near collision. Running into a whale, a creature which is generally supposed to be able to sleep near the surface of the water, can be serious for lighter, glassfibre boats, as was demonstrated by the serious holing of the French yacht *Charles Jourdan* in the 1989/90 Whitbread Race, but for our steel boats it was never a worry. *Group 4* had hit a whale on the first leg, with no harm to the boat – or to the whale so far as anyone could tell. When *Coopers & Lybrand* ran into their whale though, they were disturbed to see a trail of blood and guts streaming out in their wake. For a while, there was sadness on board, as it was impossible to know whether the whale had survived the collision or not.

Aboard all the boats, reports indicated that the last drops of excitement, emotion and competition were being squeezed out of the Challenge. In a few weeks it would all be over and, plainly, conversations on board in the relative relaxation of trade winds sailing often turned to the next stage of everyone's lives. Some were anxious about work or homes, some desperately keen to get back to their families but, as Julian Wells, of *InterSpray* told us: "Without exception we are all enthusiastic about seeing England again."

The day after *Coopers & Lybrand*'s collision with the whale, 30 April 1993, is a day that I will never forget. In the late afternoon *Heath Insured* was making easy progress in about 15 knots of wind, spinnaker flying. With the warmth of the afternoon, the on-watch crew were on deck in T-shirts and shorts or swimming trunks. Conditions were not hard, not exceptional. It was good, balmy weather. Dinner was being prepared below decks. After letting the spinnaker pole go forward, those on deck – Adrian Rayson, Carol Randall and Samantha Brewster – saw Bill Vincent, the forty-six-year-old carpenter from Bath, who had crewed with them all the way round, go overboard.

That evening, on my way to bed, the phone rang. It was the duty race officer, who told me that he had just received a message from *Heath Insured*. Adrian Donovan had a message in code for us and was sending it in five minutes. I knew it had to be something very serious indeed. Each skipper had a code to use in the event of anything he or she had to communicate to us that we wouldn't want the world to know, but it would only be used in grave circumstances.

I asked him to call Captain Drummond and Greg Bertram and the three of us hurried over to race headquarters, where we deciphered the message that Bill Vincent had been lost over the side. The telex relayed the news briefly but, in a report sent an hour later, Adrian told us in detail what had happened. His message was as follows:

"*Heath Insured* was broad reaching at 8 knots plus, with full main and heavyweight tri-radial spinnaker in 14–16 knots of breeze on a course about 335° True, about 220 miles south of the equator. I was down below. The deck crew, including Bill, had just eased the spinnaker pole forward a couple of feet, with Bill on the downhaul. Literally three minutes later, Sam Brewster saw him move quickly to the pushpit, put his foot up on the rail and dive overboard. She shouted "Bill!" and then screamed "Man overboard." Carol Randall was also in the cockpit having a break from the galley when the spinnaker pole move instruction went out. Bill was finishing a cigarette and she joked with him about enjoying a drag before working the winch.

"Bill Vincent entered the water at 1730 hours Zulu, water temperature 28°C. Within thirty seconds a danbuoy was launched by the skipper Adrian Donovan, GPS man overboard button pressed and the spinnaker dropped, with the boat already rounded up to the wind. We searched the area for two hours until dark. Conditions were south-easterly, Force 3–4, moderate swell, few white horses. We put two crew, Samantha Brewster and Dave Spratley, on the second spreaders. We also had lookouts in the pulpit, port and starboard sides of the boat and both quarters.

"Initially, I returned to the area of the first danbuoy and proceeded along a reciprocal course and launched a second danbuoy about a quarter of a mile further down this track. Using these two as data points, we then searched up and down the course line in about a 400-yard corridor for about twenty minutes. I then started a box search using 0.1-mile legs east and west of the course line, which was later extended to 0.2-mile legs. All this was done under power at five to six knots, so we quickly covered a large area. Using the GPS man overboard button as a north point datum, I then ran a box search south-east by south-west, progressively biasing this to the west of the original course line. As darkness fell, we ran with all navigation lights and deck floodlights on to make ourselves a prominent visual target.

"About two-and-a-half hours after the incident, I returned to the positions of the danbuoys and recovered both on board. I then positioned the boat four miles to the west of the GPS man overboard point and then, as now, steamed slowly along north-east/south-west lines in a down-current (given as approximately 1 knot), downwind area, searching with a spotlight."

With the water temperature so warm, Bill could have survived in the water for twelve or more hours had he been able to keep afloat, or had wished to. My heart went out to Adrian. I visualised the crew of *Heath Insured*, searching in absolute silence up and down lines that criss-crossed, to cover every part of that area. Darkness falls suddenly in the tropics; there is only the briefest of twilights, and I could imagine the feeling of helplessness they would have as the sun dropped below the horizon and the odds of finding Bill suddenly lengthened.

Some of the other yachts nearest to *Heath Insured* were informed, and *InterSpray* and *Nuclear Electric* immediately turned round and motored towards *Heath Insured*'s position to help but as they were over ten hours away it was soon clear that there was little they could do to help. We thanked them and asked them to resume sailing. By dawn Adrian saw that continuing the search was pointless. There was nothing more they could do and reluctantly, with immense sadness, they hoisted their sails and let draw to rejoin the race after seventeen hours of searching.

There seemed no adequate explanation for why Bill had dived over the side. Adrian reported to us: "Bill was obviously disturbed about something and over the last week had become withdrawn and had lost his appetite. Various members of the crew, including myself, had chatted to him at length but without finding out anything specific. Over the last two days he had seemed to be in better spirits. From myself and the rest of the crew, please give his wife Pauline and the boys our sympathies and deepest condolences. Tell her we made all efforts to find him and from knowing him closely over the last eight months we are at a loss to understand the reasons for what has happened."

Bill's loss staggered us and the tragedy was all the more shocking because it had happened on the last leg, the one that although tactically demanding, was plain sailing. As organisers, we had done all we could to make sure that the training had been carried out to emphasise and re-emphasise safety procedures and had done all we could to ensure the safety of everyone. There was no way we could prevent someone from taking their own life and never expected it. As well as sadness, I felt a bitterness that it had put a blight on a successful event and that in turn led to my having a feeling of guilt about looking on it selfishly. I found out later that sadness, selfish anger and guilt were shared by many of the crew.

Our contingency plans had to go into operation at once. Pauline Vincent had to be told. So did the sponsors, the Heath Group. Through-out the race, Helen Wybrow had done a fantastic job of contacting relatives when anyone was ill or had been injured, usually letting them know within a few hours. Our system was prompt and efficient. The Heath Group also had excellent communications with the families of the crew, and throughout the race two of their staff in London, Mavis Chapman and Jackie Kaprou, relayed information to families, sent news-letters back and forth and were there at any time to talk to or reassure people back home. They would also play a part in the counselling that lay ahead, not only for Bill's family but for the crew of *Heath Insured*.

Greg Bertram and I prepared to go to Bristol to see Bill's wife Pauline, first contacting the local police and telling them what had happened. They are experts at breaking news such as this and we agreed a rendezvous with a PC and WPC. Greg and I drove there in the early hours, met the police at seven o'clock that morning, and all went to Mrs Vincent's house to break the news.

Years back, I had lost a crewmember over the side in an accident aboard *Great Britain II*, in the Roaring Forties, so it was the second time I'd had to break such devastating news. It is a terrible experience. However, we decided it was best not to tell her that Bill had been seen diving over the side; whether or not it was a deliberate action was something for a court of inquiry to decide. All we could say was that Bill had been lost. Greg and I left shortly afterwards, much shaken, leaving Pauline to be comforted by the WPC and, later, her sister, Margaret.

The next day, a press release had to be issued. For the same reasons we hadn't been able to tell Mrs Vincent exactly what had happened, we could not state publicly how and why Bill had gone over the side. Thus the press statement was rather ambiguous. We said that it had been in daylight, in fairly light weather, that Bill had been in swimming trunks and that he wasn't wearing a harness or lifejacket. It was immediately obvious to some yachting journalists that this was a highly irregular incident. There was no reason for Bill to have been wearing either a harness or lifejacket in daylight in those conditions, but equally there was no reason why anyone should have fallen overboard or not been quickly recovered. Some people hinted at what might have happened, citing suicides attached to other round the world yacht races, such as Nigel Tetley, who hanged himself, Donald Crowhurst, who stepped off his yacht *Teignmouth Electron*, and Alexei Grischenko, the Russian co-skipper of the Russian yacht *Fasizi* in the last Whitbread Race, who also hanged himself.

Some days later, we took the advice of Mavis Chapman from the Heath Group, who had come to know Pauline Vincent well over the last eight months. Mavis's advice as 'auntie' to the yacht's crew was to alert her to what we really knew had happened. After a conversation between myself, Mavis and Pauline's sister, we decided to tell her all that the on-watch crew had seen. Again, I went to visit her, telling just the bare facts, not dramatising them in any way. I was amazed at her strength. She knew that a huge part of her life had suddenly been extinguished, yet she was determined not to go to pieces. After the shock, she began to think of her two sons and of how they might get on with their lives. I left Pauline and her sister later that day beginning, I hoped, to work out how to rebuild the pieces.

On board all the other boats there was shock and bereavement. Everyone had known Bill and now they grieved for his loss. They thought about what it would have been like had it been one of them: a cabin-mate, perhaps, or someone on the same watch – a terrible absence they would have to go on living with as intimately as if that person were still on board. Messages of sympathy were sent from each of the boats to the crew of *Heath Insured* and to Bill's widow. Richard Tudor quoted the first verse of fellow Welshman Dylan Thomas's moving poem 'And death shall have no dominion':

> And death shall have no dominion.
> Dead men naked they shall be one
> With the man in the wind and the west moon;
> When their bones are picked clean and the clean bones are gone,
> They shall have stars at elbow and foot;
> Though they go mad they shall be sane,
> Though they sink through the sea they shall rise again;
> Though lovers be lost love shall not;
> And death shall have no dominion.

On 30 April, *British Steel II* became the first of the British Steel Challenge fleet to cross the equator and, a few days later, the first to cross her outward track and thus complete a circumnavigation of the world. There were lavish celebrations on board and more homage to Neptune, now spiced with the possibility that theirs might be the first boat across the line in Southampton. By the next day, all nine others had crossed the line but were spread out across a front of 600 miles.

Vivien had taken an earlier gamble to stay to the east of the fleet in order to get better winds and it had not paid off, so when *Coopers & Lybrand* crossed the equator they glumly saw themselves in tenth position. Tactically, this was fascinating because, although spread, in distance to go the entire fleet was separated by just one hundred miles. *British Steel II* led from *Group 4*, but *Commercial Union* had run eastwards and within a few days of crossing the equator had pulled about twenty miles ahead of John Chittenden. *Nuclear Electric* was taking the inshore route on the basis of historical information: *Gauloises II* had taken a similar route on a past race from Cape Town to Holland and it had paid off. They reckoned to do the same, but soon discovered from their GPS that instead of the 1-knot counter current shown on their routeing chart, they had a full 2 knots of current against them. All that could be done was to pray that it was an eddy *Nuclear Electric* would pass through, for with *Group 4*'s crew generating greater boatspeed on this leg a gamble was imperative.

Within another two days, the fleet had entered the doldrums which were moving northwards and were now between about 4°N and 10°N. The band of calms was narrowest to the west and most of the boats opted for a westerly route. The only exception was *Heath Insured*, in last place since losing Bill. They chose to take an easterly route in an attempt to

Right Rites of passage for Steve George and Paul Egan (kneeling)
as *Rhône Poulenc* crosses the line.

catch up. Unhappily, this tactic was to be a failure and Adrian and his crew dropped even further behind. At the time, talk in England was of how the demoralised crew had given up the fight but here supporters and observers were wrong. *Heath Insured*'s crew were still fighting on; that was part of their coming to terms with what had happened. A report from Adrian Rayson told us: "The crew have been determinedly jocular and have thrown themselves back into the business of racing the boat. Behind closed doors it might be different but generally laughter bounces off the walls of the galley and ribald comments flit around the deck."

Once the steady trade winds had petered out, they were replaced by grey skies with high, heavy clouds and occasional squalls. Squalls had to be tracked by eye or by radar because they were sometimes the only wind the boats might get for a day. Just as they had done on the first leg, the crews had to attempt to hitch a ride on the 40 or 50 knots that would arrive suddenly. On *Nuclear Electric* one such squall struck with unexpected force. The on-watch crew could see it moving towards them and managed to change headsails in time but they had only just begun to reef the mainsail when the wind and rain met them. The squall peaked at 53 knots and brought with it spectacular thunder and lightning. After being knocked flat by the force of wind, they struggled to drop the mainsail altogether and flew along at ten knots under staysail alone.

Pride of Teesside had a similar experience and, after battling with foresail and main, they generated a surge of speed – 13–14 knots – that hurtled them past *Rhône-Poulenc*. *Group 4* was laid flat in a squall as well, leaving the crew who rushed up on deck to wonder fleetingly if the boat might be sinking, while on *Coopers & Lybrand* a particularly fierce squall cause a spinnaker pole to break its fitting and a genoa which was tied down on deck to be shredded by its jagged edges. "The whole lot ended over the side, damaging the guard rail and anything else in its way, wrecking the sail beyond repair," Matt Steel-Jessop remembered.

However, tropical storms are unpredictable and just as often the wind and rain would sit tantalisingly on the horizon, moving nearer and then stopping, just out of reach. Rising heat in the boats added discomfort to the anguish of being becalmed in the doldrums. Nothing could be done to speed the boats when there was no wind and that, in turn, added to the frustration of wondering if rivals elsewhere were getting better winds.

Top right The fleet at the Victoria and Alfred Waterfront in Cape Town, under the shadow of Table Mountain. From the left, *Pride of Teesside*, *InterSpray*, *Rhône-Poulenc*, *Nuclear Electric*, *Hofbräu Lager*, *Heath Insured*, *Coopers & Lybrand*, *Commercial Union*, *Group 4* and *British Steel II*. CR

Right Chay Blyth, Helen Wybrow and Andrew Roberts, the founding members of the Challenge team. BP

Rhône-Poulenc got a good start out of Cape Town and sped northward with the trade winds, recording one of her best performances of the race. SE

Above Yvonne Flatman goes up the mast of *British Steel II* to check for chafe at the spinnaker halyard. RH
Right Ian MacGillivray of *Pride of Teesside* goes for a dip in the tropics, attached to a spinnaker halyard for safety. AC

King Neptune's traditional initiation ceremony for crew on *Group 4* (top) and *Hofbräu Lager* (above right) who had not crossed the equator before involves being covered with a vile concoction of food and being accused of their crimes. MO'R/HL

Above left In a calm moment Rebecca Slater gives her skipper, Pete Goss, a haircut aboard *Hofbräu Lager*. HL

Top left Rhône-Poulenc finished in fifth place on the leg and eighth overall. MP
Right InterSpray had the misfortune to fall behind the main pack and lose the westerlies to
finish two days behind *Group 4*. MP
Above Back home to Ocean Village, Southampton, after eight months, the winners of the
fourth leg, the boys from *Group 4*. BP

Above Counting them all in, Chay Blyth gives his crews a traditional champagne salute at Ocean Village. BP

Below Family reunions at last aboard *InterSpray*. MP

Facing above left On the last leg seventeen minutes was all that separated *British Steel II* from second placed *Commercial Union*. MP

Facing above right The whole fleet went out to escort *Heath Insured* up Southampton Water. MP

Facing Hofbräu Lager fought out a lengthy battle with *Coopers & Lybrand* who won by only nine minutes. MP

Close into the African shore and its shoal waters, the leaders continued to play a tense game of cat and mouse. Once there, it was difficult to get an offing, for when the wind rose it generally headed the boats, then fell away again in the afternoon. One by one, the fleet was drawn into shallow waters off the African coast. That course also drew them into busy shipping lanes, where the boats were objects of curiosity to the freighters and cargo ships that steamed by them. Some came very close, prompting John Chittenden to remark that he felt "like a tortoise on a motorway".

Commercial Union had been passed by several ships and after the desperation of the smokers aboard who had run out of cigarettes threatened to get the better of them, they called a passing Portuguese tanker and asked if they had any cigarettes on board. Eric Gustavson, "an inveterate pipe-smoker" recorded it thus: "They were most apologetic and said that if only we had let them know a little earlier they could have launched their boat and brought some over to us. We thanked them and thought no more about it for five minutes. When we looked again at the stern of the tanker it was apparent that it was turning in a circle. This great boat turned and came alongside one hundred yards away, where they threw over the side an inflated bin liner which contained four hundred cigarettes."

Coopers & Lybrand also had a close encounter with a ship which had altered course to get a better look at them. Matt Steel-Jessop had a long conversation with the captain on VHF radio, who finally asked if they were all right or if they needed help of any kind. Matt replied that they were fine, they were sailing in a race and had all the latest equipment, including GPS satellite navigation gear. The captain's response was to ask, rather sheepishly, if Matt could give him an accurate position, as his ship had antiquated electronics.

The only yacht that did not stick close to the coast of Africa was *Hofbräu Lager* because Pete was taking a chance on getting a flyer through the Cape Verde Islands. Richard Tudor also chose to take a different route to the rest of the fleet, angling westwards by degrees and more or less splitting the distance between the main fleet and *Hofbräu Lager*. Within days the wind had come round to the north and each of the inshore boats in turn could head back out to the deep waters of the Atlantic without risking loss of boatspeed. Slowly, they began to made progress, tacking against the building north-east trade winds of the northern hemisphere, until the fleet converged again. Positions swapped each day and sightings were frequent as eight of the fleet were concentrated across a hundred

John Chittenden, the skipper of *Nuclear Electric*, holds aloft the British Steel Challenge Trophy for the race he and his crew deservedly won. BP

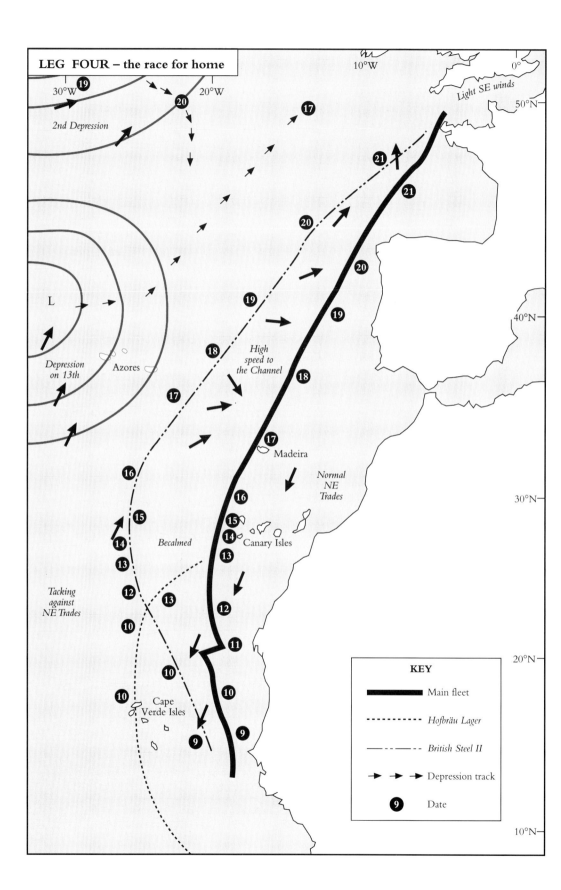

mile front. It was amazing racing and one of the most memorable points of the race was when, on 6 May, *British Steel II* and *Nuclear Electric* crossed tacks after 3,000 miles' racing. The boats were so close that *Nuclear Electric*'s crew had the satisfaction of yelling 'starboard' to get *British Steel II* to yield to her right of way and go round her stern.

It was interesting to watch the fleet's progress: how they hugged the coast instead of going out, then moved out, all the while holding close to the north-easterlies. *Commercial Union* was leading by a few miles from *Group 4* but on 8 May, *Group 4* came back at them and passed. Three days later, *Group 4* was leading by a small margin from *Nuclear Electric* and *Commercial Union* was third. Then *British Steel II* stole forward and pushed them down to fourth place.

Back in February, while the boats were out doing battle, I'd had doubts about whether the last leg would provide a close enough finish or offer spectators plenty of drama. The first leg, after all, had spread out appallingly and as everyone's relatives were coming down to see the boats in this time and were wanting to know precisely when to expect them – not to mention the phenomenal publicity that was building up – I wasn't too keen to have a straggling finish. One idea mooted was that the boats stop at a port, maybe in the Channel Islands, before the final dash to Southampton, somewhere where they could muster and restart to finish in close succession, all in daylight. This had been been received with dismay by the crews when I put it to them and I quickly dropped the idea. Had I known then, had I even imagined that the racing after thousands of miles could be so close, I wouldn't have worried.

While making their way off the coast of Senegal at a distance of about fifty miles, *Group 4* spotted a fishing boat at anchor. The crew of the fishing boat were waving. Possibly they were in distress. Mike Golding had a dilemma. We had previously warned the skippers of the possibility of pirates off this part of Africa and this is one of the classic ways that yachts are lured into danger. On the other hand, maritime law states that a vessel should always go to the aid of a stricken vessel if possible and Mike was a little way past the boat when he decided to turn back and go to their aid, no matter what lay in store. He approached cautiously but as *Group 4* got nearer they saw the fifteen fishermen looking "dishevelled and miserable and quite incapable of any piracy", as David Cowan put it. Communication was difficult between two crews who did not understand each others' language, but it was made clear that their engine had broken down a week ago, their signal flares had brought no response and that they were out of food. Mike's crew made up a box of food, including biscuits and dried milk and sent it over. There was little else that they could do to help but they sent a message to Falmouth Coastguard, who coordinate international maritime rescue in that area, giving their position and details of the fishing boat's plight. When they left to continue the race, the Senegalese crew wished them good luck. Later, we heard from Falmouth that the owner of the fishing boat had known about its difficulty but hadn't been able to afford to do anything about it.

By the time the fleet converged on 13 May, it was clear that *Hofbräu Lager*'s tactic had not worked, but what was most interesting was that, although *British Steel II* had lost ground initially, they had ultimately gained by their move. It put them in a very threatening position, for when east-going depressions of the North Atlantic came through later, as they almost certainly would, *British Steel II* would be able to sail freer and probably faster.

We had received notice of a lost container between Africa and the Canaries and telexed the fleet to warn them of the danger. Containers have been known to float semi-submerged on the surface of the water, and hitting a corner of one at six or seven knots could well hole even a steel yacht. In fact, *Coopers & Lybrand* came across a boat drifting near the Canaries that was thought to have been holed by a container. She was a catamaran named *Zeeman*, in which the Dutch yachtsman Henk de Velde had been attempting to sail single-handed round the world. Vivien diverted to see what help she could give but when she got close she could see that there was no-one aboard. Henk had been taken off some days earlier by the crew of a passing ship.

West of the Canary Islands, calms fell over the fleet again. An Atlantic depression had passed the Azores on 14 May and moved east, bringing strong south-westerly winds. As that met the north-easterly trade winds it created a void where there was almost no breeze at all. The boats sailed into it and lay there becalmed for the best part of two days. On the results sheets we saw the good speeds they had been making fall as if they had run up against some physical obstruction. Average speeds on 13 and 14 May were between 2.6–3.2 knots and when the wind did fill in, *Commercial Union*, then in fifth place, got it first and sailed ahead of her rivals. Within a day, she had won back fourth placed *Nuclear Electric*'s seventy-eight-mile lead over them. Soon *Nuclear Electric*, too, got wind and by the next day she and *Commercial Union* found themselves in joint first place.

Once clear of this windless area, all except *Heath Insured* had come under the influence of the Atlantic depression and, later, a similar successor. Further east, *Heath Insured* suffered and her crew felt as *Commercial Union*'s had on the first leg: that anyone at the back always seems to get different and worse weather patterns. From then on it was impossible to make up distance on the others and as the final week of the race unfolded, we saw them drop further and further behind.

For the others, though, the two Atlantic depressions meant strong south-westerly to north-westerly winds and they recorded impressive average speeds of 9 knots for six consecutive days, from 16–20 May. As before, sails went up and came down, a spinnaker was hoisted only to be replaced later that day by a lightweight one, or a heavyweight one. Reports made it pretty plain it was hard work and tense racing but at the same time the excitement conveyed itself. At race headquarters, we matched that. The overall winner, as well as the placings all the way down the line to *Commercial Union* and *British Steel II*, were still in the balance. Public enthusiasm and anticipation were growing as well, as could be seen from press reports and from the number of people who called the British Telecom results service every day.

Although *Hofbräu Lager* had rejoined the main body of the fleet, *British Steel II* was all the while working westwards, chasing after the winds of those building Atlantic depressions. From plotted tracks on our computer it was plain that Richard was still tracing a parabola to the west that he felt would maximise his boatspeed and perhaps speed him towards the Western Approaches to Britain on a fair wind, while others had a more acute wind angle. To an extent this worked, for between 13–17 May the depression centred over the Azores moved north-eastwards, giving him favourable winds and a tremendous average boatspeed of nine-and-a-half knots.

In the midst of the fleet, *Commercial Union* was in first place, with *Group 4* very close behind, followed in a relatively short area by *British Steel II* and *Nuclear Electric*. Not much further back were *Hofbräu Lager* and *Coopers & Lybrand* and *Rhône-Poulenc. Heath Insured* were now some way behind. Yet even with steadier, fresher winds, places changed constantly. By 21 May, when the fleet was a day from rounding Ushant and entering the English Channel, *Group 4* moved past *Commercial Union* who could see them getting past, little by little, about six miles away. That day the crew of *Commercial Union* blew another spinnaker and a combination of that and just plain good sailing by the boys on *Group 4* gave her a tenuous lead of twelve miles by the time the fleet's positions were given the following morning. By then, *British Steel II* had converged with the rest of the fleet after her chase westwards and when she did, the two Richards came more or less face to face. *British Steel II* trailed *Commercial Union* by just six miles and, as the boats passed by the tip of the Breton coast, they were able to have a tacking duel.

Group 4 managed to lengthen their lead and on form so far in this leg it seemed likely that she would be first into Southampton. Since the fleet had picked up the strong westerlies south of Madeira, *Group 4, British Steel II, Commercial Union* and *Nuclear Electric* had been within fifty miles of each other. It was still close, but now the westerlies petered out and were replaced by light and variable winds, mostly south-easterlies. Being in strongly tidal waters added another important consideration: there were the tidal gates at Portland Bill and the Needles at the western end of the Isle of Wight to add to the calculations. It was near spring tides, and even if the leaders were to arrive there first, they would be held back by hard-won and crucial hours if the tide there turned against them.

As the boats diverged up the English Channel, *British Steel II* and *Commercial Union* chose to take a southerly route, keeping towards the French side and engaging in a match-racing duel. Separated by only a few miles, they kept a close eye on each other, as did *Nuclear Electric* and *Rhône-Poulenc* and, some way further back, *Coopers & Lybrand* and *Hofbräu Lager*. The importance of interpreting weather information was critical to the leg result and it was at this point that a furore developed about some yachts that were obviously getting advice and additional information from on shore.

As a principle, outside assistance to yachts was not allowed by the racing rules, but the practical interpretation of that rule can be difficult and, with such private aids as satellite communications, even harder to police. Throughout the race, race headquarters updated the positions of yachts, together with current courses and speeds made good four times a day so that anyone calling the British Telecom fax service could follow the progress of the fleet. However, the crews of the boats themselves were not privy to such detailed information on the tactics of their rivals. There were the twice daily position reports from each of the yachts and each day we let the fleet know individual boats' course and speed made good. Over the last week of the race, it was obvious that at least one of the yachts was benefiting from the updates British Telecom broadcast on land.

Observance of the rules about weather information rested entirely on the integrity of the skippers and there was really no way that any allegations of cheating could be proven. Yet feeling naturally ran high. There was a lot at stake and the finish was very high-profile indeed. None of the skippers wanted to cheat or be seen as cheating. It was a sensitive issue and after communicating with all the skippers, we clarified the narrow interpretation of the rule that banned outside assistance and they agreed that they wanted no relaxation of the rule. What alternative was there? All that could now come from a protest about tactical advantages gained by extra information would be a long public wrangle after the race, the implications of which might even end up stretching back to earlier legs. The information being sent had to stop and we were assured, without having to point any fingers, that it would.

Overnight on 22–23 May, *Group 4* held on to their lead. Mike Golding nervously monitored the boats behind and in the dawn of 23 May made his final approach to the Solent on the last of the ebb tide at the Needles. In the grey light of the early morning, his euphoric crew made their way eastwards, joining the equally triumphant supporter boats, turning upwind into Southampton Water to cross the line at 0633. They docked at Ocean Village to an astonishing reception. "There were . . . tears of joy, thousands of waving hands and smiling faces on the quay," David Cowan recalled, "a thunderous fusillade of fireworks, 'God Save the Queen', and at last we were able to throw ourselves into the arms of our loved ones. And there were more tears, and then champagne . . . until we felt as if we might roar up into the sky like the fireworks and explode with sheer joy and excitement."

Less than an hour later, Richard Merriweather sailed across the line in *Commercial Union* to a fitting reception for a crew that had suffered such misfortune in the early part of the leg. Again they had pushed hard, had raced consistently and outdone the best efforts of the pursuing *British Steel II* over the last day-and-a-half. Like the crew of *Group 4*, indeed like all the others to come, *Commercial Union*'s crew looked dazed with euphoria and high emotion. Less than seventeen minutes behind them came *British Steel II*, finishing with the same unconcealed delight, the disappointments of their earlier legs left behind. For all but *Group 4* and *Nuclear Electric*, the desire to win above all was rightly eclipsed by the phenomenal achievement of having sailed round the world the hardest and most difficult way possible.

The day turned from the grey haze of the early morning into a warm sunny day, almost a repeat of the kind weather we had been favoured with on the day of the start eight months before. *Nuclear Electric* was still to finish, and the slender difference in elapsed time that separated her from *Group 4* had become complicated in justifiable claims for redress. *Nuclear Electric* was entitled to forty minutes for diverting to go to the aid of *Heath Insured*, and *Group 4* could claim one hour and forty minutes for going to help the Senegalese fishing boat. The eight-hour lead *Nuclear Electric* had had in Cape Town had been eroded and by the time John Chittenden's crew reached St Alban's Head, east of Weymouth, they had less than eight hours to make the finishing line and win overall.

In the early morning, *Group 4* had caught the last of the ebb tide. By mid-afternoon the favourable flood tide was waning, but it still had the power to help *Nuclear Electric* towards the finish. With less than an hour separating the two boats after over 28,000 miles of racing, it was as nail-biting a finish as any ocean yacht race has ever seen. Had the tide at the Needles been foul, *Nuclear Electric* might well have been held up; their deadline could have passed. But as it was, they had judged it right and *Nuclear Electric* sailed up Southampton Water to cross the line at 1219, accompanied by a large flotilla of yachts and motorboats, full of supporters and well-wishers. The most enthusiastic reception of all was reserved for her. Aboard the boat, the joy of having won was mixed with relief: the efforts of the past eight months and the nervous tension of guarding a slim lead constantly for over a month were over at last.

Close behind her came *Rhône-Poulenc*. She finished at 1241, having had probably her most successful leg. For the thousands of spectators who had gathered at Ocean Village we could not have contrived a better finish, for later that evening *Coopers & Lybrand* and *Hofbräu Lager* fought out the last of a lengthy battle, during which they had close-tacked up the coast, match-racing each other. The duel was won by *Coopers & Lybrand*, but only by nine minutes. *Pride of Teesside* was not far behind and finished at just after 11 o'clock that evening, less than two hours after Vivien and Pete. I was ecstatic: in a race this long and this hard it was almost unbelievable to have eight of the ten boats finish in less than seventeen hours.

InterSpray arrived two days later. Just over a week before, she had been lying fifth, just astern of the leaders and many of the spectators and supporters were wondering what had gone wrong. *InterSpray* had quickly dropped back to ninth place during the last week of the leg and it was the depressing, familiar story – that the boats at the back never seem to get as favourable weather as those at the front. As they drifted back, so the depression to the west that had benefited the fleet with strong westerlies moved away and *InterSpray* was marooned at the back, while in front the others swept north-eastwards towards the English Channel. Paul Jeffes and his crew finally finished on 25 May at 1448.

For the unfortunate crew of *Heath Insured*, their problems were compounded even further by the weather. She did not get westerlies and instead had a long hard slog against continuing north-easterly trade winds. Tacking up the rhumb line was a tedious business and it was disheartening to know the others were finished, on shore, celebrating. All the same, *Heath Insured*'s crew held up until, at last, on 21 May they got fair winds and sped towards Southampton in the early hours of 27 May.

All the crews of the nine other boats set out down Southampton Water to greet her. That spontaneous gesture of welcome and fellow feeling for what *Heath Insured*'s crew had been through sums up the camaraderie of the British Steel Challenge which the spirit of full-blooded competition did nothing to destroy. It was also a very emotional time for most of the crews. Not only did that mark the very end of the Challenge, when the crews would split up for good, but it marked their recognition of, and sadness about, an incident that could so easily have happened on their own boat. *Heath Insured* finished at 1049 to cheering and celebrations that rivalled the reception four days earlier. The crews were overwhelmed and so were we. The British Steel Challenge had worked, it was a success, and here were ten boats in fine condition and 140 experienced ocean racers to prove it.

There is a postscript to the story of the race. For many of the crews that took part in the British Steel Challenge, the experience changed their lives dramatically in practical ways. Some had to seek jobs, some determined to go about making a change in their way of life or career that earlier they had just thought about. Some returned to families and friends with a new perspective; others told me that they returned to find relationships changed unalterably, but that their achievement and its reward of satisfaction justified those changes. Many are still paying off debts accrued over the years of training and sailing, but none that I have spoken to of their feelings about the event would ever think of themselves as a customer, nor ever question whether the costs or the sacrifices or the endurance were worthwhile.

From my own perspective, of course, the British Steel Challenge was a fantastic success, on its own terms as well as a business enterprise. It has changed attitudes to sailing and it has altered, in the eyes of the majority anyway, the perception of ocean racing as an elitist sport that can only be done by the professional or the wealthy amateur. The achievements of a perfectly representative selection of ordinary people, whose only common denominator was the ambition and determination to do something difficult and extraordinary, to my mind stands for everything that is unconquerable about team spirit and co-operation. If my solo voyage in 1970 was the impossible voyage, then this one was ten times more impossible. Yet all but one man returned safely.

It was my privilege to have known everyone who sailed on the British Steel Challenge. Andrew, Helen, Greg, Alastair, Captain Drummond, Chris, Gara and all the others on the Challenge team made possible the opportunity to sail round the world the wrong way, but we know only too well that without the initiative and resolution of those crewmembers it could never have been the close run race or the successful event that it was.

There still are cynics who ask why on earth anyone would pay £15,000 to endure such privation and hardship. It seems they cannot understand what the British Steel Challenge was really about for the people who took part. The answer to silence them all – yet again – is that the crews for the Ocean Challenge are already being trained, and the same boats will sail again for Cape Horn, the Southern Ocean and beyond in 1996.

Arrival Times
Race Leg: 4 – Cape Town to Southampton

Yacht Name	Status	Arrival Time GMT	Leg Time DDD HH MM SS	Placing
01: *Group 4*	Finished	23 MAY 06:33:58	035 19 33 58	1st
02: *Commercial Union*	Finished	23 MAY 07:27:27	035 20 27 27	2nd
03: *British Steel II*	Finished	23 MAY 07:43:32	035 20 43 32	3rd
04: *Nuclear Electric*	Finished	23 MAY 12:19:40	036 01 19 40	4th
05: *Rhône Poulenc*	Finished	23 MAY 12:41:51	036 01 41 51	5th
06: *Coopers & Lybrand*	Finished	23 MAY 21:08:44	036 10 08 44	6th
07: *Hofbräu Lager*	Finished	23 MAY 21:17:08	036 10 17 08	7th
08: *Pride of Teesside*	Finished	23 MAY 23:13:30	036 12 13 30	8th
09: *InterSpray*	Finished	25 MAY 14:48:03	038 03 48 03	9th
10: *Heath Insured*	Finished	27 MAY 10:49:12	039 23 49 12	10th

Additional Information:

The Southampton protest committee noted that, in the event, yacht positions would not be affected by any claim for redress and that no yacht had made a claim for this reason. The provisional results for Leg 4 and the Race overall, i.e. *Group 4 Securitas* wins the Infolink Leg Trophy and *Nuclear Electric* wins the Challenge Trophy, are therefore confirmed

Final Race Results: Combined Times

Yacht Name	Status	Combined Time DDD HH MM SS	Placing
01: *Nuclear Electric*	Finished	151 11 49 11	1st
02: *Group 4*	Finished	151 13 59 36	2nd
03: *Hofbräu Lager*	Finished	152 15 45 56	3rd
04: *Coopers & Lybrand*	Finished	154 17 59 56	4th
05: *Pride of Teesside*	Finished	155 16 06 48	5th
06: *InterSpray*	Finished	156 14 09 10	6th
07: *Heath insured*	Finished	157 10 29 18	7th
08: *Rhône Poulenc*	Finished	159 04 07 22	8th
09: *Commercial Union*	Finished	159 17 26 13	9th
10: *British Steel II*	Finished	163 00 25 07	10th

DDD HH MM SS – Leg time/combined time expressed in: days, hours, minutes, seconds

BT Race Results Systems Data. © British Telecommunications plc, 1992/93

THE CHALLENGE FLEET 67 FT ONE-DESIGN
YACHT SPECIFICATION

Rig	*Bermudan Cutter Rig*	
LOA	*67ft*	*20.42m*
LWL	*55ft*	*17.76m*
Beam	*17ft 3in*	*5.26m*
Draught	*9ft 3in*	*2.82m*
Top of mast from waterline	*85ft 3in*	*25.98m*
Height of mast above deck	*79ft 5in*	*24.20m*
Displacement	*33 tons*	
Ballast keel	*12 tons*	
Sail Area		
(inc 100% foretriangle)	*1932 sq ft*	*179.49 sq m*
Main	*926 sq ft*	*86.02 sq m*
Genoa	*1480 sq ft*	*137.49 sq m*
Spinnaker	*3780 sq ft*	*351.17 sq m*
Accommodation		
Berths	*14 (6 cabins)*	
Saloon	*1*	
Galley	*1*	
Heads	*2*	
Drying/Oilskin room	*1*	
Chartroom/Deckhouse	*1*	
Engine		
Type	*Mermaid Ford 6 cylinder naturally aspirated diesel*	
HP	*120 hp*	
Generation	*2 × 110 amp hours alternators (Bat. capacity 800 amp hours)*	
Electrics	*24 volt*	
Watermaker	*Aquafresh 800ED*	

Fuel	*418 gal*	*1900 lt*
Water	*242 gal*	*1100 lt*
Instruments	*Autohelm ST-50 Series*	
Decca	*Navstar 2000D*	
Satnav	*Navstar 2000S*	
GPS	*Navstar XR4*	
SSB Radio	*Skanti 8400S*	
VHF	*Skanti 3000*	
Radar	*Raytheon R20x*	
Mast	*Proctor Masts*	
Sails	*Hood*	
Winches/Deckgear	*Lewmar*	
Standing Rigging	*Norseman-Gibb Dyform*	
Running Rigging	*Marina*	
Construction		
Hull	*50B Mild Steel*	
Deck	*316 Stainless Steel*	
Designer	*David Thomas*	
Working drawings	*Thanos Condylis (C & S yacht designs)*	
Builder	*DML Devonport Yachts*	

HULL PROFILE

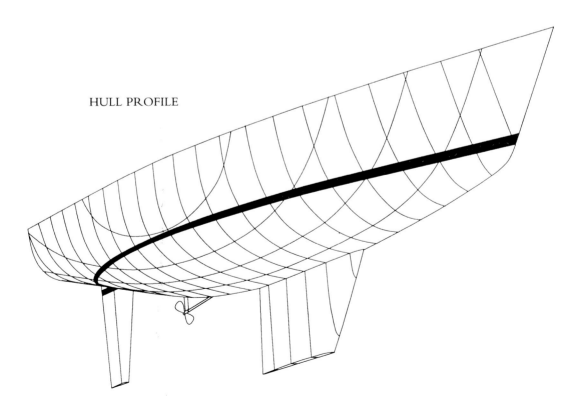

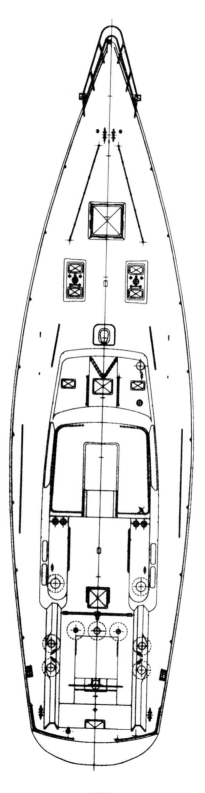

DECK LAYOUT

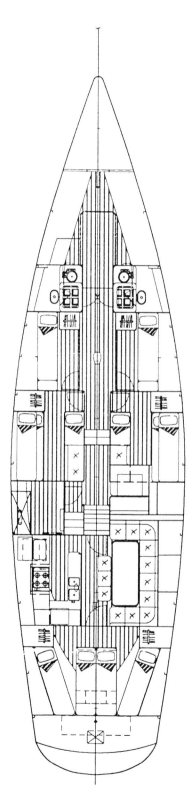

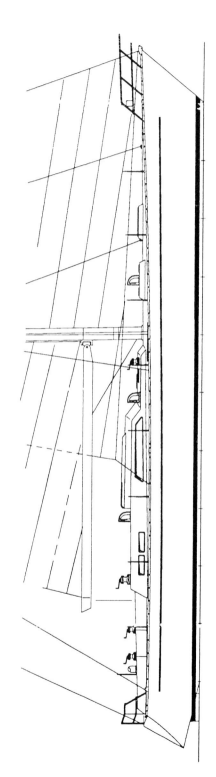

GENERAL ARRANGEMENTS

APPENDIX TWO

SKIPPERS AND CREWS

Yacht COOPERS & LYBRAND

Skipper Vivien Cherry **Date of birth** 1 July 1959
Occupation environmental engineer
Sailing experience raced a South Coast One-Design from 1982–8 and a Sigma 33 from 1989–90. Delivered a 40-footer to Portugal and returned with the OSTAR Race in 1988. Took part in the Scottish Islands Race in 1986 and 1987, the Australian Three Peaks Race in Tasmania in 1990 and trained a novice crew for the 1989 Fastnet Race.

Crew Brian Bird, 52, butcher; Robert Faulds, 30, shop manager; Richard Griffith, 50, company director; Geraint Lewis, 30, computer systems analyst; Maarten Malmeberg, 23, student; Neil Skinner, 34, HGV driver; Matthew Steel-Jessop, 30, computer network manager; Paul Titchener, 30, accountant; David Turner, 33, financial consultant; Samantha Wood, 23, student
Crew for one or two legs Mike Bass, 23, electrician; Ann de Boer, 27, account manager; Shane Dickson, 44, bank manager; Murray Findley, 63, company president (USA); Gary Hopkins, 36, local government manager; Phil Jones, 29, steel worker; John Kirk, 51, outdoor activities instructor; Paul Shephard, 40, fitter; Martin Wright, 35, investment manager

---

Yacht NUCLEAR ELECTRIC

Skipper John Chittenden **Date of birth** 23 June 1940
Occupation Master Mariner
Sailing experience dinghy racing, inshore and offshore racing on IOR yachts between 1970–85, cruising across the Atlantic, 1989/1990 Whitbread Round the World Race as skipper of the maxi *Creighton's Naturally.*

Crew Martin Bayfield, 33, banking systems consultant; John Cox, 50, company director; Nick Edgington, 33, computer systems consultant; Chris Head, 47, sub-sea engineer; Nigel Janes, 22, student; Roy Meakin, 25, lifeguard; John Nash, 42, building services engineer; Richard Rollinshaw, 46, baker; John Tillish, 40, company director;
Crew for one or two legs Martin Barker, 31, maintenance craftsman; Martin Clarke, 37, Nuclear Electric employee; Douglas Foulds, 31, instrument mechanic; David Johnson, 57, schoolmaster; Nick Lupton, 29, shift operations

manager; Liz Macdonald, 35, administrations assistant; Nick Marshall, 23, electrical craftsman; Bill Mew, 33, mechanical craftsman; John Pollard, work study assistant; Bill St Leger, 36, fire fighter; Neil Stewart, 50, shift charge engineer; Gretta Thomas, 30, corporate press officer; Peter Thomas, 54, production procurement manager; Steve Yates, 32, nurse

---

Yacht: HEATH INSURED

Skipper: Adrian Donovan **Date of birth**: 14 February 1957
Occupation: Master Mariner and charter yacht skipper
Sailing experience: Skipper of 40ft yacht in the Caribbean, a 72ft yacht in the eastern Mediterranean, instructor with Britannia Sailing School in 1988, Solent School of Yachting 1988–9 and Sailing South West 1989–90. Two-handed Transatlantic Race, 1990. Antigua Race Week, 1991.

Crew: Adrian Arnold, 50, company director; Samantha Brewster, 25, student; Arthur Haynes, 47, manager; Kenneth Pearson, 42, farmer; Graham Price, 36, sound engineer; Carol Randall, 34, journalist; Godfrey Owen, 29, personnel manager; Adrian Rayson, 37, company secretary; David Spratley, 28, sales manager; Bill Vincent, 46, carpenter; Lisa Wood, 35, care assistant; Stuart Smith Warren, 45, steel worker
Crew for one or two legs: Jonathan Goodall, 47, public relations officer; Steve Stamp, 38, operations engineer; Philip Streeter, 32, turner; Richard Walker, 26, accountant

---

Yacht: GROUP 4 SECURITAS

Skipper: Michael Redvers Golding **Date of birth**: 27 August 1960
Occupation: operational sub-officer (watch commander), Royal Berkshire Fire Service.
Sailing experience: Four transatlantic crossings. Circumnavigation of the world following Drake's route in a 33ft catamaran. Entered 1983 Azores and Back Race (1st in class), 1988 OSTAR Race (3rd in class) and 1989 Round Britain and Ireland Race. Also cruised to Azores, Canaries and Cape Verde Islands. Had built and was campaigning his own 40ft trimaran at the time he applied as a skipper in The Challenge. Has sailed 50,000 miles racing and 12,000 miles cruising

Crew: Gary Ashton, 28, warehouse manager; John Carter, 38, computer manager; Simon Clarke, 28, chartered accountant; Rob Coles, 36, printer; David Cowan, 53, teacher; Donald Deakin, 53, company director; Trevor Harvey, 38, engineer; Tony Hill, 28, dentist; Nick Jubert, 41, company director; Tony Marsden, 56, construction technician; Michael O'Regan, 27, trainee accountant
Crew for one or two legs: Kevin Handley, 35, operations manager; Martin Hall, 25, Group 4 sergeant; Richard Palmer, 51, personnel and recruitment manager; Simon Littlejohn, 28, freelance photographer (3 legs); Jim Barrett, 40, technical security manager

Yacht: HOFBRÄU LAGER

Skipper: Pete Goss **Date of birth**: 22 December 1961
Occupation: sail training instructor
Sailing experience: 1984 Three Peaks Race (1st in class), 1986 Two-handed
Transatlantic Race (2nd in class and awarded the Royal Naval Sailing Association
Trophy for outstanding seamanship), 1987 Three Peaks Race (2nd in class), 1989
Round Britain and Ireland Race (1st in class). Instructor at the Joint Services Sail
Training Centre in Plymouth from 1983–8, when he joined the British Steel
Challenge as training skipper.

Crew: Andrew Hindley, 45, account manager; Tristan Lewis, 25, computer
engineer; Brian Lister, 56, insurance broker; Jonathan Myers, 28, doctor; Roger
Pratt, 47, director, advertising agency; Steve Rigby, 25, unemployed; Rebecca
Slater, 27, nursery nurse; Mark Steadman, 29, maintenance manager; Jack
Gordon Smith, 45, market gardener; Pippa Welch, 29, computer programmer
Crew for one–three legs: Mike Calvin, 35, journalist, the *Daily Telegraph*;
Kenneth Ellis, 53, trout fishery owner; John Giddings, 37, fitter; Michael Kay,
45, manager; James Lees, 29, construction buyer; Tricia Smith, 32, teacher; Jim
Toseland, 33, personnel manager

Yacht: INTERSPRAY

Skipper: Paul Jeffes **Date of birth**: 6 April 1953
Occupation: Naval architect
Sailing experience: 1978 Round Britain and Ireland Race, skipper of racing
yacht between Scotland and Antigua in 1979, 1980 Three Peaks Race, 1982
Round Britain and Ireland Race, racing in Scottish Series and Scottish offshore
points series 1983–9.

Crew: Patrick Brockman, 30, project manager; Paul Buchanan, 31, account
manager; Juliet Connell, 50, air stewardess; John Davis, 52, petrol distributor;
Carlton Dodd, 39, investment marketing; Duggie Gillespie, 26, chartered
surveyor; Dominic Matthews, 48, financial adviser; Jeff Plummer, 45, oil
technician; Richard Scott, 38, HGV driver; Alison Smith, 25, unemployed;
Brian Warr, 43, engineering maintenance fitter; Julian Wells, 42, vet
Crew for one or two legs: Ruth Colenso, 26, graduate trainee; Barry Ford, 31,
electrician; Paul Gelder, 46, journalist, *Yachting Monthly*; Roger Peek, 48, British
Steel treasurer

Yacht: PRIDE OF TEESSIDE

Skipper: Ian MacGillivray **Date of birth**: 21 April 1956
Occupation: sailing instructor
Sailing experience: two Atlantic crossings in own boat, dinghy and local offshore races in a quarter-tonner; Mate to Challenge training skipper, Pete Goss

Crew: John Bagley, 56, agronomist; Gary Bailey, 47, director; Andrew Chamberlain, 24, satellite scientist; Les Dickinson, 50, property sales; Ramin Dilmaghanian, 26, civil engineer; Helen Griffiths, 22, student; Phil Harvey, 28, investment assistant; Robert Milnes, 29, doctor; Kate Twyman, 28, software engineer; David Wallbank, 29, engineer
Crew for one or two legs: George Backhouse, 57, farmer; Ian Bibby, 29, engineer; David Donkin, 32, accident prevention manager; John Hooper, 43, solicitor; Sue McKichan, 32, researcher (3 legs); Beverley Mulvenna, 33, lawyer; Richard Oliver, 55, banker; Keith Snell, 43, welder

Yacht: COMMERCIAL UNION ASSURANCE

Skipper: Richard Merriweather **Date of birth**: 17 April 1966
Occupation: professional yacht skipper
Sailing experience: yacht deliveries in the Caribbean, sailing instructor, Southern Ocean circuit on a three-quarter tonner, race skipper of a J35 in 1987, skipper of an Oyster 53 from 1988–9, skipper of a Bénéteau 40 in 1991 Antigua Week, skipper and manager of the sail training project *Spirit of Scotland*, a replica 1850s pilot schooner, between 1991–2.
Skipper for leg one: Will Sutherland

Crew: Roger Boyd, 28, technical sales; Peter Coop, 36, business development consultant; John Gibson, 34, company director; Eric Gustavson, 52, plastic surgeon; Andrew Stevenson Hamilton, 28, insurance broker; Tony Jones, 54, company director; Jim Kinnier Wilson, 34, solicitor; Mark Lodge, 28, ceiling fitter; Alison McKichan, 30, market researcher; Jonathan Norton, 24, insurance broker; Sue Tight, 35, management consultant
Crew for one or two legs: Marco Cullen, 29, operations assistant; Vince Hughes, 26, production caster; Stewart Hood, 43, data processing manager; Denis Skillicorn, journalist; Keith Taylor, 47, flooring contractor; Yvonne Taylor, 46, management accountant; Jonathan Wilson, 29, electrical engineer

Right, from top left The Challenge skippers: Vivien Cherry; John Chittenden, Adrian Donovan; Mike Golding; Pete Goss; Paul Jeffes; Ian MacGillivray; Richard Merriweather; Peter Phillips; Richard Tudor; *Nuclear Electric*, the overall winner, arrives at Southampton. (all MP)

Yacht: RHÔNE-POULENC

Skipper: Peter Phillips **Date of birth**: 1 May 1935
Occupation: former police officer, operations manager at Victoria Marine Services in Devon.
Sailing experience: 1978 Round Britain and Ireland Race, 1979 Azores and Back Race, 1979 Fastnet Race, 1980 Single-handed Transatlantic Race, 1981 Two-handed Transatlantic Race, 1982 Round Britain and Ireland Race, 1983 Plymouth-Vilamoura-Plymouth Race, 1984 Single-handed Transatlantic Race, 1985 Round Europe Race, 1986 Two-handed Transatlantic Race, 1986 Round Ireland Race (current record holder), 1987 Azores and Back Race (overall winner), 1987 Round Europe Race, 1988 Single-handed Transatlantic Race, 1989 Blue Riband Transatlantic crossing record.
Skipper for leg one: John O'Driscoll

Crew: David Brydon, 30, futures trader; Justine Cotton, 23, student; Valerie Elliott, 50, teacher; Suzanne Emerson, 28, computer programmer; Nick Fenner, 29, solicitor; Tony Fowler, 43, property developer; Campbell Mackenzie, 60, doctor; Daniel Sailor, 60, prison officer; Rod Street, 47, property renovator; Simon Walker, 25, student; Jerry Walsingham, 39, sales manager
Crew for one or two legs: Nicholas Atha, 38, transport manager; Paul Egan, 27, electronic engineer (3 legs); Steve George, 44, purchasing manager; John Haynes, 51, barrister; Jane Laycock, 28, process technician; Angus Mackenzie, 24, printer

Yacht: BRITISH STEEL II

Skipper: Richard Tudor **Date of birth**: 26 July 1959
Occupation: sailmaker
Sailing experience: co-skipper and navigator on Atlantic crossing. 1983, 1984 and 1985 Fastnet Races, 1986 and 1988 Three Peaks Race, 1988 Swan World Cup, 1987 and 1989 Swan European Championships, 1988 and 1990 Round Ireland Race, co-skipper and owner of a Contention 33 sailed in most ISORA Races.

Crew: David Arthur, 46, company director; Nigel Bray, 30, builder; Kevin Dufficy, 46, training consultant; Yvonne Flatman, 31, trading standards officer; Marcus Gladwell, 30, fisherman; Rob Haine, 36, chartered surveyor; Michael Martin, 52, management consultant; Patrick Quinn, 54, company director; Mike Sherwood, 48, electrical engineer; Giles Trollope, 43, company director; Steve West, 45, company director
Crew for one or two legs: Louise Broadbent, 26, salesperson; Richard Davies, 30, shift engineer; Nicola Handley, personal assistant; Harry Heathcock, 45, electrical design engineer; Sandra Hill, 25, auditor; Clare McKernan, 28, technical officer; Keith Mundell, 33, design engineer; Michael Smith, 42, senior shift supervisor

APPENDIX THREE

SAFETY AND NAVIGATION EQUIPMENT

The British Steel Challenge class 67ft one-design yachts were provided with the safety equipment required by the appropriate statutory bodies and those elected bodies considered appropriate by the organisers of the British Steel Challenge, such as the Ocean Racing Council and the Royal Ocean Racing Club.

Lifejackets

These are manufactured by Baltic in Sweden and inflate automatically on immersion in water. Each crewmember was provided with one and each yacht had two spares. The lifejackets have a built-in safety harness with crutch straps to stop it riding over the wearer's head in the water. The automatic inflation proved unsatisfactory in the race, as the jackets kept inflating while the crews were working on the foredecks.

Lifelines

Those we used are also manufactured by Baltic in Sweden. There is a standard lifeline attached, with two Gibb safety hooks at each end.

Personal EPIRBs (Emergency Position Indicating Radio Beacons)

These models, named PLB 7, were manufactured by Sea Marshall and are now marketed by Musto Ltd. The beacon gives off a signal if the wearer is immersed in water and transmits on 121.5MHz. Each crew had one, and every yacht had two spares. We found, however, that the early models we used suffered because of the damp conditions.

Man overboard alarm

This is an automatic unit that picks up the signal from the personal EPIRB described above and sounds an alarm. It works in conjunction with a 121.5MHz direction finding unit, which picks up the signal from the EPIRBs to give a directional fix on the person in the water.

Personal strobe light

A manually operated strobe light was given to each crew and two spares given to each yacht. These gave a very bright light that would be visible from afar and reflect powerfully from waves if the wearer were to fall overboard at night.

Yacht EPIRBs

Those we used are manufactured by Lo-Kata. They operate on 406MHz & 121.5MHz and send a signal to satellites relaying the position of the unit. This would have been vital information if a boat had had to be abandoned at sea by the crew.

Liferafts

We used liferafts manufactured by RFD. Each yacht has two eight-person rafts and one six-person raft – a capacity 50 per cent greater than we needed in order to comply with Department of Transport regulations. The emergency pack sealed inside was supplied to the E pack specification devised by the Royal Ocean Racing Club, and the raft had a double floor.

Danbuoy markers

There were two of these per yacht, fitted with flags and flashing lights. If someone were to go overboard, this piece of equipment was the first to be thrown over the side to mark the location of the crewmember.

Survival suits

Generally speaking survival suits are not designed to be worked in and are intended to extend life in very cold water, should a helicopter or ship have to be abandoned. They have a double skin insulation system and an integral lifejacket, so they tend to be bulky and relatively uncomfortable to wear for long periods.

A spin-off from the work on survival suits was the recent development of immersion suits, or dry suits. While immersion suits are designed to be worn for relatively long periods and facilitate work, they do not have insulation and the neck and cuff seals may not be totally waterproof. They will therefore extend life in very cold water for only a short time.

Prior to the start of the British Steel Challenge Race the Musto immersion suit was not in full production and there remained areas of doubt about how long the suit would stay watertight in really heavy conditions. If development of the immersion suit had been five or six months more advanced, the crews would probably have been supplied with these as well as conventional foul weather gear.

Safety policy for yachts taking part in the 1992/1993 Whitbread Race specify that competitors must have these immersion or survival suits.

Lifebelts

There were two horseshoe-type lifebelts per yacht, fitted at the port and starboard quarters of the pushpit.

Flares

We used flares manufactured by Pains Wessex. Each yacht had the following issue:

12 red rockets (for distress at night)
4 orange smoke flares (for distress during daylight)
4 white hand-held flares (for collision warning)
White rockets
Hand-held red flares

Electronic equipment

Each yacht had a set of Autohelm ST50 instruments marketed by Raytheon and all the instruments were repeated in the cockpit. Together they provided boatspeed, distance, windspeed (true and apparent), angle to the wind and sea temperature.

Magnavox MX100 GPS

We issued two of these per yacht. The Global Positioning System allows a yacht's position to be determined to an accuracy usually within metres by automatic fixes between several satellites. One of each yacht's GPSs interfaced with the Autohelm ST50 instruments and one interfaced with the INMARSAT standard C telex so that we could ascertain the yacht's speed, course and position.

Raytheon R20X radar

These are standard Raytheon units with a range of 20 miles.

Skanti 3000 VHF radio

Again, this is a standard unit, with an aerial at the masthead and on the radar mast aft.

Skanti 8400S Single Sideband High Frequency radio

This standard 400 watt unit used an 8m whip aerial and was to used to communicate over long distances. It was interfaced with the weatherfax computer to relay signals from which weather maps could be printed.

Mascot Standard C telex

These were supplied by STC (now Marine Technology International Ltd). This standard unit was interfaced with one GPS to provide the position fixing that we could tap in on back in England.

APPENDIX FOUR

THE POWER:
ENGINE, GENERATOR
AND SAILS

The engine and generator

During the early design studies of late 1988 and early 1989, most computations of main engine and generator makes were considered in relation to their reliability, efficiency, weight, fuel consumption and ability to run at large angles of heel.

Historically, in long distance races such as the Whitbread, separate generators had provided endless problems. Some yachts even elected to have a very lightweight main engine and two gimballed generators while others, such as *Flyer*, elected not to have a generator.

At that time, only a limited number of generators which would run for long periods at large angles of heel were available at affordable prices. Things had changed since then and we had to consider the pros and cons of using generators in the British Steel Challenge.

There are two main categories of 240-volt generators: those that run at 1,500rpm and those that run at 3,000rpm. The 1,500rpm types were reliable but heavy and the 3,000rpm types tended to have highly stressed engines running at maximum revs to drive air-cooled alternators. This means they are prone to problems in the tropics. The lightweight generators crank shafts available then were not strong enough to belt-drive the watermaker pump.

For our purposes a 240-volts supply was neither necessary nor desirable. No proven, compact, standard 24-volt generator was readily available, so the decision was made to go for a robust and proven reliable main engine, belt-driving two 110 amp m.o.d. standard 24-volt alternators and a watermaker pump.

We chose a Ford Mermaid six-cylinder unit. A single 110 amp alternator would have provided adequate electrical output, but two 'washable' (splashproof) alternators provided a significant safety factor. A spare smaller alternator is carried as is a spring starter, with which the engine could be started in the event of electrical failure.

The engine also drove the watermaker, an Aquafresh 800ED, which produced between 75 and 120 litres per hour depending on the temperature and, hence, the salinity of the water.

Sails

All the sails were built by Hood Sailmakers in Lymington, of Dacron★. The full specification is as follows:

Mainsail

Crosscut in 8.5oz with 8.5oz crescent, 3 reefs, 4 Battens and 2 overhead leech lines. Area 84 sq.m. Weight 106 kg.

No 1 Genoa

Bi-star construction in 8.0oz and 7.3oz warp Dacron with multi purchase leech line and heavy duty hanks. Area 137 sq.m. Weight 61 kg.

No 1 Yankee

Crosscut in 9.8oz Dacron with overhead leech line and hanks. Area 98 sq.m. Weight 79 kg.

No 2 Yankee

Crosscut in 9.8oz Dacron with overhead leech line and hanks. Area 60 sq.m. Weight 52 kg.

No 3 Yankee

Crosscut in 10.2oz Dacron with wire luff. Area 32 sq.m. Weight 23 kg.

Forestaysail

Crosscut in 10.2oz Dacron with hanks. Area 42 sq.m. Weight 38 kg.

Storm staysail

Crosscut in 13.0oz Dacron with hanks, head and tack strop. Area 23 sq.m. Weight 29 kg.

Trysail

Crosscut in 13.0oz Dacron with slides to fit mainsail track. Area 32 sq.m. Weight 32 kg.

Light spinnaker

Tri-star construction in Hood Nylon with webbed on rings. Area 351 sq.m. Weight 38 kg.

Heavy spinnaker

Tri-star construction in Hood Nylon with webbed on rings. Area 357 sq.m. Weight 45 kg.

Promotional spinnaker

Tri-radial construction in Hood Nylon with webbed on rings. Area 357 sq.m. Weight 45 kg.

Tri-star asymmetric reaching spinnaker (A.R.S)

Tri-star construction in 2.2oz Nylon with reinforced clew, tack and leech. Area 270 sq.m. Weight 50 kg.

This sail is in a Squeeza spinnaker sock for easy handling in bad weather.

★ Dacron is a trademark of DuPont.

APPENDIX FIVE

TOTAL DRIED FOOD
STORES AND SUPPLIES

FOOD ITEM	PACK SIZE	LEG 1	LEG 2	LEG 3	LEG 4	GRAND TOTAL
Melco	2.27kg	76	176	158	94	504 = 20160 pints!
Orange	500g box	183	295	288	294	1060 = 26500 litres!
Grapefruit	500g box	149	217	193	192	751 = 18775 litres!
Applejuice	500g box	10	39	0	0	49
Bread mix (white)	2.27kg	34	41	76	50	201
Bread mix (brown)	2.27kg	21	20	52		93
Plain flour	1.5kg	21	4	33	22	80
Scone mix	3.5kg	10	12	20	17	59
Beef chunks	5kg	47	13	23	25	108
Chunky chicken	5kg	23	62	41	23	149
Beef curry	2kg	13	28	45	41	127
Minced mutton	5kg	23	63	41	31	158
Minced chicken	5kg	0	0	16	14	30
Bolognaise	2kg	70	111	83	60	324
Chilli	2kg	54	106			160
Vegetable curry	2kg	34	78	22	22	156
Sweet & sour chicken	2kg	63	99	69	50	281
Mince onion & gravy	5kg	6	64	0	0	70
Chicken supreme	2kg	15	70	0	0	85
Curry with chicken	2kg	36	34	12	12	94
Lamb curry	2kg	4	0	18	6	28
Cheese onion pasty	2kg	25	37	19	11	92
Vegetable chilli	2kg	6	26	2	1	35
Chunks onion & gravy	5kg	0	1	50	20	71
Lasagne pasta	3kg	0	5		8	13
Minced beef	5kg	0	23		0	23
Suet pastry mix	2.27kg	26	48	45	26	145
Pasta plain spirals	3kg	21	56	12	24	113
Macaroni	3kg	20	24	16	13	73
Long spaghetti	3kg	8	38	13	15	74
Pasta shells	3kg	9	26	19	15	69
Tri colour spirals	3kg	2	9	10		21
Tri colour animals	3kg	2	9	3	2	16
Mashed potatoes	5lb	53	75	62	48	238
Mixed vegetables	5lb	32	72	59	26	189

Peas	7.5lb	33	57	62	53	205
Sliced onions	5lb	16	58	29	23	126
Chocolate delight	24ptn	24	53	44	33	154
Strawberry delight	24ptn	29	35	43	37	144
Banana delight	24ptn	19	47	2	20	88
Cherry cheesecake	24ptn	7	55	18	19	99
Appleflake	2kg	32	33	41	25	131
Crumblemix	3.5kg	7	19	6		32
Custard	3.5kg	23	78	26	20	147
Butterscotch delight	24ptn	8	32	29	17	86
Peach delight	24ptn	30	22	50	32	134
Creme caramel	24ptn	6	20	12	6	44
Raspberry delight	24ptn	7	18	0	0	25
Pastry mix	3kg	2	9	6	3	20
Sponge mix	3kg	27	3	28	32	90
Chocolate sponge mix	3kg	0	2	42	9	53
Blackcurrant cheesecake	24ptn	1	33	24	7	65
Marmalade	454g	6	31	0	3	40
Strawberry jam	340g		22	42	34	98
Apricot jam	340g		30	22	7	59

Interesting facts on usage during the British Steel Challenge

ITEM	QTY
Toilet Paper	1140 rolls
Duct Tape	343 rolls
Sikaflex	131 tubes
Fuel Filters	136
Running Rigging	24,000 meters 18mm
Split Pins	4200
Multi Purpose Cleaner	260 ltr
Fuel	£15,500 worth
Winch Pawls	680
Winch Pawl Springs	1554
Nav. Light Bulbs	194
Internal Halogen Bulbs	220
Batteries (Torch etc)	3500

APPENDIX SIX

EXTRACT FROM
THE RACE RULES

SAFETY (IYR Fundamental Rule B) It shall be the exclusive responsibility of each skipper to decide whether or not to start or to continue to race.

1 RULES

1.1 The Race shall be governed by:

    1.1.1 The International Yacht Racing Rules, current on 1 May 1992.

    1.1.2 The International Regulations for Preventing Collision at Sea when specified in Leg Sailing Instructions.

    1.1.3 The British Steel Challenge Safety Regulations which include the Department of Transport Sail Training Code of Practice and ORC Special Regulations Category "O".

    1.1.4 The British Steel Challenge one-design class rules.

    1.1.5 The International Telecommunications Union Regulations.

    1.1.6 The Notice of Race.

    1.1.7 These General Sailing Instructions.

    1.1.8 Leg Sailing Instructions.

    1.1.9 In the event of conflict these Sailing Instructions shall prevail over the Notice of Race and Leg Sailing Instructions shall prevail over these Sailing Instructions.

1.2 IYR Rule 26: The Race is a Category C event.

1.3 Alternative penalties (affecting IYR 52.1 or IYR Rules Part IV). When code flag "I" is flown by a yacht a lesser penalty may be applied by the Protest Committee.

    1.3.1 Notice of Race 7.11 and 7.12 shall apply to a yacht which infringes a rule of Part IV or which touches a mark.

    1.3.2 A yacht which acknowledges infringing a rule of Part IV or acknowledges touching a mark shall, at the first opportunity, display Code Flag "I" for at least one hour. She shall display it again when finishing the Leg and keep it displayed until it is acknowledged by the Race Committee.

1.4 IYR Rules of Part IV shall apply until sunset on the day of the Start of each Leg. Thereafter, they shall cease to be applicable and shall be replaced by Part B (Steering and Sailing Rules) of the International Regulations for preventing Collisions at Sea. Approaching the finish IYR Rules of Part IV shall again apply, between the times of sunrise and sunset, when yachts enter a circle radius 20 miles centred on the outer distance mark of the finishing line.

1.5 At the start of each leg the engine shall not be run for any purpose between the Preparatory signal and 6 hours after the Start except as permitted by Fundamental rule A and Rule 55.

2 THE COURSE

2.1 The course for the Race is Round the World leaving Cape Horn and The Cape of Good Hope to Starboard and the following to Port:

    a. Position 52 deg 00min South 120 deg 00min West.

    b. Kerguelen Isles (49 S 69 E).

    At the start of the Race and at its end yachts are to pass between Hurst Castle and the Isle of Wight.

2.2 The Race will Start and Finish at Southampton as detailed below. The Race will have 4 Legs with STOPOVERS at Rio de Janeiro, Hobart and Cape Town. Details of Starts and Finishes will be contained in individual Leg Instructions. The dates planned for each Start are contained in Part I of the Race Notice.

2.3 The first Leg will start 12:00 BST on Saturday 26 September 1992. The Starting Line will be off Gilkicker Point near Southampton. The last Leg will finish at Southampton.

3 STANDARD STARTING PROCEDURE

3.1 THE START. Starting signals will be in accordance with IYR Rule 4.4 System 1. Details will be contained in Leg Sailing Instructions.
    3.1.2 *Round the Ends Starting Rule* may be used.
3.2 RECALLS (Individual Recalls Affecting IYR Rule 8.1)
    3.2.1 A yacht which starts prematurely and which fails to return wholly to the pre-start side of the Starting Line will incur a time penalty of not less than 2 hours.
3.3 *Radio at the Start* The Race Committee will use VHF radio at the start to inform competitors of yachts recalled, postponements etc. However, Radio information is provided as an aid, the provision or failure of this aid shall not form part of any protest.
3.4 GENERAL RECALLS (General Recall Affecting IYR Rule 8.2 and 8.4.1)
    3.4.1 After a General Recall, the first substitute will be hauled down accompanied by a sound signal 1 minute before the warning signal (10 minute gun) for the restart.
3.5 POSTPONEMENT OR CHANGES
    3.5.1 The Race Committee will, if possible, announce any postponement of the Start on the VHF Channel designated in the Leg Sailing Instructions with the expected duration of the delay
    3.5.2 When Flag L is displayed on the Principal Committee Vessel, yachts should stand by to receive written instructions from a boat which will also fly Flag L.
3.6 PENALTY ROUTING FOR NEW SAILS (Notice of Race para 5.13)
A yacht issued with a new sail will:
a. Start the next leg with the remainder of the Fleet (and continue with them for a short coastal 'spectators benefit leg' if any)
b. She will then be required to proceed separately to round one or two special marks before following the course of the race

4 CONDUCT OF THE RACE

4.1 PROTESTS (Affecting IYR Rule 68. See also Part VII of Notice of Race)
    4.1.1 As well as flying Flag B a protesting yacht should inform the Race Committee on VHF before leaving VHF range that she has a protest and the name of the yacht protested against. This is to be followed by a Radio report to Race Headquarters (see Notice para 7.6). A yacht acknowledging an infringement by displaying Code Flag "I" should report by radio to Race Headquarters.
    4.1.2 On finishing a Leg a protesting yacht should display Flag "B". Protests in writing shall be made on the RYA form, accompanied by a fee of £500, which will be returned if the protest is not adjudged to be frivolous, shall be handed in at the Race Office within 24 hours of the protesting yacht finishing the Leg to which the protest applies.
    4.1.3 A protested yacht which flies Flag I shall hand in a brief written report within 24 hours of arrival.
    4.1.4 Protests will be heard at the end of each Leg by a Protest Committee as soon as possible after the yachts concerned have finished.
    4.1.5 Penalties. See Notice paras 7.11 and 7.12.
4.2 TIME LIMIT
There is no time limit for completing a leg, however the next leg will start on the published date. Skippers whose yachts are lagging well behind should consider retiring from that leg and motor-sailing to make up sufficient time to start the next leg with the remainder of the Fleet. This would improve their scoring for the aggregate points trophy. Race HQ and Sponsor should normally be consulted.
4.3 RETIREMENTS
A yacht which retires from any Leg of the Race must inform Race Headquarters and the Duty Yacht of her Group as soon as possible. A yacht which has retired should wear her ensign. See Annexe A (Notice of Race 6.3) about entering a port in an emergency.
4.4 ENSIGNS AND SPECIAL FLAGS
    4.4.1 Ensigns may be worn up to the warning (10 minute) signal and after finishing and when Part B of the International Regulations for Preventing Collisions at Sea are applicable (see 1.6 above). Ensigns should not be worn when IYR Rules of Part IV are applicable.
    4.4.2 However ensigns may be worn when racing, if in the opinion of the Skipper, it is necessary to show the nationality of his yacht (for example, on approaching a Country's Territorial Waters).

4.4.3 Each yacht shall display The British Steel Challenge (Class Flag) prominently (on the backstay if possible), from the time the yacht leaves her berth on the day of each start until sunset after the start. She shall display it again when she enters the finishing area defined in 1.6 above.

4.4.4 BT pennant shall be displayed continuously at sea and in harbour.

4.5 RULES COMPLIANCE

Declarations on the official forms supplied with the Leg Sailing Instructions are required at the end of each Leg.

4.5.1 On completion of each Leg, the Committee will require selected yachts to be in measurement trim for freeboard checks. Such checks will be carried out within 48 hours of finishing and each yacht will be checked at least once during the Race.

4.5.2 All yachts shall be prepared to submit to simple scrutiny whilst underway and racing if requested by a Committee Vessel flying The British Steel Challenge Flag. Such checks will be carried out within 48 hours of finishing and each yacht will be checked at least once during the Race.

4.6 POSITION REPORTS AND ETAs

4.6.1 The accurate position of each yacht is required to reach Race Headquarters at the least every 24 hours (see para 8.3). Under normal circumstances this will be done automatically but should this not occur yachts are responsible for ensuring that positions are passed by another route. Any suspicion of inaccurate or misleading position reports or unreasonable delays in reports will be investigated by the Race Committee.

4.6.2 *Leg Finish Reports* Yachts shall report as follows:
  a. To Race HQ
  i. ETA when 100 miles to go.
  ii. On crossing the line giving exact time.
  b. To Local Yacht Club as directed in Leg Instructions.

4.7 INJURY TO CREW OR DEATH REPORTS

Should any crew member be injured or killed the Skipper must:

a. Report to Race HQ immediately with a follow up report within 4 hours and thereafter at least every 12 hours until the situation stabilises.

b. Hold an enquiry on the same day and compile a written report which includes:

i. Written and signed statements by the Watch Leader and all witnesses.

ii. His own statement.

c. The report is to be given to a BSC Committee Member on arrival in port.

5 DUTY YACHT

5.1 Leg Sailing Instructions will nominate each yacht in turn as Duty Yacht. Duty starts at 12:00 GMT and is for 24 hours. Before handing over at the end of the previous Inter-Yacht routine the off-going yacht must obtain confirmation that her successor has satisfactory communications. Should the yachts become very spread out Race HQs will divide them into 2 groups with a Duty Yacht in each.

5.2 An inter-yacht communications schedule is established so that yachts may exchange information of mutual interest, use the services of another yacht to relay their position or other reports, pass reports to the duty yachts and receive relayed messages from shore.

5.3 All yachts are to establish communications with the Duty Yacht during the twice daily inter-yacht schedules and are encouraged to participate in the exchange of information.

5.4 *Duties* Duty Yachts shall carry out the following duties:

1. Maintain a constant Watch on 2182 KHZ using the Watch Alarm. If communications are bad on this frequency 4125 KHZ or 6215 KHZ should be used instead.

2. Control the inter-yacht schedule for her group.

3. Maintain an up to date record of the positions of all the yachts in her group.

4. Make a daily report to Race HQ (see para 5.5).

5. Act as shore Radio link for any yacht with communication problems.

6. In the event of general INMARSAT C failure:
  a. listen to Portishead traffic lists twice daily and alert yachts for whom there is traffic.
  b. collect in all yachts positions every 12 hours.

7. If the Duty Yacht decides it is appropriate she should listen to local traffic lists when approaching stop over ports on behalf of yachts in her group.

8. In the event of an emergency the duty yacht shall act as local co-ordinator until other arrangements are made.

5.5 *Daily Report to Race HQ* This report is required to keep Race HQ up to date and informed of events at sea. It will normally form the basis for the daily press release. The following points should be covered:

1. Duty Yacht position, course and average speed.
2. Weather.
3. *List* of reported problems and defects (Race HQ can ask individuals for details).
4. Communications – problems, need for 2 groups.
5. Newsworthy items – including "life afloat".

5.6 All yachts should contribute to this report.

6 INTER-YACHT COMMUNICATIONS

6.1 *Calling schedules and times* The twice daily one hour schedules begin at 11:00 and 23:00 GMT. The Duty Yacht shall control as follows:

Frequency (KHZ)

Minutes past the hour	Group 1	Group 2	
00–20	2056/2638	8297	NOTES
20–30	4146	2056/2638	1. Use 2056 during legs 1 & 4
30–45	6224	4146	Use 2638 during legs 2 & 3
45–59	8297	6224	2. Use VHF 72, 77, 6 or 8 if within range

6.2 The first 5 minutes of each of these periods shall be used to pass Distress or Safety messages and for passing yachts position reports.

6.3 Duty Yacht may alter above schedule if needed. Keep Race HQ informed.

6.4 If possible medical advice/discussion should be transferred to an alternative inter-ship channel.

6.5 If Duty Yacht judges it appropriate to use VHF for inter-yacht routine she should announce the Channel in her opening call on each of the listed MF and HF frequencies.

7 COMMUNICATIONS BETWEEN YACHTS AND ASHORE

7.1 The primary communication link is INMARSAT C which provides continuous TELEX type communication via satellite. INMARSAT C also offers a world-wide Distress Service. The Secondary link is HF RT via Portishead as well as via local Coast Radio stations using HF, MF or VHF.

7.2 *Operational use of INMARSAT* The following messages should be sent via INMARSAT and BSC will meet the charge:

   7.2.1 *From yachts*
   – GPS position every 12 hours (autofix).   – Distress, Safety & Medico traffic.
   – Daily sitrep from Duty Yacht (para 5.5)   – Response to Race HQ or Local HQ message.
   – ETA & Finish time (para 4.10).   – Urgent messages.
   7.2.2 *To yachts*   – From Race HQ – Daily position summary.
   7.2.3 INMARSAT should not be used within 10 mins of autofix time.

7.3 *Other uses of INMARSAT* Inmarsat is available as required for non-operational traffic such as: Messages to and from Sponsors.
Personal messages to and from crewmembers.

   7.3.1 BSC will not bear the cost of these messages. It should also be noted that limited yachts batteries may make rationing of "out messages" necessary.

7.4 *Use of HF RT via Portishead* Messages will be routed through Portishead for any yachts believed to be out of touch on both INMARSAT and also Inter-Yacht Net. Portishead is also available for telephone conversations.

   7.4.1 Portishead will include any traffic for BSC yachts on a nominated daily Traffic list. At the end of this list Portishead will call "CQ BRITISH STEEL CHALLENGE YACHTS" and listen for incoming traffic. Times will be in Leg Instructions.
   7.4.2 In the event of any Yacht being unable to read INMARSAT and not be in touch with the DUTY Yacht she should report the fact to Race HQ by any possible route and read Portishead. Extra daily times may then be arranged.
   7.4.3 In an emergency yacht can call Portishead at any time to pass traffic.
   7.4.4 Sponsors' and personal messages can also be passed through Portishead. Again BSC will not bear the cost.
   7.4.5 Frequencies and procedures for calling Portishead are in the Maritime Radio Services Guide section 5. Propagation Forecasts providing recommended frequencies and best times will be included in individual Leg Sailing Instructions.

8 SAFETY AND DISTRESS

8.1 The mounting of a successful operation to assist a yacht in distress is dependent on her accurate position being known and her distress message getting through.

8.2 The nearest yacht to a casualty will often be the quickest and frequently the only means of providing assistance or rescue. It is vitally important that yachts keep in close touch with each other and report even minor problems in case they should unexpectedly worsen.

8.3 Yacht positions will automatically be transmitted from their GPS via INMARSAT to Race Headquarters who will re-broadcast all positions daily. Should a yacht's position not arrive, Race Headquarters will send an appropriate message to it and to all other yachts. If the automatic link is found to be defective the yacht concerned is to report its position twice daily to Race Headquarters via the Duty Yacht or any other means.

8.4 A yacht requiring assistance should:
    a. Transmit on INMARSAT in distress mode.   b. Activate EPIRBS if urgent.
    c. Send amplifying message to Race HQ via INMARSAT or another yacht.
    d. Broadcast on 2182 KHZ using normal distress or Urgency procedure preceded by the automatic alarm signal. If no response repeat on 4125 KHZ and 6215 KHZ.
    e. If no acknowledgement is received message must be passed on HF RT to Portishead or other Coast Radio Stations.

8.5 Distress sent via a. and b. will reach Race HQ via Falmouth Coast Guard and the extensive international Rescue organisation. They will also reach MRCCs in the Yachts area.

8.6 Race HQ will acknowledge any distress messages received and inform all other yachts.

8.7 Race Headquarters will initiate emergency action in conjunction with Falmouth Coast Guard.
    i. If there is any doubt about the safety of a yacht
    ii. On the request of a yacht if at any time she is in need of assistance

8.8 In an emergency situation the Duty Yacht (see para 5.4.8) should act as local area co-ordinator until other arrangements have been made or the nearest yacht takes over. The Duty Yacht must also determine if the emergency is genuine and not one triggered by accidental activation.

8.9 The greatest care must be taken to avoid false alarms by accidentally triggering off INMARSAT or EPIRBS. Any false alarm or suspicion of one must be reported at once to Race HQ.

9 SUMMARY OF YACHT COMMUNICATIONS

9.1 Weather	FAX HF	– Choice of Shore Stations (ALRS 3)
	Storm Warnings	– HF RT from ditto – also Forecasts & Warnings from Coast Radio Stations
9.2 INMARSAT	From yachts to Race HQ	– 12 hourly GPS (automatic) – Daily Sitrep from Duty Yacht – Urgent Messages – ETA and Finish report
	Race HQ to Yachts	– Daily Position Summary
	Personal & Sponsor	– They pay. Battery power limit
9.3 INTERYACHT HF RT or VHF		– 11:00 and 23:00 GMT (Duty Yacht i/c) – Message relay if no INMARSAT – Keeping in touch
9.4 HF RT with Portishead (Yachts not in touch para 7.4.2)		– Read daily BSC Traffic Lists then Portishead takes yacht traffic (see para 7.4.1)
9.5 2182 Distress		– Constant auto alarm
9.6 Local Coast Radio		– When approaching Finish (as in Leg Instructions)

NOTES

1. If any Yacht is not in touch on INMARSAT or on Inter-yacht net Race HQ may ask Portishead to provide a twice a day communication link (para 7.4 et seq).

2. Duty Yacht should read traffic lists on behalf of her Group if all are out of touch on INMARSAT and also perhaps when there is a need to read Coast radio approaching a stopover port (para 5.4.6 and 5.4.7).